Uncontrolling Love

Essays Exploring the Love of God

with Introductions by Thomas Jay Oord

Edited by Chris Baker, Gloria Coffin, Craig Drurey
Graden Kirksey, Lisa Michaels, and Donna Ward

SacraSage

SACRASAGE PRESS

SacraSage Press
San Diego, CA 92106
Uncontrollinglove.com
© 2017 uncontrollinglove (Thomas Jay Oord)

Essays in this book draw from or build upon Thomas Jay Oord's book, The Uncontrolling Love of God: An Open and Relational Account of Providence (Downers Grove, Ill.: Intervarsity Press Academic, 2015).

Interior Design: L Michaels
Cover Design: Hammad Khalid
ISBN 978-0692884942 (Print)

Printed in the United States of America

Library of Congress Cataloguing-in-Publication Data

Chris Baker, Gloria Coffin, Craig Drurey, Graden Kirksey, Lisa Michaels, and Donna Ward. Editors.

Uncontrolling Love: Exploring the Uncontrolling Love of God, with Introductory Essays by Thomas Jay Oord / Baker, Coffin, Drurey, Kirksey, Michaels, Ward. Eds.

ISBN: 978-0692884942

SacraSage

dedicated to seekers everywhere

who want to ponder, experience, and express

uncontrolling love

Contents

SECTION ONE

SECTION TWO

SECTION THREE

SECTION ONE

Introduction:
Who God Is

Thomas Jay Oord

The editors have helpfully divided this book into three sections of essays. This first addresses God's nature. The second offers essays on God's action. The final section includes essays on creaturely responses to God.

The ideas in the three overlap. In fact, many essays could have easily been placed in another section. Given my views about theology, it's difficult for me to think about one section topic without considering the other two. I have difficulty considering God's nature, for instance, and not also thinking about divine actions and creaturely responses. The three categories profoundly interrelate.

Dividing the book into three sections has the advantage, however, of focusing our thoughts and perhaps going deeper into each subject. In this spirit, I am writing brief introductions to the three. While the essays speak for themselves, my introductions provide a lens through which readers might approach the essays. My intros also provide me the opportunity to present key ideas from *The Uncontrolling Love of God: An Open and Relational Account of Providence* (IVP Academic), which is the book that sparked these writings in the first place. Along the way, I also explore ideas I didn't mention in the book.

Note of Appreciation

Before I go further, I want to express appreciation to the editors and essayists. It's an honor, joy, and privilege to have the ideas of my book taken seriously. In many cases, essayists expanded my ideas or explored notions I had not addressed. I thank them for their kindness and exploratory spirit!

The editors have been working on this project for some time. The essays were first published online in 2016 as blog pieces. The Uncontrolling Love website was created for the essays, and disseminating completed the blogs through social media sparked lively conversations. Chris Baker managed the site, while Gloria Coffin, Graden Kirksey, Cameron McCown, Lisa Michaels, and Donna Ward edited the essays for the site and book. Craig Drurey functioned as the general leader of the project team. I am grateful to each for their work, encouragement, and comradeship.

God's Nature

Back to the theme of this first section: "Who God Is." I was tempted to begin by talking about how theologians make claims about God's nature. I was going to talk primarily about Scripture, reason, and experience, and then throw in quotations from famous thinkers who speculate about the nature of God. But I decided that approach might be boring. If you care about how theologians frame a doctrine of God's nature, I encourage you to read various books on theological methodology.

I want to focus, instead, on my proposals about God's nature in *The Uncontrolling Love of God*. I suspect that will be more interesting to readers. Most essays placed in this section address those proposals directly, others do so indirectly.

Perhaps my central idea is the claim that love comes logically first in God's nature. By 'first,' I don't mean God's attributes line up, like dominos, and love comes first in that line. By the phrase 'comes logically first,' I mean we should think about God's other attributes in light of love. Love comes first conceptually.

When our ideas about God's attributes seem to clash with love, I think we should reformulate them in ways that harmonize with love. As I see it, our ideas about God should be oriented around the belief that Charles Wesley expresses in his hymn, when he writes, "thy nature and thy name is love."[1]

For instance, some theologians assume power or 'sovereignty' comes first in God. Consequently, they say God has the power *not* to love. To put it another way, because they believe God's sovereign will comes first, God can choose not to love.

By contrast, I think love logically comes before power, in God. Among other things, this means I don't think God can choose not to love. Because love comes in God's nature logically before choice, God must love. God is free to choose *how* to love but not free to choose *whether* to love.

I'm not the first theologian to say love comes first in God's nature, although we who say this seem to be in the minority. Nor am I the first to say God must love, although this statement may also strike some people as unusual.

I don't know of anyone else, however, who adds the particular content I add to saying love comes first in God's nature or that God must love. I call my view 'essential kenosis.' And it seems appropriate to talk about essential kenosis when discussing who God is.

Essential Kenosis

Taking Philippians 2:1-13 as my touchstone, I believe God's love is necessarily self-giving and others-empowering. This means that God *must* self-give and others-empower, because it is God's nature to do so. God's loving gifts are "irrevocable," to use the Apostle Paul's language.[2] In fact, I think the majority of the Bible is interpreted well when essential kenosis is our hermeneutical lens.

Essential kenosis says, therefore, that God *cannot* override, withdraw, or fail to provide the power of freedom, agency, or existence to creation. Consequently, God cannot control creatures or creation. That's right; I'm saying God *can't* control others, not just *won't* control. To put it another way, God's love is essentially uncontrolling.

Most kenosis theologians think God voluntarily chooses to self-give and others-empower. Most say God *usually* self-limits and decides to allow space to creatures to act freely. Jürgen Moltmann is a good representative of this view. Voluntary self-limitation entails that God could choose to un-self-limit at any time. In kenosis theologies like Moltmann's, sovereign choice to self-limit comes first in God's nature.

By contrast, essential kenosis says God is *involuntarily* self-limited. God is *self*-limited, in the sense that no outside force, power, or authority limits God. God's loving nature shapes divine action such that God cannot control others.

Because as the Apostle Paul would say, God "cannot deny himself," I claim that God cannot control others.[3]

Essential kenosis provides advantages that are great and wide-ranging. Many essays in this section explore them. The advantage of essential kenosis I discuss most in *The Uncontrolling Love of God* is its importance for solving the central conundrum in the problem of evil.

The God who must love and cannot control others is *not* morally responsible for failing to prevent evil. The God of essential kenosis *can't* prevent evil by acting alone. So God is not to blame. This solution to the problem of evil is not just big for the scholarly community and theology nerds. It's a big deal for everyday people who wonder why a loving and powerful God doesn't prevent suffering. According to essential kenosis, God doesn't even 'allow' suffering, because God can't stop it acting alone. Therefore, God's not culpable for the genuine evil in our lives.

I could say more about God's nature and essential kenosis. But I hope my introduction sets the stage for the excellent essays in this section. Many go deeper into these issues or explore them in a wider context. There is some great writing in this section!

Enjoy!

Endnotes

1. Wesley, Charles, *Come, Oh Thou Traveler Unknown* (1742, reprint, The United Methodist Hymnal 1989), 386 (page citation is to reprint edition).
2. Rom. 11:29 (NIV).
3. 2 Tim. 2:13

The Jesus Lens:
Seeing God through Jesus

Will Albright

Much like the ant would struggle to comprehend and explain the existence of humanity, our theorizing upon the divine is often little better than the ant theologians who ponder the existence of the gods who trounce above their hilly abode. It is logically conclusive: finitude struggles to comprehend infinitude. In this vein, God is mystery. Knowable, for God has been made known through God's own mighty acts, but not wholly explainable. This, then, is why the most prominent of theologians—the writers of Scripture—predominantly employ the use of metaphor to explain God.

Herein lies a conundrum of biblical interpretation. What should be taken literally and what should be taken metaphorically? Swaying too far to either side leaves us off-kilter. The result is not only an unbalanced faith, but one that is unbiblical. When practicing theology, particularly in the Christian tradition, it is imperative that theology be biblical. We must have a canon, a standard of measure by which to rule our theology. It is my assertion that Jesus, particularly the Jesus found in the four canonical gospel accounts, provides us the lens through which we are to practice theology and interpret Scripture. This essay focuses primarily on theorizing divinity through the biblical narrative of divinity incarnate.

And the Word became flesh, and dwelt among us, and we saw His glory, glory as of the only begotten from the Father, full of grace and truth . . . For of His fullness we have all received, and grace upon grace. For the Law was given through Moses; grace and truth were realized through Jesus Christ. No one has seen God at any time; the only begotten God who is in the bosom of the Father, He has **explained** (Greek *exegeomai*, "to expound or to reveal") Him.[1]

Scripture informs us that God is revealed through the person of Jesus Christ. Jesus, in whom, "the fullness of Deity dwells in bodily form," expounds, or more fittingly exegetes, God's very nature and essence.[2] Jesus is our hermeneutic principle, the very lens, through which we interpret the Godhead proper. Through the lens of Jesus, we see who God is—God's character, nature and essence. Therefore, it is imperative to filter any Christian theological discussion through the life and actions of the incarnate God.

The story of Jesus calming the sea is a favorite of preachers and Christians alike. Very often, it is used as a proof text to demonstrate God's control over God's creation. Typically, it is taught as follows: Have faith, we are encouraged (or admonished). Look! God is in control! What have we to fear with a God who controls even the wind and the waves? Therefore, do not let the storms of life cause you anxiety. Do not doubt that God is God, and God is in control. Certainly there are many who find comfort in this sentiment.

But, for a moment, I would like to rethink this common interpretation. My focus, then, is on the inquiry of the disciples: "Who then is this, that even the wind and the sea obey Him?"[3] First and foremost, this passage is indicative of who Jesus is, namely, God in the flesh. The overall purpose of this passage is to reveal Jesus as the incarnate God, and the truth of this—to me and many others—is undoubtable and not up for question.

Rather, let us rethink the response of the elements. What is the nature of their obedience? Do the wind and the waves obey because God controls them, forcing them into submission? Or, are the elements fulfilling their creaturely duty of responding harmoniously to the Creator? I would advocate the latter. At first glance, it may seem that I am splitting hairs or merely playing a game of semantics, but there is a significant distinction between the two. Obedience is only obedience if one responds willfully in subjection to the will of the one in authority. If Jesus were controlling the elements, it would be difficult to infer their response as obedience. Here, the same created matter that responded obediently to the God speech of Genesis 1 responds accordingly to the voice of its Creator.

Granted, the discussion thus far has been centered upon the response of wind and waves, subjects without volition. One could certainly, and rightfully, ask what this has to do with us, with people. It seems to me that if God is willing to act this way towards the wind and the waves, how much more so is God inclined to act uncontrolling towards those who bear God's image? It would be my assertion that God acts with the influential power of love, and not dictating power of force or control, when dealing with every aspect of creation. God is delicate, graceful, and artful in dealing with creation, not forceful and/or manipulative. For many, a God who does not control is weak. To say that God is not controlling is to somehow make God an invalid. Yet, when we examine those in our lives who are controlling, we often find their controlling tendencies arise out of weakness and insecurity. Our God, the maker of heaven and earth and of all things visible and invisible, is not weak.

Very often we view God as a sort of grand puppeteer—making this one to jiggle and that one to dance, all on cue. I wonder, however, if this analogy isn't all wrong. I wonder, instead, if it wouldn't be better to analogize God as the master conductor instructing the various sections to respond on God's signal—this section then the next, rhythmically responding and harmonizing with excellence. I wonder if God isn't instead this great music maker, teaching all creation to play and sing along to the melody of love. God speaks: "Listen. Do you hear it? Do you know the tune? Join with me. Let us make music in the key of divine love!"

Will Albright serves as Discipleship Pastor at Hope Fellowship in Chestertown, MD. He is a licensed minister and ordination candidate in the Assemblies of God. He has earned a BA in Theological Studies and an MA in Spiritual Formation.

Endnotes

1. John 1:14, 16-18 (ESV, emphasis mine).
2. Col. 2:9
3. Mark 4:41

Infertility and Essential Kenosis

Teresa Baker

I wish you were my mommy. That would be so fun!"
These words, spoken by a seven year old parishioner at a church game night, have become familiar to me over the past two decades. In this case, it was mostly a liter of root beer and a frosted cookie talking, but I have heard these words hundreds of times. In most cases, they come from a kid dreaming about a mother who is a grown-up playmate instead of an authority figure. For years, I found these statements humorous and adorable. But at age 27, things changed when my husband and I began trying to conceive our own child. Not long after the decision to grow our family was made, the words began to hurt.

Month after month went by and there was no pregnancy. We did all of our research and followed all of the right steps. Still nothing happened. We tried for years. Soon, it seemed as though everyone around us was having babies. We were struck by the realization that we did not have as much control of the situation as we thought we did. But if we weren't in control of our own reproduction, who was? "God" felt like the obvious answer—at least to most of our friends and family.

"God's timing is perfect."

"It will be your turn soon."

I heard these words over and over again. Sometimes it seemed near constant. I was to believe that God timed everything out and apparently let people take turns pro-creating, but I found it *hard* to believe. Why would a loving God want me to suffer so much heartache while I waited on his perfect timing for my 'turn'?

As I tried to wrestle with the meaning behind all of the pain, I began to wonder if this meant we were to adopt or foster a child. Was adoption God's plan for our family? Maybe, but thinking about this theologically began to make less and less sense. If God had *planned* for us to be infertile so that we would adopt, did he also cause a young woman somewhere to be in a desperate situation for the sake of growing *our* family? Did God cause a family to fall apart or to be unable to care for their kids so that we might find a way to add to our household? Could God really be the author of all that pain?

Although the voices all around insisted that God was in control of every aspect of this situation, I knew deep down it couldn't be so. Thomas Jay Oord's discussion of essential kenosis has helped me work through the struggle of God's role in our infertility situation. Our infertility remains medically unexplained. There are numerous factors that all have to line up in order to conceive a child, and most of the entities involved in this process have God's necessary gift of free agency. God's divine love allows freedom. That freedom may lead to much heartache.

But the good news of the free agency afforded us by God's love is that we are free to participate in the redemption and restoration that God has for this fallen creation. I don't think God caused our infertility any more than he causes parents to be unable or unwilling to raise the children they birthed. But the two situations can collide when people understand that the pain and heartache are not caused by God but by free-agency. That same free-agency invites us to work with God to change the heartache into rejoicing. One day my husband and I may give birth to our own child, or foster or adopt a child, or invest our time and money in the lives of children who need us in some other capacity besides parenting. Whatever happens, I am thankful for a God who gives us choices and invites us to participate with him in redemption.

Teresa Baker is a co-pastor at Columbus Community Church of the Nazarene alongside her husband Chris. She previously served as a children's pastor in Upstate New York. She also enjoys her job as a cook at a local high school.

Timeless Eternity
or Temporal Existence

Vaughn Baker

I am fascinated by watches and clocks.

Perhaps the intricate movement fascinates me, movement easily seen if the watch face is clear. I like to look into its 'skeleton'—the wheels, gears and mechanisms for measuring time.

Time itself fascinates me. I read Jules Verne as a teenager, and I tried to imagine what it might be like to time-travel. The idea is central to scores of present-day books and movies.

In college, I began reading theological books by John Stott, J.I. Packer, and C.S. Lewis. I don't recall reading anything in them about tensions between genuine freedom and absolute foreknowledge. I do remember thinking if God was omnipresent in space, He could likewise occupy all points of time at once.

I had not yet read Boethius during this period, nor had I heard of him, but I began to think as he did: we can reconcile genuine creaturely freedom with God's exhaustive foreknowledge by thinking of God as being eternally timeless.[1] The key was to imagine God experiencing all moments simultaneously, at once.

Eventually my thinking moved away from the Boethian model. Divine timelessness created more problems than solutions. In particular, creaturely freedom was hard to understand. The problem of evil was difficult, too. I couldn't imagine how a timeless God has real give-and-receive relations of love with time-full or temporal creatures.

My "re-think" of the timeless God began when taking a class in seminary. In that class, I was exposed to the writings of Charles Hartshorne, John Cobb, Schubert Ogden, and Alfred North Whitehead. These process thinkers taught that reality is in process. Life is less about 'arriving' than about 'becoming.' They said reality is fundamentally constituted by relationships, and these thinkers introduced me to alternative interpretations of God's attributes.

During this time, I also read about a 'hybrid' theological perspective. It was then called free-will theism, and later open theism or open theology. Being hybrid, open theology embraces some classical notions such as God's omnipotence and creation *ex nihilo,* but open theology affirms general sovereignty, not determinism. Advocates of open theology say absolute divine sovereignty and libertarian creaturely freedom are incompatible. God cannot be in complete control if creatures are genuinely free.

What stands out most, however, is this. Open theology rejects the usual view of God's foreknowledge. Like the process thinkers, open theologians say God knows all there is to know. The future, however, does not yet exist to be known. Because the future is open, creatures are genuinely free to choose. What creatures decide, and even chance events, offer new information to God.

Open theology says the creatures are genuinely free and enjoy a give-and-take relationship with God and others. God makes this freedom possible by self-giving or emptying (kenosis), as the Apostle Paul puts it in Philippians 2. God is affected by others (is passible) and God's experience changes (is mutable), yet God's essential nature is unchanging.

God being affected by others also implies God's experience is temporal, in the sense of being time-full rather than timeless. God is not the exception to moment-by-moment existence but the supreme exemplification of it. In short, thinking God is in time draws me closer to the biblical witness about God and His providential care and love.

Augustine said he knew what time was . . . until you asked him. He also said God created time when God created the universe. God made the sun, moon, stars and our planet, said Augustine, and by these objects we measure years, months, days, hours, minutes and seconds.[2]

While we can agree with Augustine that God created everything, this doesn't mean temporal experience is bound by the movement of physical bodies, not even at the sub-atomic level. My watch, for instance, measures time. It doesn't create it. If my watch is running five minutes slow, this doesn't mean time has slowed down. Even planetary bodies, e.g., our moon and earth are slowing down. Does this slowing of creation mean that time is itself slowing down? Hardly, if by the time we mean the experience of duration. Time is more than metrics!

Scripture suggests genuine relationships existed before the creation of the world, but it says nothing about God being timeless in all respects. The Bible is very clear about God being love. I am among many who think God is essentially loving and relational throughout all eternity. I cannot imagine how a timeless God, whose existence would be nonrelational, unaffected, and unchanging, could love others perfectly.

In fact, the idea that God creates out of nothing, *creation ex nihilo*, suggests some kind of time or sequential experience of duration for God. A timeless being cannot create a temporal existence at some point 'in time' and remain timeless. A temporal God, however, could create at any point of time.

I further have difficulty imagining how a timeless God could relate to a temporal world, including ongoing creation, providence, miracles and the incarnation. In other words, the doctrine of divine timelessness offers me no help in understanding God's providential governance of the world.

In, *The Uncontrolling Love of God*, Thomas Jay Oord says, "God's ongoing presence in all moments of time is time-full, not timeless."[3] I agree. He goes further and says, "essential kenosis takes the time-full reality of existence and God's time-full existing as crucial for understanding why God cannot foreknow or prevent genuine evil."[4] I also agree.

If God exists everlastingly in time, the future is open even for God. This view is starkly different from conventional theology's interpretation of eternity, with its closed future. Nicholas Wolterstorff notes, "at least some of [God's] aspects stand in temporal order-relations to each other. Thus God, too, has a time-strand. His life and existence is itself temporal."[5]

In sum, open and relational models of God affirm a time-full God. God experiences time analogously to how my watch measures time: moment by moment. That makes a whole lot more sense to me than the idea that God is timeless!

Vaughn Baker, an Elder in the United Methodist Church, has served Methodist congregations both in Texas and in Ireland. Vaughn completed his doctoral studies at the University of South Africa where he argues that dynamic concepts of God, such as those

found in open theology, better serve theology in understanding, articulating, and defending the mission of the Christian church.

Endnotes

1. Boethius, *The Consolation of Philosophy*, ed. James T. Buchanan (New York: Frederick Ungar, 1957).

2. Augustine *Confessions*, 11,14

3. Thomas Jay Oord, *The Uncontrolling Love of God: An Open and Relational Account of Providence* (Downers Grove: InterVarsity Press, 2016), 173.

4. Ibid.

5. Nicholas Wolterstorff, "God Everlasting," in *God and the Good: Essays in Honor of Henry Stob*, ed. Clifton Orlebke and Lewis Smedes (Grand Rapids: Eerdmans, 1975), 181-203.

Uncontrolling Love:
Tailor Made for All Creation

Rick Barr

The great American philosopher Josiah Royce died 100 years ago, in September of 1916. Known both for his prolific academic output and his friendship with the much better known William James Royce, he was nearly forgotten a few decades ago but has made a significant comeback in recent years. He was not only an academic philosopher but also a public intellectual, taking in the society in which he found himself and shaping constructive reflections for society at large.

The book, *Sources of Religious Insight*, is one of those reflections.[1] I am borrowing from it to provide a framework for my approach to understanding Thomas Jay Oord's challenging new book. Royce defined his understanding of insight as, "knowledge that makes us aware of the unity of many facts in one whole, and that at the same time brings us into intimate personal contact with these facts and with the whole wherein they are united."[2] True insights need to be both comprehensive, reflecting a broad sense the world, and personal, providing personal orientation in that world.

The Uncontrolling Love of God is a book filled with Roycean insights. From the beginning pages, one can feel the heartfelt reflections of a deeply committed follower of The Way who has been gifted with a critical mind and a passionate interest in truth. The following will highlight three of Oord's insights that I see as most significant.

We live in a universe filled with both regularity and randomness. The interplay between these two enables the rich dynamism we experience in this world.

In this, Oord is consistent with current scientific understanding. At the most fundamental level of physics, the past never completely determines the present or the direction of the future. At the same time, chaos does not reign supreme. Regularity is present at all levels. The interplay between chance and necessity, randomness and regularity, freedom and determinism plays out in all we encounter.

In this dynamic universe, there is beauty and value but also destruction and suffering. Both goodness and evil are real aspects of reality. Evil, in particular, presents a profound conundrum. For if God is able to prevent evil and fails to do so, God cannot be good. God is good; therefore, there must be a sense in which God's sovereignty is limited. In light of this theological tension, Oord addresses the issues of God's action in the world and challenges our understanding of divine sovereignty.

By answering this challenge, Oord articulates his first significant insight. God, traditionally viewed as sovereign of the universe, does not control events. Additionally, God does not know how all events will turn out, nor does God providentially determine what will happen. For Oord, God is understood as 'open and relational.' Creator and creation impact each other. The relationship is a two-way street with both sides having the freedom to act and respond.

The second insight presenting itself in Oord's book is his fair, generous presentation of the options available for understanding divine providence. Oord lays out a continuum with one end representing the reformed tradition of an omnipotent and omniscient God who views all that is as subject to divine decree. At the other end, God is ultimately a mystery and God's ways are not our ways so any knowledge in the finite realm is irrelevant.

Oord's position is a middle way between the extremes, advocating an understanding of God as 'essentially kenotic,' reflecting God as uncontrolling love with and for creation. In presenting each alternative, historical and current representatives of each are highlighted noting the salient points with a sympathetic tone. In doing so, he represents what Royce would call the "community of interpretation" or "the beloved community" where each interpreter engages sympathetically with the other.[3] Those with whom disagreement is held are represented as participants in the community of truth, seekers whose perspectives are appreciated and viewed as gifts. We are all fellow travelers and seekers. Recognizing this, even if more implicitly than explicitly, is Oord's second insight.

Within this open/relational model of God's providence, Oord presents his most significant insight. It is deceptively simple—what he terms essential kenosis. God is love, "self-giving, others-empowering love."[4] This is the foundational understanding of who and what God is. God does not choose to love. God does not subordinate love with any other attribute. Instead, all that God is flows from this fundamental eternal essence. As he states, "God must love."[5]

But here is the important twist. Any limitations are due to the underlying nature. It is neither a voluntary limitation nor an external limitation from without. To rephrase, love does what love is. "God necessarily loves, but God freely chooses how to love each emerging moment."[6] Love is always appropriate to specific, unique contexts, "tailor-made for each creature."[7] For Oord, creation is fundamentally relational with freedom and self-organization working together in an emerging complexity. It is through these relationships, creature to creature and also with the uncontrolling relationship with God that the world evolves. For Royce, there is nothing that is that is not known by God. For Oord, there is nothing untouched by the uncontrolling love of God. In a sense, to be is to be known and to be loved. But that also means that suffering, any and all suffering, is God's suffering. This is true for Royce and for Oord.

There are more insights, big and small within this very compact book. As someone who has been involved in the science and religion dialogue for over a decade, I have selected these three because they represent common features of the dialogue. Science and faith come together through deliberate acts of interpretation by individuals with different life experiences, different sets of values, and different skill sets. The dialogue reaches out to others with different perspectives— truth seekers whom Royce called the hidden church. Oord is part of that dialogue and his insights are substantial and appreciated.

Rick Barr is co-founder and acting Board Secretary of WesleyNexus, Inc., a nonprofit organization dedicated to the dissemination of sound information about the dialogue between science and religion within the Wesleyan tradition. He received an MA degree from Wesley Theological Seminary in 2015 majoring in Systematic Theology with a concentration in science and religion. He has over thirty years of experience in information systems management, currently acting as an IT Audit Manager for CEB Global, a best practice insight and technology company. He lives in Damascus, Maryland with his wife Jean, and he is a member of Damascus United Methodist Church.

Endnotes

1. See Josiah Royce, Josiah. *Sources of Religious Insight* (New York: Octagon Books, 1912), 3-34.

2. Royce, 5-6.

3. Josiah Royce. *The Problem of Christianity* (Washington, DC: The Catholic University of America Press, 2001), 125.

4. Thomas Jay Oord, *The Uncontrolling Love of God: An Open and Relational Account of Providence* (Downers Grove: InterVarsity Press, 2016), 159.

5. Oord, 161.

6. Oord, 162.

7. Oord, 166.

The Psychology of Humble Love

Roger Bretherton

The Humility of God

In 1978, the existential theologian John Macquarrie wrote a short book with an unusual title, *The Humility of God*. As a systematic theologian, he viewed it as his duty to think of Christianity as a whole. Every doctrine of the Christian faith, he asserted, implied every other. We can start thinking anywhere, and it will eventually lead to everything else. With this in mind he took the unassuming notion of humility and stretched it into every corner of the faith: creation, incarnation, redemption, consummation, and so on. Having done so, he concluded with a view of God as,

> . . . *no self-centred absolute, no unmoved and unmovable mover, no unfeeling impersonal principle, not even a lonely monarch distantly presiding over the universe, but a Father yearning for his creatures, a Father who is most fully revealed in the suffering crucified Saviour. And the fact that he too can be touched and affected certainly does not make him any less God or any more adorable, but rather more so. The God of Christian faith, we could say, is great enough to be humble.*[1]

With a few caveats, perhaps, it's the kind of statement I can imagine Thomas Jay Oord writing. A God in whom love is more fundamental than power. For what is a God of uncontrolling love, if not a God of humility?

The Psychology of Humility

At this point I need to come clean. I am a psychologist, not a theologian. Or, to put it more accurately, I am a *professional* psychologist but an *amateur* theologian. Nevertheless, I still dare to entertain the notion that occasionally, like the detectives of Christie and Conan Doyle, an amateur can see patterns and make links that may elude the laser-like focus of the expert.

For the last few years I have been conducting research in the psychology of humility. It's quite a new field, only bursting to life in the last decade or so. Prior to this, most psychologists thought it was almost impossible to study humility in the real world—partly because measuring it is so tricky.[2] If someone gives themselves a ten out of ten for humility on a rating scale, we are more than justified in viewing their self-assessment with suspicion. For quite some time, therefore, humility tended to be studied as a void, an emptiness. It was the absence of narcissism, arrogance, boastfulness, or self-enhancement. Humble people, it was thought, lacked something.

In a sense this is true. Diminished self-focus is certainly one of the hallmarks of humility and has been denoted in numerous ways: self-forgetfulness, un-selving, the quiet ego. All of these refer to the delightful ability of humble people to put self-concern aside when the situation requires it. They do not allow their egos to get in the way.

But in recent years we have become more aware of the positive aspects of humility. The humble are not charisma vacuums. In fact, they make a profound contribution to the people around them, and this is what makes them so winsome as friends, leaders and employees.[3] They know how to listen, no matter how critical or unflattering the conversation may be. They know how to care, because they see other people without bias or distortion and can accurately recognize strength and vulnerability. The fundamental gift of humility, psychologically speaking, is that it acts as a gateway to professional, spiritual, and ethical growth. Humble people are learning people.[4]

Humility . . . and its Discontents

It is therefore interesting to note that one of the major biblical passages that acts as a lynchpin for Thomas Jay Oord's essential kenotic theology is also a passage commending humility. The apostle Paul begins the second chapter of Philippians with an endorsement of humility over selfish ambition and then erupts into a great hymn, stressing that Christ not only emptied (*kenoō*) himself, but also humbled (*tapeinoō*) himself.[5] For Paul, the emptying of Christ and the humility of Christ are closely aligned.

The apostle, however, is not citing these self-giving, other-enhancing qualities in a vacuum. He has urgently practical reasons in mind. As always, his apple of application never falls too far from the tree of doctrine, and in this case it could be that he is writing to avert the fracturing of the Philippian church. His final greetings suggest that two influential and beloved women, Euodia and Syntyche, are in conflict.[6] His talk of self-emptying and humility is no doubt aimed at averting the potential escalation of the situation. Humility is essential to the future of the congregation. It would appear that we psychologists are only just catching up with Paul in recognizing the central role of humility in the life and health of human communities.

In recent history, however, several critics have taken issue with the Christian virtue of humility. Nietzsche famously rewrote the eleventh verse of Luke chapter fourteen to read: "He who humbles himself wants to be exalted."[7] Camus, on the other hand, satirized the group cohesion that comes about through humility with the chilling words, "all together at last, but on our knees with heads bowed."[8] For both of them, humility was suspect. For Nietzsche, humble submission was a resentful performance designed to ingratiate the powerful. For Camus, the promotion of humility was principally a device by which the church suppressed the life of the individual and enforced obedient conformity.

They are not alone in querying the validity of humility as a human good. Some evolutionary psychologists of religion are fond of the refrain that religions teach that God demands submission from his worshipers, under threat of execution or exile, just as a tribal chief requires unswerving loyalty from his tribesmen. Submissive followers are more easily controlled, compliant, and convenient. Presumably this is what a controlling god, like the leader of any totalitarian regime, would want from his followers. In other words: God wants us to be nice, because he is nasty.

Kenosis and Character

This is where essential kenotic theology can help us. It rescues us from the master-slave morality in which God needs us to be weak, so he can be strong. By illuminating self-giving, other-enhancing love as the essential nature of God, Thomas Jay Oord frees us from viewing God as an undeniably powerful, but questionably loving, dictator. God, he claims, cannot be unloving and still be God. If I could extend the assertion further, I'd add: . . . *nor can God lack humility and still be God.*

God wants us to be loving, because he is loving. He wants us to be humble, because he is humble. Unlike him, we are not essentially so and therefore must trust that God knows the ultimate power of an infinitely patient, eternally persistent, humble love. We are confronted with a choice between force and humble love, a choice keenly felt by Dostoyevsky when he wrote:

> *Always decide to use humble love. If you resolve on that, once and for all, you may subdue the whole world. Loving humility is marvelously strong, the strongest of all things, and there is nothing like it.*[9]

Essential kenotic theology is therefore good news for psychologists like me, concerned with the development of character and virtue. It offers, to my mind, perhaps the best theological rationale for Christian character development imaginable. It applies not just to love and humility, but to hope, wisdom, patience, gratitude, and so on. It addresses not just the problem of evil but the problem of good, and in doing so offers hope that one day the character of heaven will indeed cover the earth.

Roger Bretherton is Principal Lecturer in Psychology at the University of Lincoln (UK). His extended research programme looks at positive qualities of character such as humility, gratitude, forgiveness and love, in various contexts: church, business, health and education.

Endnotes

1. Macquarrie, J., *The Humility of God.* (London: SCM Press, 1978), 71.
2. See Davis, D. E., Worthington Jr, E. L., & Hook, J. N., "Humility: Review of measurement strategies and conceptualization as personality judgment," *The Journal of Positive Psychology* 5(4) (2010): 243-252.

3. See Collins, J. C., "Level 5 leadership: The triumph of humility and fierce resolve," *Harvard Business Review* January (2001): 66-76.

4. See Chancellor, J., & Lyubomirsky, S., "Humble beginnings: Current trends, state perspectives, and hallmarks of humility," *Social and Personality Psychology Compass* 7(11) (2013): 819-833.

5. Phil. 2:3, 6-8 (NIV).

6. Phil. 4:2

7. Nietzsche, F. W., *Human, All Too Human* (The Complete Works of Friedrich Nietzsche 3), trans. G. J. Handwerk (Redwood City, CA.: Stanford University Press, 1878/2001), 68.

8. Camus, A. *The Fall* (J. O'Brien Trans.). Harmondsworth: Penguin, 1956) 100.

9. Cited in Worthington, E. L., *Humility: The quiet virtue.* (Philadelphia: Templeton Foundation Press, 2007)

A Better Love:
The Evolving Shape
of Postmodern Theologies

Tim Burnette

The idea that theology is both imaginative and constructive has been contoured by the late Harvard Divinity School Professor, Gordon Kaufman. He wrote, "All theology, in its attempt to analyze, criticize, and reconstruct the image/concept of God, is an expression of the continuing activity of the human imagination seeking to create a framework of interpretation that can provide overall orientation for human life."[1]

I tend to share his sentiments here, but with perhaps a more poststructuralist hermeneutical sensibility than he might have embraced when he first penned those words. He proposed this methodology in response to the looming potentiality of a nuclear holocaust and perhaps, in so doing, hit upon a recurring apocalyptic theme that still has relevance in our 21st century context: the need for an imaginative, constructive theological response to the looming threats of our day, including things like the ecological crisis, global poverty, totalitarian political regimes, refugee crises, systemic racism, and the list goes on.

By imaginative, I mean that it is crucial for our theologies to risk the adventure of innovation in conversation with (or perhaps even in the face of) classical interpretations of various doctrines, in light of the enfolding narrative relationship that humanity has had with its great religious traditions. By constructive, I mean that in embracing a posture that inhabits the radically deconstructive hermeneutical moves of the postmodern era, we must attempt to cataphize out of the inherent apophasis that has seemingly engulfed modern notions of truth. That is, we must give valuable and beauty-full interpretations of reality that correspond with what we continue to observe in disciplines like theoretical physics and work together with those disciplines to craft theologies that speak formative words of life and liberation to a planet in desperate need of a hope for today.

It seems to me that Thomas Jay Oord's work in *The Uncontrolling Love of God* has succeeded insomuch as it has attempted to do just that: it has given us an imaginative construction of the doctrine of God's providence through the lens of a non-coercive, kenotic form of love. When I first encountered Tom's work, I was struck by his ability to build bridges between camps when it came to thinking about God, as he emphasized the primacy of love more than theologians who prioritized other characteristics like God's holiness, creativity, power, mystery, or judgment. And, as he parsed out his understanding of love, what separated him from even other open and relational theologians was that he proposed that the reality of God's love is as inherently vulnerable as it is essentially kenotic. Whereas many theologians who hold to kenotic forms of theology emphasize God's self-emptying nature as some kind of onto-mutation into a Christ-form, Oord has suggested to us that this self-emptying is *actually* God's nature.

This idea is both novel and relevant for Christians in the 21st century who are searching for ways to continue onward in the tradition that has been given to them, while not having to divorce themselves from their experience of the actual world in which they live. Much of western (especially postmodern neo-reformed and other foundationalist forms of) theology since the Reformation has tended toward constructions of God that force adherents to profess things about God's nature and activity that have become indefensible in a post WWII culture. The sufferings of many have left us with historically unique questions about the reality of God in the 21st century, and much of theology has moved from questions of existence/non-existence to other alternative discourses surrounding our God-constructions. True to this multiplicitous fashion, Oord promises that his proposition produces, "A model of providence that includes randomness and regularity, free will and necessity, goodness and evil, and more. This model would emphasize that God loves all creation steadfastly because God's nature is uncontrolling love."[2]

Let us be clear here what he is preserving, where he is innovating, and why it matters. Tom has here in his proposal accomplished a few things important to the discipline of theology. First, he has engaged the historical interpretations of the tradition in placing his view in conversation with both Scripture and historical theology. Second, he has engaged contemporary scientific views of the world including cosmological randomness, as well as current philosophical notions of creaturely freedom. As he has done this, he has embodied what every theologian since the end of modernity should attempt: transdisciplinarity. He has set his God-talk in a much more expansive setting by engaging other schools of thought, and this type of engagement has no doubt sharpened his thinking as he puts forth his constructive account of God.

He has also innovated by delving deeper into kenotic theological discourse by saying, "God's kenotic love logically precedes divine power in the divine nature. This logical priority qualifies how we should think God works in and with creation."[3]

Whereas many theologies have emphasized certain big "O" qualities like omnipotence or omniscience, Tom has opted for omnibenevolence in light of God's omnipresence. As is characteristic of most panentheistic theologies, the omnipresent portion of his understanding implies God is 'down, in and through' (immanent), not 'up there and out there somewhere' (interventional). It is this relationality that has, in Tom's mind, let God off the hook for allowing things like evil, because God's vulnerability is necessary for the possibility of a true loving relationship with the world. While I might find my points of difference, we need more theologians like Tom.

In an era where we are seeing the decline of Christianity in the West and more and more anti and pseudo-intellectual forms of the faith becoming combatant in the public sphere; more than ever, we need fresh, imaginative, constructive ways of translating God for the 21st century. Tom's proposal of a love-centric, uncontrolling God can give those in search of a more vibrant theological imagination the option of not only a better love, but a transmutable theology attuned to an ever-evolving world.

Tim is a writer, process philosopher, theopoetic, artist, and contemplative working for a more Beauty-full future in the Disciples of Christ in Santa Barbara, CA. T:@timothytalk

Endnotes

1. Gordon D. Kaufman, *Theology for a Nuclear Age* (Manchester: Manchester UP, 1985), 26.

2. Thomas Jay Oord, *The Uncontrolling Love of God: An Open and Relational Account of Providence* (Downers Grove: InterVarsity Press, 2016), 152-153.

3. Oord, 162-163.

Trust and Love:
A Causal Relationship

Kaitlyn Haley

I sat in a stiff backed wooden chair; a counselor with kind, generous eyes sat across from me. I felt my back hunching under the weight of the embarrassment discovered when theological theory meets raw human pain and proceeds to shatter the image I had once perceived of God: the one I had once called my best friend. A two-month mission trip to India left me questioning the theological concepts I once held to be true. It left me emotionally and interpersonally wrecked. The combination of reverse culture shock, the reality of extreme poverty, and academic theological education caused me to become callused toward religious experience. The mere suggestion of experiential religion felt like a slap to the face.

The word trust was among the greatest offenders to my emotional unrest. Many Christians find great solace in the concept of trust. We try to use trust to comfort those who have experienced loss, but unless it is born from love; trust is the result of mistaken and, at times, abusive ideas about God. We might say, "We don't understand God's ways, so we just need to trust. God is in control."

Perhaps we say such things because, for us, trust has a starting place of sovereignty and is a basic duty of the Christians' journey much like obedience might be. This is because, as Thomas Jay Oord explains in his book, *The Uncontrolling Love of God*, such ideas begin with the concept that God's will logically precedes God's love. If we think in this way, God becomes a being who, perfectly in control, is worthy of trust because of this control. So, despite the suffering and evil we see in world, God is still worthy of trust, because God is in control and God's ways are beyond our human understanding.

For my college-sophomore-self, this concept of trust was the farthest thing from comforting. Because my concept of trust was tied to my ideas about God's sovereignty, I lost all logical reason to trust God. I no longer found God trustworthy.

The ideas found in Thomas Jay Oord's book can help to restore believers who find themselves questioning the trustworthiness of God by reconstructing a view of trust that begins and ends with love. When we question God's trustworthiness, it may seem that we are questioning something essential to God's nature. But if we maintain that God's love logically precedes God's will, and we begin to explain suffering in the world not through God's sovereignty but instead through limitations God experiences, God being in control can no longer be the source of our trust. If we begin with God's nature being love, God does not remain untrustworthy but is rather trustworthy because of the nature of God's relationship with creation.

My own journey has led me to believe that God is still trustworthy even if God is not in control in the traditional ways we have often understood God to be. If God's fundamental nature is love, God is trustworthy not because God is sovereign or because God is in complete control, but rather because God perfectly loves. By thinking in this way our language of comfort might change from, "simply trust: God is in control," to, "simply trust: God has, is, and will continue to sacrifice all because God loves us."

Our concept of God then shifts from a removed being, able to save but unwilling to do so, to a loving relational being, capable of and willing to sacrifice to the point of death for creation.

Humanity then finds itself trusting God not out of obligation or an assurance that God is in control but rather out of a deep and relational love. Today, several years after my India experience, I find myself trusting God because I find myself in a relationship of love with God. We might call trust based in love a relational trust. This trust is not based on a relationship in which God withholds critical understanding from the other, for the sake of power, but rather on the belief that God will continue to act in loving, relational ways, regardless of the immaturity of the creation. Instead of trusting a superpower that we will never comprehend, we trust a loving being capable of relationship and loving sacrifice. We trust a being that will continue to be present to creation through all its pain and endurance of evil, who then guides the creation to participate in love.

Kaitlyn Haley is a second year Master of Divinity student at Nazarene Theological Seminary in Kansas City. Before graduating with a bachelor's degree in Christian Ministry, Kaitlyn grew up in California and Washington State and currently enjoys visits to see her parents who reside in Honolulu, Hawaii. When not studying, Kaitlyn enjoys music, theater, party lights and fireflies (a recent discovery since becoming a Missouri resident). She is always game for deep conversations or belting show tunes.

The Ideal-less God

Justin Heinzekehr

G rowing up in a rural, evangelical Mennonite church, I heard two things very clearly: God wanted us to be nonviolent, and God would ultimately intervene to punish the violent and reward the peaceful. I never really understood how those two statements fit together. What use is it to practice nonviolence if you expect God to eventually annihilate your adversary? A nonviolent, noncoercive God seemed much more consistent with the Christian ethics that I learned from my peace church tradition. Process theology helped me see nonviolence as a way to engage the world rather than prove my superiority over the world. I headed off to graduate school to learn more.

I soon realized that I had a slightly different theological perspective than my professors and peers. I often heard an argument similar to the one that Thomas Jay Oord makes, "because genuine evils occur and God always loves, we are right to infer that God must not be able to coerce to prevent genuine evil."[1] This argument assumes that, in the face of evil, real love means being coercive, if possible. According to this logic, the only reason that God wouldn't exercise violence in these situations is that God is unable to do so. The implication that follows is that, for us humans who *are* able to act coercively, violence *is* sometimes a necessary response to evil. As a Mennonite and a pacifist, I found this very odd. Here I was, learning about a supposedly nonviolent theology, only to find it being used to justify human violence. To me, it wasn't necessary to stress the fact that God *couldn't* use coercion, because I already believed that violence was a less effective strategy than nonviolence in the long run.

I soon realized, however, that I *did* have to grapple with the silence of God in the face of evil. Even if we don't believe that a violent response to violence is ever justified, why isn't God obviously intervening in the world in a creative, nonviolent way? If we hold up the ethics of Jesus . . . or Gandhi . . . or Martin Luther King Jr. as the ideal, then we should expect God to actively confront injustice. How is it that God embodies perfection and yet tolerates such an imperfect world? In the end, the peace churches (and any Christian interested in nonviolence) need something to bridge our ethical ideals and our theology.

From a Mennonite perspective, we could flesh out a pretty attractive God based on Oord's concept of essential kenosis. Let's say, for instance, that God, as an "omnipresent spirit with no localized divine body,"[2] works in the world by calling creatures to intervene in situations of evil or injustice. When a teacher stops one student from bullying another, or a firefighter saves a toddler from a burning house, these are examples of creation embodying the spirit of God. We could see God's hand in all the nonviolent movements of history and blame violence or injustice on someone's failure to live up to the divine calling. It's attractive, because it aligns God with our ideas of goodness and love, removing any culpability for evil or violence. And, it places *us* on the right side of history. To the extent that we are carrying out God's calling, we are on *God's* side.

I can appreciate that vision of God, and I think it's possible to hold that theology with integrity. But there is also a danger, one that the peace churches have fallen into more than we care to admit. Namely, if your portrait of God matches your self-portrait too closely (even if it's a very nice portrait), it becomes difficult to hear criticism or entertain another perspective. For example, when Mennonites emigrated to the United States and Canada from Europe, they were too busy thinking about how they had faithfully avoided military conscription to consider whose land they were occupying. Until very recently, Mennonites have tended to see themselves as automatically aligned with God's call toward non-coercive love. The problem is the assumption that we know in advance what nonviolence or non-coercion means.

I'm attracted to Oord's idea of essential kenosis, because it stabilizes the ideals of love and nonviolence that I hold to be central to Christian faith. But what if nonviolence itself needs to be *destabilized*? I'm not advocating a step away from nonviolence. Instead, I wonder if nonviolence in the deepest sense might require us to challenge our own ideals and assumptions *about* nonviolence. To that end, I have also appreciated another stream of process theology that talks about God in terms of emptiness or space—a slightly different, and in some ways more traditional, way of thinking about kenosis. The benefit here is that God is not equated with any particular ideal. God's call is not toward a pre-established idea of love but provides a scaffold upon which the world could construct diverse forms of love.

Perhaps essential kenosis can accommodate this way of thinking, too. After all, I agree with Oord on the basics. It seems clear to me that the nature of God is not to suddenly intervene in metaphysical or natural laws. I agree that the idea that God has *chosen* to limit Godself is unconvincing. So, in the end, the only addition I would make is to our definition of non-coercion or love. Love not only works for the good of the beloved but also provides space for the beloved to define his or her own good. The non-coercive God is not hovering over us with a specific set of directions but is encouraging us to tap into our own creativity without knowing where it will lead. In many cases, this kind of creativity may demand that we rethink our assumptions about what 'good' is. This is non-coercion at its deepest. If God is Love, it's not because God doles love out to us but because it is through God that we are led to discover new ways of loving.

Justin Heinzekehr is Director of Institutional Research and Assessment and Assistant Professor of Bible and Religion at Goshen College. His research interests include process philosophy, Anabaptist-Mennonite theology, and political theology. His forthcoming book, Socialism in Process (edited with Philip Clayton), explores theoretical and practical connections between socialism and process thought.

Endnotes

1. Thomas Jay Oord, *The Uncontrolling Love of God: An Open and Relational Account of Providence* (Downers Grove: InterVarsity Press, 2016), 185.
2. Oord, 178.

On the Question of
God's Relationship to Morality

John Daniel Holloway, III

There is a theist maxim of uncertain origin that states, "If God does not exist, everything is permitted."[1] Claimed here is a connection between theism and morality, so that morality cannot exist without God. As those like C. S. Lewis claim, our sense of morality is evidence of the existence of a moral God. Without God determining what is moral, we can have no concrete moral compass, and so everything is permitted.[2] Philosopher and sociologist Slavoj Žižek criticizes this maxim and reverses its proposal, saying instead, "It is precisely if there is a God that everything is permitted."[3] We find this to be true in a surprising way when we look at the way many theologians explain God's relationship to morality. Daniel Heimbach, for example, addresses the issue of the violent actions of God, in the Bible, by saying that what is immoral for us can be moral for God, and even that what is immoral on our own authority becomes moral by the authority of God:

> Because God defines morality for us and not the other way around, it must therefore be that God acting as a bloodthirsty warrior is sometimes morally justified; and it must also be that at those times fighting on God's side on crusade terms, allowing no surrender, showing no mercy and sparing no one, is also entirely justified.[4]

Similarly, when asked if it was moral for the ancient Israelites to enact genocide, Tremper Longman said, "Yes, by definition it was moral. I may struggle with it, but God defines morality—what is right and what is wrong. If it is initiated by God, it is moral."[5]

While the theology here is admirable in its emphasis on the divine-human distinction, it is wholly inadequate. It is true that we should not make God in our image, or constrict God to our frame of reference, but to make God out to be arbitrary and capricious is to make way for the very idolatry that is to be avoided. If God is *entirely* unpredictable in essence, God becomes entirely malleable. If God is capable of anything, God can be used to justify anything. The danger of this theology cannot be overstated. Not only has it been used throughout history to justify atrocities, but it can be (and if history is any indication, will be) used to do so again.

If killing a child is morally wrong, it should not be considered morally right if God does it. If all you need to render an act moral is divine sanction, then morality is relativized and rendered meaningless, becoming a concept completely adaptable to human perversions. History is full of examples of humans construing their atrocious actions in such a way that they can claim divine sanction. If we are good at anything, it's justifying to ourselves our sinful actions. If all we need in order to justify ourselves is to construe our actions in such a way that we can claim divine sanction, then everything is permitted.

Thomas Jay Oord offers a more promising alternative on the issue. Rather than saying, "God determines morality, so that if God does something evil it is good because God does it," he claims that goodness is necessarily part of God's nature, so that God cannot do anything evil but only does what is good. There is a standard of morality that God cannot violate precisely because it is in God's nature to be good, and God cannot be something God is not. As Oord says,

> God did not arbitrarily choose the laws of nature and standards of morality. And God cannot supersede them. But the standards of morality or laws of nature neither exist independent of nor transcend God. They emerge from God's loving interaction with creation, as God acts from an eternal and unchanging nature of love.[6]

God acts morally, not because God submits God's self to the standard of morality, but because God is moral in nature. Thus, to speak of morality is not to speak of something that is arbitrary, for God acts in accordance with the divine will, and the divine will is always and forever good, never evil.

Oord offers a promising theological perspective on the problem of God's relationship to the good, and we would do well to follow his lead. For God there can be no suspension of the good, no disregard for what is just and right. With God we can always expect goodness. This does not, however, answer the question of whether or not we can know the divine standard of goodness. How we can know what is ethical, just, right, good, and moral is a question that still must be addressed.

Roberto Sirvent addresses this question by advocating a "shared moral standard" between God and humans. Our sense of morality, he says, "must apply to God because it is the only one we know."[7] He explains:

> Too much "mystery" in the divine moral plane would render the divine-human relationship quite problematic. If God is in fact a relational God, then a shared moral language is necessary not only for God to appeal to us, but to relate to us in any meaningful matter as well.[8]

Sirvent claims that we have to take our moral standard seriously as revelatory and so applicable to the divine understanding. He assumes, however, that we have a clear moral standard. He quotes John Barton, who says, "If we want to know what it would be like for God to be good, then we look to a good human being and extrapolate that person's moral qualities on to the divine plane."[9] Is this not creating God in the image of the human? Are we not then doing exactly what Feuerbach said, projecting our ideals onto the absolute and then calling it God? Sirvent does acknowledge these problems, but says we can't help it.[10] We need a moral standard, and it is far too problematic to say God has a different one, so we have to affirm a shared divine-human moral standard. I ask, do we actually have a moral standard? Is it not just as complicated to speak of morality as it is to speak of divinity? A sense of morality is not the same as a moral standard handed down to us in neat, systematical form, from which we can draw conclusions, and to which we can point when we do theology. As John Caputo states,

> Obligation happens. . . . I am not its judge, its law, its personal door-keeper. . . . I cannot get on top of it, scale its heights, catch a glimpse of its rising up. . . . When I am obliged I do not know by what dark pow-

ers I am held. I only know/feel/find myself caught up, in the midst of obligation.[11]

Our moral sense is not a program or a syllabus. It does not reveal to us its inner workings or a comprehensive vision of its depth and scope. We do not have a clear standard by which we can measure and understand divinity. I accept that we must hold God to the same moral standard to which we hold humans, but that is not to say we know always and in every situation what that standard is, and thus what the divine will is.

We must take seriously human finitude and human frailty and their implications for moral understanding. As sinful, finite humans how can we arrive at a settled understanding of what comprises goodness? We can say that to speak of morality is to speak of God, but how do we speak of morality?

John Daniel Holloway, III is a graduate student at Union Theological Seminary in New York, NY. He is Secretary-treasurer of the International Society for Heresy Studies, and he holds a B.A. in biblical and theological studies from Regent University. Additionally, he is a musician, a reader, a beer-drinker, and a lover of film.

Endnotes

1. On the maxim's origin, see Slavoj Žižek, "Christianity against the Sacred," in *God in Pain: Inversions of Apocalypse* (New York: Seven Stories Press, 2012), 43.

2. See C.S. Lewis, *Mere Christianity* (New York: Macmillan Publishing, 1952), book one.

3. Slavoj, Žižek, film, *The Pervert's Guide to Ideology* (2012), directed by Sophie Fiennes.

4. Daniel R. Heimbach, "Crusade in the Old Testament and Today," in *Holy War in the Bible: Christian Morality and an Old Testament Problem*, eds. Heath A. Thomas, Jeremy Evans, and Paul Copan (Downers Grove: InterVarsity Press, 2013), 190.

5. Tremper Longman, quoted in William L. Lyons, *A History of Modern Scholarship on the Biblical Word* Herem (Lewiston: The Edwin Mellen Press, 2010), 153–154.

6. Thomas Jay Oord, *The Uncontrolling Love of God: An Open and Relational Account of Providence* (Downers Grove: InterVarsity Press, 2016), 49.

7. Roberto Sirvent, *Embracing Vulnerability: Human and Divine* (Eugene: Pickwick Publications, 2014), 59.

8. Ibid., 62.

9. John Barton, *Understanding Old Testament Ethics*, 41, quoted in Ibid., 47.

10. Sirvent, 56–59.

11. John D. Caputo, *Against Ethics: Contributions to a Poetics of Obligation with Constant Reference to Deconstruction* (Bloomington: Indiana University Press, 1993), 6–7.

Love Is an Ultimate

Darren Iammarino

The view that "God is love"[1] is the deepest understanding expressed in the New Testament. In his book, *The Uncontrolling Love of God*, Thomas Jay Oord expounds on this understanding, highlighting God's loving nature as essential to his being and not as the product of choice. Oord writes:

My answer says the standards of morality and regularities of existence derive from God's loving nature. God's nature is eternal, without beginning or end. God did not create or choose the attributes of the divine nature. And God cannot change them because the divine nature is immutable.[2]

Process Theology—including my own version, Cosmosyntheism—may be capable of providing some unique twists on the above notion of God as love and God as immutable, which could reduce some ambiguity that I feel still persists within open theism.[3]

I suggest that rather than understand God *as love*, we shift to speaking of God as *in love*. If all things are within God—the doctrine known as panentheism—and God is within Love, then all things are ipso facto in Love as well—*paneneros* or perhaps *panenagape*. This makes at least one important—albeit generic and abstract—component of love *separate from but related to God's eternal nature*, but also properly an ultimate or a component of ultimate reality itself.

God *in* love is analogous to the gravitational pull of two heavenly bodies. The attraction of two or more bodies extends far beyond the physical reach of the matter comprising the objects. In much the same way, the gravitational influence of Love radiates out like earth's magnetosphere embracing, protecting and drawing bodies, entities, and objects into a state of togetherness. Love pulls all things into a kenotic state of self-giving or a sharing of information. The force field of love is the endless renewable catalyst, binding the two ultimates (God and a World) together in a ceaseless creative dance, much like the Indian concept of *lila* or the cosmic play of the gods.

The shift being suggested here is to modify the notion that God's eternal nature is love and that God, being immutable, cannot change this. In its place is the belief that God is, literally, *in* love. God is in the pull of *eros*/creativity, an ultimate that vacillates endlessly between pulling all things into a state of togetherness and then apart again for a moment of partially determining self-creativity. Eros exists automatically, in the process view, where God has never been alone; instead, there has always been God and some World, or other, of simplistic finite particles akin to the subatomic particles of today's physics. If there has always been a plurality of entities, then there has always been *eros*.

The question becomes, if God is love, then *in what sense* precisely? If not eros, then philia? Agape? Perhaps even storge? What sort of love is God? If he were truly unconditional love, then why are all his covenants conditional and on a *quid pro quo* basis, at least in the Tanakh? Why is one group of people singled out as chosen? Why are only certain individuals worthy or ritually pure enough to enter the tent of meeting and the holy of holies? Why is the policy of herem (God sanctioned genocide?) enacted in Jericho? The Torah expresses clear conditions for being worthy to be in God's 'loving' presence.

This line of argument can be extended into the New Testament as well: slavery is accepted,[4] the role of women is hardly equal,[5] and even Jesus has an inner circle who are given special instruction not for outsiders.[6] If God is love, he does not seem to fit the typical *agape* model, so what term best describes his love?

The best version of God that we can find, expressing his character throughout the Bible as a whole, is *storge*. After all, is he not *Abba*? Storge is a family oriented love and affection. God is consistently described as our heavenly father, but surprisingly, the use of *storge* is limited in Scripture.[7]

Our father would and should protect us from getting raped or blown up by bombers. Why can my biological father do this, but God cannot? This uncontrolling love seems to run the risk of being more unworthy of worship than the process-relational solution of multiple ultimates that imposes a fundamental and necessary limitation on God. Oord states:

Creation differs from God in that free creatures are free both in deciding whether to love and in deciding how to express love. They do not have eternal natures in which love is preeminent and necessary. Because of this, for instance, creatures can choose sin and do evil. God's nature is love, however. This means God can neither sin nor do evil. But God can both want to love us and love us necessarily because love is essential.[8]

I fully concur that creation, including humans, are capable of freely deciding to love and how they want to express it, but I would add that God *must also be free to love or not, at least in terms of philia, storge, and agape.* It would seem very odd if we can do what God cannot (i.e. choose not to love.) It is true, as Oord masterfully summarizes, that Anselm, Aquinas and others have noted that logical contradictions are not genuine limitations on God's sovereignty, but choosing not to love does not seem logically contradictory. Choosing not to love is a far cry from making a stone so heavy that even God himself cannot lift it, or changing the past.

Isn't choice the fundamental aspect of genuine love? If one had no choice but to love, could we call this perfect love at all? I agree that, "In fact, I believe it is impossible to worship wholeheartedly a God who loves halfheartedly," but a God who cannot choose *not* to love seems, perhaps, halfhearted.[9]

Another phrase Oord frequently uses is, 'other empowering love.' I like this phrase, but if we are to be true to it, does not other empowering love suggest at least a degree of acceptance of what different peoples and cultures have experienced concerning ultimate reality? A quick survey of the world's religions makes it clear that there are genuinely diverse beliefs concerning the object or objects of religious ultimacy, as well as the nature of salvation from the human condition.

How can we incorporate religious pluralism within the framework of *creatio ex nihilo* and a one ultimate system? I just do not see how one can do this without resorting to the Trinity in some bizarre way like S. Mark Heim did or ranking religions like Hegel did or saying that on the esoteric level they are all the same, the approach of the perennial philosophy.[10] However, the claim that there always have been multiple components comprising ultimate reality allows for a genuine plurality of views to be correct and also to do justice to currently popular metaphors like ecosystems for understanding the God/World relationship.

I believe Oord's response to this question can be found in the following.

The other view standing near essential kenosis says external forces or worlds essentially limit God. This view gives the impression that outside actors and powers not of God's making hinder divine power. Or it says God is subject to laws of nature, imposed upon God from without. God is caught in the clutches of exterior authorities and dominions, and these superpowers restrict sovereignty. This view seems to describe God as a helpless victim to external realities. Some criticize this view as presenting a 'finite God' because outside forces or imposed laws curb divine activity. Many wonder how this God can be worthy of worship. While I think we have good reasons to think God's power is limited in certain respects, this view places God under a foreign authority. This God is too small.[11]

However, the real question for me is not whether this God is too small, but whether this picture of multiple religious ultimates is the most accurate to our current accounts of religious experience, to global religious scriptures, and to current science.

Darren Iammarino is a process theologian and professor of humanities and religious studies at San Diego Mesa College where he teaches world religions, New Testament and Old Testament. His most recent book, Religion and Reality: An Exploration of Contemporary Metaphysical Systems, Theologies, and Religious Pluralism, explores many of the themes covered in the above material and can be found on amazon. He can also be reached on Instagram: @driammarino

Endnotes

1. I Jn. 4:8 (NIV).
2. Thomas Jay Oord, *The Uncontrolling Love of God* (Downers Grove: IVP Academic, 2016), 49.
3. Darren Iammarino, *Religion and Reality: An Exploration of Contemporary Metaphysical Systems, Theologies, and Religious Pluralism* (Eugene: Pickwick, 2013).
4. Eph. 6:5-8, I Tim. 6:1-2
5. Eph. 5:22, I Tim. 2:11-15, I Cor. 11:2-10
6. Mark 4:10-12
7. 4 Macc. 14:13-15:13, Rom. 12:10
8. Oord, 162.
9. Oord, 68.
10. Cf. S. Mark Heim, *The Depth of the Riches: A Trinitarian Theology of Religious Ends* (Grand Rapids: Eerdmans, 2000); Hegel, *Lectures on the Philosophy of Religion* (Oxford: Oxford University Press: 2006); Huston Smith, *Forgotten Truth: The Common Vision of the World's Religions* (San Francisco: HarperOne, 1997).
11. Oord, 164.

Why Relational Theism Really Matters

Tyron Inbody

N othing happens that is not the will of God."
    This claim is the reassurance offered by many Christian pastors and counselors and friends in times of horrible suffering. It is also the logical conclusion of classical Christian theism.

An aunt dies at age 45 of uterine cancer, a teenage daughter is killed by a drunk driver in a head on collision, a housing bubble bursts and you lose your house and retirement plan at age 55, a plane crashes because of birds sucked into an engine, genocide is carried out in Syria—these are horrible events. But for many Christians these are not chance or meaningless events, because God willed them. Therefore, we should accept them and give thanks to God for these moments of apparent evil. God willed them, and God's will is always good.

These events are not genuinely evil; the evils are only apparent.[1] They are part of God's perfect plan. They have their place in the infallibly good will of God and so are not genuine evils (our lives would not have been better off without these as moments in God's will).

As hard as this assurance is to accept in moments of suffering, we are assured they are not meaningless, even though we cannot discern the purpose now or even ever. This, I am convinced, is the most powerful difficulty—the most powerful argument *against* accepting the teaching of classical theism.

The problem is this: although divine determinism may be logically possible and compatible with our freedom, it is not plausible if we believe in genuine freedom. Freedom is not merely the absence of external coercion (a gun to my head).

Freedom means we are active agents, among other agencies including God, in what happens in our lives.

Consequently, many Christians are left with a dilemma: either give thanks for what we cannot give thanks for, or conclude there is no God who is compatible with human freedom. Atheism often springs from this very quandary, and here I agree with the atheists. Why believe in and worship such a God?

The fact is, however, that there is a concept of God which avoids this impasse. It is more biblical, more theologically sound, and more compatible with our lives as we live them daily. The heartbreak is that most Christians are not aware of this more plausible concept of God.

My argument is that Thomas Jay Oord's *The Uncontrolling Love of God* (along with other versions of relational theism) provides a genuine alternative, superior to classical theism. This is a matter of life and death in the theology and practice of pastors, counselors, and members of the Christian community. I say this for three reasons:

First—a Christian view of creation

Relational theism, open theism, and process theology are consistent with the beliefs and experience of the Christian life. What possible difference could intercessory prayer make, if God is aseity, nontemporal, impassible, and controlling—if all things are already 'actual,' 'decided,' or 'real,' in the life of God? Furthermore, what can love mean apart from essential relationship, mutual response-ability between God and us? Love by definition means reciprocity and requires a degree of freedom. An unfeeling, unmoved being cannot love in any meaningful sense of the term. Classical theism empties the love of God of any meaning.

An implication of relational theism, with significant succor for personal and pastoral counsel, is that not everything that happens is the will of God. A notion of creation with a degree of freedom, particularly evident at the human level, is that openness to the future, novelty, emergence, chance, randomness, and luck are elements in a creation that moves from divine possibility to creatural wellbeing and meaning.

Why did my daughter die of SIDS, my mother die of cancer at 39 years of age? Why did a tornado destroy my village? Why did this bad thing happen to me?

The answer is not because God willed these for some mysterious reason.

Within the sustaining power of God of the whole creation, with the good genes we inherited and the strong family background we received, and some wise decisions we made; our lives include an abundance of good. But in a world with a degree of genuine freedom, in the process of creation from simple to complex, from minimal value to more complex meaning; a finite creation also includes chance and bad luck. There is a tragic structure to a world of creativity, novelty, and an open future.[2] Sin and tragedy intermingle with the basic goodness of life. God has a will for *every* event of the developing creation, but although God loves and lures creation; God does not control any event.

We experience pain because pain receptors are stimulated by an anomaly inside the body or violence outside the body. Body tissues become too hard or too soft because of genetic coding or stress or diet and so restrict the blood supply or burst causing strokes or heart attacks. The immune system if weakened by defective genes, diet, stress, radiation, or environmental factors; succumbs to bacteria, viruses, or causes cells to expand at an uncontrolled pace. These things occur because of the kind of world God has created, and is creating, instead of the claim that God is punishing us for Adam and Eve's sin or to educate us for spiritual maturity or, if none of this works satisfactorily, for some mysterious reason.

Second—the biblical God

Relational theism is more faithful to the full biblical witness, and especially to the christological focus of scripture, than is classical theism. To be sure, there are verses and stories that seem plausibly to imply an omnipotent controller of history and each life, along with much of the tradition of the church. Traditional theism is not at all a groundless theology. Many of the brilliant doctors of the church have advocated and defended it.[3]

But the Bible is shaped by images of God as repentant (changing direction), broken-hearted, filled with pain and sorrow, and above all loving and desiring love and human well-being in a creation that is not yet shalom.[4]

Above all, however, the life of Jesus, the incarnation, and a triune understanding of God all imply relationship *within* God and *between* God who loves the world and gives God's self to it in unconditional and uncontrolling love. This is not a God who is eternal (beyond time) but is everlasting as pure unbounded love and faithfulness, luring and responsive to the creature.

Third—conceptual plausibility

Relational theism is conceptually superior to classical theism in the light of this understanding of God.

Given the distinction between possibility, plausibility, and certainty, I admit classical theism is logically possible, at least if you can baldly assert 'compatibility' (divine omnipotence and human freedom simply are compatible—just accept it and claim it is not self-contradictory). I find this nonsense if human freedom means agency and not simply absence of external coercion.

Few Christians want to argue absolute certainty about any concept of God. Rather, the question is what kind of theism is most *plausible* in the light of scripture, experience, tradition, and reason. Traditional theism is simply spiritually and conceptually beyond my boggle point!

That God acts to promote the healing and well-being of the whole creation is clear in scripture and consistent with a good and loving God. But that God wills, causes, permits, or allows the suffering of the world seems to me to be spiritual and conceptual gobbledygook. God and we create the world together (although by no means in equal ways).

Any theology that does not enhance that co-creation, in service of the well-being of life, is incompatible with God as creator, redeemer, and sanctifier. It matters what kind of theist one is! Relational theism is not a theology just for professional theologians like Oord, Sanders, or Cobb, but for every Christian pastor, counselor, and member of the body of Christ who loves God and seeks the healing and well-being of the whole creation in the midst of genuine suffering and evil.

Tyron Inbody is Professor Emeritus of Theology at United Theological Seminary in Dayton, Ohio. He is the author of four books, including The Transforming God: An Interpretation of Suffering and Evil. He is married for 55 years, has two sons and two grandsons, and enjoys reading, world travel, photography, and any excuse to be with his grandsons.

Endnotes

1. David Griffin, *God, Power, and Evil* (Philadelphia: The Westminster Press, 1976), 21-29.
2. Wendy Farley, *Tragic Vision and Divine Compassion* (Louisville: Westminster/John

Knox Press, 1990), chap 1, and Terrence Fretheim, *The Suffering of God: An Old Testament Perspective* (Philadelphia: Fortress Press, 1984), 123-26, 146, and Jon Levenson, *Creation and the Persistence of* Evil (New York: Harper & Row, 1988), chap 12.

3. John Hick, *Evil and the God of Love* (New York: Harper & Row, 1978), chaps 3-4.

4. Walter Brueggemann, *Old Testament Theology: Essays on Structure, Theme, and Text* (Minneapolis: Fortress Press, 1992).

On the Uncontrolling Love of God

Catherine Keller

A friend describes a process she learned as a mother: "I never did try to control my kids, there were too many of them to do that. I had three children in two years, and it became very clear early on (such as day one), that control was not possible. Instead of getting in their way and trying to run their play, I had to arrive at some other mode of being with them as they are."

So she invited friends over for them to play with, and chaos mounted. But this is what she observed: "If I were willing and able to let the four or five very young children jostle, master round, explore for about 45 minutes—with the ground rules of not hurting each other or the home—if I just let them go through whatever procedures they needed to go through, they would come up with something that they loved to do together. They would arrive at some game, project, make-believe . . . That would keep them positively, joyfully engaged for up to three hours. All of them."

This is a humble parable of creation from chaos. It illustrates uncontrolling love.

Parents and all who relate in love have to 'let be.' So do good teachers, pastors, and leaders, as *Elohim* 'let be' the light. John McQuarrie defines 'letting be' as something much more positive than just leaving alone: "as enabling to be, empowering to be, or bringing into being." Thus our experience of 'letting be' may serve as an analogy of 'the ultimate letting-be.'

Love does not control. It opens up the space of becoming. The space is not without protective boundaries, not without rules.

The healthy parent is not merely permissive but constantly teaching ideals of fairness, cooperation, and creative development. This space comprises neither rampant disorder nor imposed order. It opens at the edge of chaos, without plunging into the abyss. It supports the free play of relations—and satisfies desires of both parent and children. This uncontrolling care empowers the children to construct their own 'complex self-organizing system.' At least temporarily!

If I may push our parable a bit further, the desired interplay is not about a private 'me and my God' relation but a love—open and out—into a fuller sociality. "Two or more gathered in my name."[1] In the communality of Genesis things are risky, noisy, and messy. But fresh order continues to emerge from the chaos. And while its equilibria do not last forever—"love never ends."[2]

Does God just *choose* not to interfere with our freedom? The so-called free-will defense of God's goodness and omnipotence tries that middle road: God permits, but does not cause evil, and so leaves us our freedom. This is close to the chilly deism Calvin railed against.

But usually those who hold this reasonable view also hold out for occasional special or miraculous interventions on God's part. But then: Why didn't God manipulate the vote just a bit so that Hitler would lose the election? Or, for that matter, heal my friend's little sister's leukemia? Or excise that bad gene in the first place? Or all bad genes?

The free-will defense only works if held consistently. But that is hard to do. To say God 'permits' evil for the sake of our freedom implies that God *could* step in at any time, and as far as history demonstrates, just chooses not to.

The alternative to omnipotence lies in the risky interactivity of relationship. It does not toss the creatures into a deistic void, chilled but autonomous. It continues to call them forth, to invite . . . The power of God, if it is response-able power, *empowers* the others—to respond, in their freedom.

In what sense then is the divine *powerful*? It can perhaps even be called all-powerful, if that language for the biblical God seems indispensable to some, in this sense: God has 'all the power' that a good God, a God who fosters and delights in the goodness of the creation, could have or want to have.

But the point is that this is not the unilateral power to command things to happen out of nothing and then to control them under threat of nothingness. It is another kind of power altogether, a *qualitatively different power*—a power that seems weak when dominance is the ideal.

The metaphor of "power perfected in weakness" tried to make comprehensible the difficult alternative to coercive force: the contagious influence that flows from a radically vulnerable strength.[3] Two thousand years later, we have made limited collective progress in its realization. Perhaps experiments in social democracy, in which persuasion is favored over coercion and care valued as a supreme public strength, hint at the alternative. Perhaps experiments in gender equality and nonviolent parenting are also advancing, here and there, our metaphoric reservoir.

The One who calls forth good even from the ashes of evil, a good that requires—indeed commands—but cannot coerce our cooperation, is a power that *makes possible* our response.

From On the Mystery: Discerning God in Process pp. 88-90 copyright © 2007 Fortress Press. Reproduced by permission. For a more complete treatment of the subject consider purchase of the book, which may be found at: http://fortresspress.com/product/mystery -discerning-divinity-process

Catherine Keller is Professor of Constructive Theology at The Theological School of Drew University. She's the author or editor of more than a dozen books, her latest being Cloud of the Impossible: Negative Theology and Planetary Entanglement. New York: Columbia University Press, 2015.

Endnotes

1. See Matthew 18:20
2. I Cor. 13:8 (ESV).
3. See II Cor. 12:9

All a Part of the Plan

Graden Kirksey

We've all heard the sayings before: "There's no way to understand, because God's ways are just higher than our ways." "Everything happens for a reason." "It's all just a part of God's plan."

These statements say a great deal about how we view God and God's activity in the world. I do not deny God's ways are higher than our ways; however, I would contend, what we do with this scripture is not its intended purpose.[1] These sayings paint a picture of God that says God literally has everything under complete control. Nothing goes contrary to God's desires or 'plan.' When something difficult or painful happens, we are expected to accept, even though we can't see it now, that God has preordained the event to happen to achieve His purposes.

The problem lies in what happens when we take this understanding of God and apply it to our lives. If everything is all a part of the 'plan,' then my life does not make sense, nor do the other countless horrors occurring around the world each day.

Oord calls the experiences in question "genuine evils."[2] These are events with no redeeming qualities. He says, "Some evils are character destroying rather than character building."[3]

Our challenge as Christians is not to tell a story existing on the pages of a book, no matter how holy the book may be. Our call is to spread the word given for our everyday lives; therefore, any belief we have in God must be in agreement with the lives we lead and share together.

In the case of genuine evil, we don't have the luxury of adjusting our lives. No one wants to experience hurt or pain or loss. Instead, we have to find a view of God that agrees with what we experience day in and day out.

For me, it all started in 2008 while I was in seminary. This was the year we lost our son, Josiah, to a rare genetic condition. He was our miracle, our child of promise, and he was gone. In an instant, I was forced to reconsider my relationship with God and my theology. The God I thought I understood vaporized, and I wasn't left with much. I knew facts and could quote verses; however, none of my understandings of God lined up with the very painful reality I had to face.

I would never suggest God wanted such a thing to take place, any more than I would suggest God desired the Holocaust. The Bible tells us "God is love," and there are countless events throughout history that simply cannot be attributed to God if that is true.[4]

Saying God is love is not a comment on how God has treated someone. It is a statement about His very being. God cannot choose when He loves and when He does not love. God always acts the way perfect love would act. Oord rightly states, "A perfectly loving individual would do whatever possible to prevent—not just fail to cause—genuine evil."[5] For a perfectly loving God, "even one instance of genuine evil is one too many."[6]

I'm convinced the root of all of God's action is love. How do we deal with the all-loving, all-powerful, omnipresent God who fails to deliver us from evil? That is the question resting on the lips of all who have walked the dark and lonely path of inexplicable pain or loss. Church is not always the most inviting place when we question long standing beliefs, especially beliefs concerning topics as uncomfortable as this. The default reaction is to tread water as long as possible, hoping the barrage of doubts and questions will cease.

Fortunately for the church, the questions generally do cease, but at great cost. Often, the hurt and damaged find themselves without a home, let down and dismayed. Many leave the church altogether. Others eventually fade into the background.

What if I were to say God is all-loving and all-powerful and all-knowing and omnipresent *and* He doesn't have to control everything? It may sound scary to consider at first, but I believe it is the only way to reconcile our view of God with what we all readily know to be the common human experience.

In the church, we often fear anything other than complete control will in some way weaken God. We prioritize power because it is what impresses us and, in our extensive attempts to maintain 'everything is going according to plan,' our brothers and sisters are plagued by the thought that God's desire was for them to experience their nightmares.

Consider trying to explain the divine plan behind the loss of an infant. I can tell you from experience this endeavor does not end well. Try telling a young girl her rape was God's desired path for her. The emotional and physical baggage she must carry with her the rest of her life is simply her lot as prescribed by God Almighty. Such things are unthinkable, but they are exactly the corner in which we put ourselves when we hold to this traditional view of providence.

True love does not force itself on the beloved, nor does it force the beloved to do what it desires. That is what selfishness and hate look like. "A controlling God of love is fictional."[7]

Accountability and responsibility are real. How we live and the decisions we make affect us and those around us. We aren't more important than God, but God, out of His unending love, has seen fit for us to live in such a way that matters, a way where we have the privilege to return and share His love or choose to oppose and possibly even stand in His way. A lesser god would shove us aside and show us who's boss, but not our God. Instead, He is willing to risk the hurt and the likelihood that what He desires will, at least at times, not be what transpires.

We need to understand God is not up in the clouds or on His throne with popcorn in hand awaiting His favorite parts of history to occur. He is here. He is with us. He is Emmanuel.

It is not impressive to consider God controlling His creation. Anyone can do that. However, it is amazing to see the Creator being counted among, and suffering alongside, His creation. Truly, "Greater love has no one than this."[8]

Howard Graden Kirksey IV is a computer programmer and evangelist from Tennessee. He is an ordained minister in the Church of God (Cleveland, TN) and received his M.Div. from the Pentecostal Theological Seminary. In his spare time, he studies theology, especially theodicy. He also loves spending time with his wife, Sabrina, and two children, Silas and Ella.

Endnotes

1. See Isa. 55:9 (NIV).

2. Thomas Jay Oord, *The Uncontrolling Love of God: An Open and Relational Account of Providence* (Downers Grove: InterVarsity Press, 2016), 64.

3. Oord, 25.

4. I John 4:8b

5. Oord, 67.

6. Oord, 64.

7. Oord, 181.

8. John 15:13a

Getting Our Priorities Right

Todd Littleton

How do we set our priorities in order?

Christian couples sit through pre-marital counseling. They are advised to set priorities for their marriage, their family, their future. Many will hear the tried list of priorities without much explanation: God, family, others, and self. Any one of these may become an idol if the pursuit of one undermines what is prior. But, just what *is* prior?

Small cities make decisions about what matters most. If road conditions rise to the level of an important infrastructure need, money will be budgeted for this purpose. Most often, these funds come from another area, so to fail to allocate money for roads is to declare something else as a greater priority. It would be rare, indeed, to have enough resources to meet every need. What matters most?

In *The Divine Conspiracy*, Dallas Willard explicated the Sermon on the Mount to the conclusion that learning to value others would result in a "community of prayerful love."[1] Missing *the gospel* for *the gospel of sin management* resulted in the lack of both prayer *and* love. Sometimes priorities are dependent upon one another.

Intentionally or unintentionally, everyone sets priorities. Couples, cities, and communities reveal what is important when they express their respective priorities. What if our understanding of God could impact our world more profoundly, on all levels, if we got this right? What if we took a second look at God's revelation to human beings and learned that love isn't just another attribute. Instead, love must be first.

The Scriptures reveal certain themes related to God's activity in and with the world. These came to be described as attributes—actions or attitudes characteristic of the revealed God. Many of us learned these attributes of God as a means to knowledge. We wanted to know something *about* God. But what if we took the time to know God, *Godself*, filtering these attributes through the life of Jesus, the Christ. Tripp Fuller simplifies this notion by asserting that God has to be at least as nice as Jesus.[2]

It is startling to realize that wrath and love often occupy the same plane when the list of divine attributes is given. Love does not sit atop the list. Could it be that the loving-kindness of God that leads to repentance is simply one attribute among many? Jesus de-centered the powers of the world by centering on the God who *so loved* the world.[3] How is it, then, that those who inherit that great tradition often view love as ordinary or merely one part of who God is?

Thomas Jay Oord challenges the former articulations of divine action by calling attention to what must be prior: love. Love is *not* one attribute among many. Instead, love is the priority that frames *all* other attributes. Take, for instance, the fixation on the power of God. Many modern notions of power describe a love that is in service to power. Oord paints a different picture, one of power in service to love. It is the Jesus Story.

Love as the first priority applies to the essential nature of God. Oord describes an understanding of God asserting that if God was capable of being unloving, God would cease to be God. Put differently, when we tell someone God is love, we say that God relentlessly pursues all with the goal of universal well-being. God persuades in such a way that God encourages all of creation to be self-giving rather than self-asserting. God's loving relationship to all things is prior: love itself is prior to all attributes.

The interest of this essay is to contend that a human understanding that love is prior to all priorities sets the world up for life of a different sort. Couples, cities, and communities simply provide a framework for thinking about how first priority love might form human decisions differently than the traditional, or current, view that the most important attribute of God is power.

With this in mind, maybe we would find a different starting point with those young couples coming for pre-marital counseling. Rather than asking them to map out a ten year plan, or negotiating between their different hobbies and pastimes, we could ask them to commit *first* to love, in *all* things. Love should not only be a priority *somewhere* on the list.

What if Christian involvement in politics, down to the city that is looking to set its infrastructure priorities, first asked, "What is the most loving thing I could do?"

Mapping the needs of the city, taking the most loving action into consideration, may bring a community to focus on everyone's needs rather than the needs of just a few.

Consider our churches, those communities of faith. What impact would they have in the world if their first course of action centered on what is most loving rather than what is most holy? One may discover that the most holy thing to do would also be the most loving thing conceived.

"God's ways are not our ways" is a phrase often used to help human beings accept mystery. What if, instead, this statement could be used to draw our attention to the call to love first?

Todd Littleton continues to serve as pastor with the same church in Oklahoma for more than 22 years. He has an interest in the pastor as theologian. He writes and podcasts at toddlittleton.net. In his spare time, Todd enjoys fly fishing and jeeping in the Colorado Mountains.

Endnotes

1. Dallas Willard, *The Divine Conspiracy: Rediscovering Our Hidden Life in God* (San Francisco, CA: Harper Collins, 1998), 215-269.

2. Tripp Fuller, *Homebrewed Christianity Guide to Jesus: Lord, Liar, Lunatic or Awesome?* (Minneapolis, MN: Fortress Press, 2015), 102.

3. See John 3:16 (NIV).

Randomness and the Sovereignty of God

Cameron McCown

Frequently in our lives, we encounter events that seem to be random. A tornado rips through a town that hasn't seen one in 30 years. A child is born into poverty instead of into wealth. A woman contracts cancer and beats it, only to contract cancer again.

Sometimes, however, events happen that also seem random but work in our favor. A person finds $10 lying on the sidewalk. A woman becomes pregnant with a long-desired baby when the doctor says there is no hope. A family is delayed only to discover that if they had left on time, they would have been in a serious accident.

Is there some grander design? Is someone pulling the strings? Are we at the mercy of a world that, however predictable it might be, is ultimately full of undetermined processes and events?

We attach reason to randomness, because we try to make rational sense out of a world in which we desire control. Even the most powerful among us must at some point admit we do not have ultimate power. So we turn to God. Surely God has control if we do not. Surely there is intention even in the most seemingly random events around us.

As I grapple with the notion of God's essential nature being uncontrolling love rather than controlling power, I realize that I have to let go of the idea that God sends $10 bills my way and delays me so I won't be in a wreck. I do not think God ensured I was born in America instead of Africa or sent Hurricane Katrina to destroy parts of New Orleans. I simply don't think it makes sense for me to attribute either good or bad results of these events to God.

I find it much more constructive and satisfying to admit the following: Randomness is real. Life is full of chance.

So where does this put the sovereignty of God? If randomness is real, God might not be in control. Randomness is not more powerful than God. Randomness is simply a result of the kind of world that would best respond to a loving God.

Webster defines sovereignty as "possessing supreme or ultimate power."[1] Randomness is defined as, "without a particular plan or pattern."[2] Every effect may have a cause, but an immediate cause doesn't mean ultimate intention.

Thomas Jay Oord, in his book, *The Uncontrolling Love of God*, addresses God's mightiness and power in the following way: 1) God is mightier than all others, 2) God is the only one who exerts might upon all that exists, and 3) God is the ultimate source of might for all others.[3]

For God to have ultimate power means nothing is more powerful than God. There is good reason to affirm this. Far from being powerless or weak, God can be the most powerful being but still necessarily influence the creation of a world that includes randomness.

Why would this world be the world God influences? A loving God would be intimately a part of such a world, because it's the only kind of world with which a fair and loving God can co-create. I think randomness is the epitome of fairness. So to influence the creation of a world in which fairness exists, randomness would have to be part of that creation.

To explore this more deeply, imagine you had a set of die cut so that the 5 came up more often than the other numbers. Then six people each bet a set amount on a specific number to be rolled. The person who bet on the 5 would win more than the others, because the result of the roll was not truly random. Therefore, it would not be fair.

God's co-creation with humanity includes cooperation with what God would like to do in every given moment. Determinism, design, and dictatorship therefore seem to be off the table.

Randomness, chance, and free will are part of God's nature of love that is uncontrolling, noncoercive, and others-empowering. God gives creation freedom to cooperate fully with what God would like to do, and it is up to us to respond to that calling.

✎

Cameron McCown is a graduate of Baylor University and eight-year veteran of the U.S. Army. An advocate of open and relational theology, Cameron lives in Meridian, Idaho with his wife Robin and works in the field of finance.

Endnotes

1. *Merriam-Webster, s.v.* "sovereignty," accessed May 19, 2016, https://www.merriam -webster.com/dictionary/sovereignty.
2. *Merriam-Webster, s.v.* "random," accessed May 19, 2016, https://www.merriam -webster.com/dictionary/random.
3. See Thomas Jay Oord, *The Uncontrolling Love of God: An Open and Relational Account of Providence* (Downers Grove, IL: InterVarsity, 2015), 189-190.

The Uncontrolling Love of God: A Mormon Approach

James McLachlan

L et me say immediately, this is a Mormon's view of the Uncontrolling Love of God. It is not *the* Mormon view. Although I think most Mormons would view God's love as uncontrolling, I expect that many Mormons would find my view of God's uncontrolling love unacceptable. Unlike many of our Christian brothers and sisters, Mormons have no creed. This goes back to early statements of Joseph Smith who repeatedly repudiated the idea of creeds. For example:

"I cannot believe in any of the creeds of the different denominations, because they all have some things in them I cannot subscribe to, though all of them have some truth. I want to come up into the presence of God, and learn all things; but the creeds set up stakes, and say, 'Hitherto shalt thou come, and no further;' which I cannot subscribe to."[1]

In the 19th century, Mormons did talk about something they called the 'Mormon Creed' that was simply 'mind your own business.' Yet Mormons have been tried for heresy, and there is a certain uniformity in doctrine. However, on the whole, Mormonism favors orthopraxis over orthodoxy. I say all this merely to emphasize that there is a certain fluidity to Mormon theology that creedal Christians find odd. So although the position I'm putting forth here is Mormon, it shouldn't be taken as orthodox.

In the 1960s, Mormon philosopher Sterling McMurrin claimed that Mormonism was, "in principle basically non-absolutistic."[2] This did not mean that in their everyday discourse Mormons didn't talk about God using the same absolutist terms as other Christians, only that their idea of God would not let them do so consistently. From the pulpit, Western Religions love to talk about the eternal, infinite, omniscient, and omnipotent Deity. It's language of praise for the ultimate. People often don't seem to want to take their problems to a God who has problems of His/Her own. McMurrin said Mormonism was guilty of, "lusting for the linguistic fleshpots of orthodoxy and is turning its back on its own best insights."[3]

I share much with Thomas Jay Oord's view of the uncontrolling love of God. As a young man I was deeply disturbed by the pulpit claims in my church of God's all-controlling power. It seemed to me that people were more likely to worship power than goodness. These claims seemed coupled with the claim that whenever a horrible event happened, it was all a part of God's plan and this plan would sooner or later be forced on the inhabitants of the world through a powerful apocalyptic event. Later I read the Russian Orthodox theologian Nicolas Berdyaev who dubbed this kind of thinking, "the moral source of atheism."[4] By the time I was 19 and thinking about serving a Mormon mission; I had pretty well given up belief in God. Voltaire, Mark Twain, and Ivan Karamazov made much more sense to me than what I thought was my tradition. I became a Mormon missionary at age 19, not because of any profound belief in God and Mormonism; I just loved my parents.

As a missionary, I repeatedly read Joseph Smith's 1844 *King Follet Discourse*. Smith explicitly rejected creation ex nihilo and affirmed creation from chaos contending that God, "organized the world from chaotic matter as a human being might organize materials and build a ship."[5] "Hence, we infer that God had materials to organize the world out of chaos, chaotic matter . . ."[6] In traditional forms of theism, Creation ex nihilo protects the power, knowledge, and transcendence of God. In giving up Creation Ex Nihilo, Mormons essentially give up the absolutism of God. They also give up God's utter transcendence of space and time and place God within the struggle with chaos and suffering. God calls humanity to help create a just and loving world.

In *Joseph Smith, Jesus and Satanic Opposition: Atonement, Evil and the Mormon Vision,* Douglas Davies claims, "It is this presence that poses Mormonism's strategic yet apologetic dilemma of 'otherness,' of wanting to be accepted as Christian by the wider Christian world while not accepting that world's definition of Christianity . . ."[7] Mormon theologies, even in their most conservative versions, don't see God as completely ontologically distinct from human beings. God is involved in the same struggle. Still, Mormons often want to keep some of the traditional attributes of God. But they end up redefining them. Omnipotence, for example, has been used in Mormon writings to mean almighty or all the power that a being can possess given they exist alongside other self-existing, free beings that logically limit omnipotence. Like Process Theologians, Mormons can claim that just as most creedal Christians and traditional theists place limits on omnipotence, when they define it as doing what is logically possible, this means that God is limited by the activity of other free beings. The thought seems to be if omnipotence is limited by logic by traditional theists; why not also claim that it is just as inconsistent to say that God could force beings to act against their freedom as to say that God could create a square circle. The first statement is to misunderstand freedom as the second is to misunderstand geometry. Thus God is understood as having all the power any being could have and is thus in religious terms 'almighty.'

Coupled with this is an idea that love can and will triumph over evil. Moral evil has its source in human egoism—the desire to control others. Jean-Paul Sartre characterized the basic human project as "the desire to be God."[8] This is the desire to control the freedom of others, and thus "Hell is other people."[9] A good deal of religious zeal has been spent imposing our worldview on others. This results in chaos and destruction. Ekaputra Tupamahu, in his essay for this collection, "The Decolonial Love of God," captures the problem. If we worship power and authority we seek to see that power imposed on the world. In Sartre's terms we create Hell. If, instead, we worship, love, and care; we might help God create a world fit for all Her/His children.

James McLachlan is professor of philosophy and religion at Western Carolina University. He is past co-chair of the Mormon Studies Group at the American Academy of Religion, and organizer of the Personalist Seminar. He has assisted as co-chair Levinas Philosophy Summer Seminars, in Vilnius, Buffalo, Berkeley, and Rome and is co-director of the NEH Summer Seminar on Levinas at the University at Buffalo summer 2017. His recent publications have dealt with concepts of Hell in existentialism, Satan and demonic evil in Boehme, Schelling, and Dostoevsky, and the problem of Evil in Mormonism. He is currently working on a study of Emmanuel Levinas and the existentialists.

Endnotes

1. Joseph Fielding Smith ed., *Teachings of the Prophet Joseph Smith* (Salt Lake City: Deseret, 1938), 57.

2. Sterling S. McMurrin, *Theological Foundations of the Mormon Religion* (Salt Lake City: University of Utah Press, 1964), 35-40.

3. Sterling S. McMurrin, "Comments on the Theological and Philosophical Foundations of Christianity." *Dialogue: A Journal of Mormon Thought* Vol 25, No. 1. (March 1992) pp. 37-47.

4. Nicolas Berdyaev, *The Destiny of Man*, trans. Natalie Duddington (New York: Harper and Row, 1960), 32.

5. Smith, 350.

6. *Ibid.*

7. Douglas Davies, *Joseph Smith, Jesus, and Satanic Opposition: Atonement, Evil, and the Mormon Vision* (Farnham, UK: 2010), 228.

8. Jean-Paul Sartre, *Being and Nothingness: An Essay in Phenomenological Ontology*, trans. Hazel Barnes (New York: Philosophical Library, 1948), 694.

9. Jean-Paul Sartre, *No Exit and Three Other Plays* (New York: Vintage, 1989), 45.

God and Time

R.T. Mullins

In *The Uncontrolling Love of God,* Thomas Jay Oord rejects the traditional claim that God is timeless, and instead affirms that God is in time or temporal. Oord refers to this as God's time-full existence. To more traditional Christian ears, this will sound incredible. I believe that the incredulity arises from a misunderstanding of several issues related to the nature of time and God's eternal nature. In this short essay, I seek to clear up some of these issues so that readers can more fully engage with Oord's doctrine of God.

The Nature of Time

The notion of time is a notoriously difficult philosophical issue. For the purposes of this essay, I shall note two traditional claims about the nature of time (what is time?) and the ontology of time (what moments of time exist?).

What is time? Time has traditionally been understood to have a close relationship to change. The idea here is that if there is a change, there is time. Change creates a before and an after in the world. Part of the nature of time is its constant flow of one moment after another. Christian theologians and philosophers have overwhelmingly affirmed this close relationship between time and change. There has been dissent from this opinion, which I discuss in my book, *The End of the Timeless God.*[1] For the sake of brevity, I will not discuss that dissent here. What matters for our purposes is the way Christians have traditionally understood this connection between time and change. For traditional Christian theologians, a being is in time if it undergoes change. A being is timeless if it does not change in any way, shape, or form.

What moments of time exist? Traditionally, Christians have affirmed a position called *presentism*. Presentism says that only the present moment of time exists. The past no longer exists, and the future does not yet exist. This can be contrasted with a view called *eternalism*, which says that the past, present, and future moments of time all exist equally. On presentism, the present exhausts all of reality. All that exists, exists at the present. Whereas on eternalism, things exist at other times, and those times are just as real as any other moment.

Eternalism is fairly new in Christian history. Most Christians did not consider it a live option for theology until after Einstein's theory of relativity became mainstream. In fact, I am not aware of any major Christian theologian who denies presentism prior to the 1800's. Presentism has a long track-record in Christian history, and has had a major influence on the way Christians have articulated their theology. This influence continues today with the rise of relational and open theism.

What is a Timeless God?

With the brief statement on time above, we can start to understand a bit about God's relation to time. As I said before, Christians have traditionally claimed that God is timeless. What did they mean by this? Christians have traditionally said that God exists in a timeless present that lacks a before and after. What does this mean? Well, recall the close connection between time and change. Christians have traditionally wished to say that God cannot change. As such, God cannot have a before and after in His life. God experiences His life all at once in a present that is sort of like ours, but in a timeless present that lacks a before and after.

Here is another traditional way to state divine timelessness. God is timeless if and only if God a) never begins to exist, b) never ceases to exist, and c) lacks succession. The 'lacks succession' claim is essential to God being timeless. Beings that exist in time experience a succession of moments. We experience one moment after another. If God is timeless, God does not experience one moment after another. Instead, He enjoys all of His life at once in a timeless present that lacks a before and after.

What is a Temporal God?

The claim that God is in time has caused some controversy in the 20th and 21st Centuries. I think most, though not all, of this controversy is due to a basic misunderstanding of the claim that God is in time. For instance, some theologians worry that if God is in time, then God is not really eternal. This is false. Those who affirm that God is temporal, affirm that God is eternal. What they deny is that God is *timelessly* eternal. All it takes for a being to be eternal is for that being to have a life that never begins to exist and a life that never ceases to exist.

Recall from above that for God to be timeless is to say that God a) never begins to exist, b) never ceases to exist, and c) lacks succession. Those who say that God is temporal affirm (a) and (b), thus affirming that God is eternal. However, temporalists deny (c). To say that God is temporally eternal is to say that God never began to exist and can never cease to exist. God is an eternal being, from everlasting to everlasting.[2] However, God does have succession in His life. God experiences one thing after another. For example, God the Son was not always incarnate. At one point in time, God the Son took on human flesh to redeem a lost humanity. The incarnation is a new moment in the life of God. God does not experience His life all at once in a timeless present. Instead, God experiences a succession of moments just like we do. This is the temporal God that Oord wishes to affirm.

Divine Temporality and Oord's Time-full God

Affirming divine temporality does not automatically commit one to Oord's doctrine of God. Divine temporality simply claims that God is an eternal being that enjoys new moments in His life. Theologians who affirm that God is temporal differ on various aspects over the nature of God and Christian doctrine. In concluding this essay, I wish to point out a few different ways a divine temporalist might differ with Oord so that readers can begin to see ways to engage with Oord's theology. In particular, I will focus on differences over God's relationship to creation.

One of the most prominent divine temporalists, William Lane Craig, holds that God is not essentially temporal.[3] Instead, Craig affirms that God is timeless without creation and temporal with creation. What this means is that God can freely choose to become temporal. In the act of creation, God becomes temporal by taking on change and succession in the triune life. For Craig, the act of creation is contingent, which means that God did not have to create a universe at all. It is only in the free act of creating a universe that God becomes temporal.

I affirm something called the Oxford school of divine temporality.[4] On the Oxford school, God is essentially temporal. God did not become temporal at the moment of creation since God is always temporal. God cannot choose to become temporal since it is part of His nature. God can no more chose to be loving than He can chose to be temporal. It is simply part of the divine nature. However, the Oxford school agrees with Craig that God is free to create a universe or free to not create anything at all. On my doctrine of God, God existed without creation from everlasting to everlasting as Psalm 90 affirms. At the moment of creation, God freely enters into the history of the universe that He has created. This is a new moment in the life of God. It is the first of many new moments as God continually works with His creation to bring it deeper into the love of the triune life.

Oord's doctrine of God is closer to the Oxford school than Craig's, yet there are differences worth noting. Like the Oxford school, Oord affirms that God is essentially temporal. However, Oord disagrees with both schools over the nature of creation. On Oord's understanding, God is free to create many different kinds of universes, but God must create a universe of some sort. It is not possible for God to exist without a universe of some sort. If I understand Oord correctly, this doctrine of creation is an entailment from God's essential loving nature. It is not an entailment from God's essential temporal nature.

So readers who are interested in engaging with Oord's theology further can consider different accounts of divine temporality without affirming all of Oord's theology. However, readers must grapple with the nature of love, and contemplate whatever the entailments of love might be for all of Christian thought and practice.

R.T. Mullins is a research fellow and director of communications at the Logos Institute for Analytic and Exegetical Theology at the University of St Andrews. When not engaged in philosophical theology, he can often be found at a metal show.

Endnotes

1. R.T. Mullins, *The End of the Timeless God* (Oxford: Oxford University Press, 2016).

2. See Psalm 90 (NIV).

3. William Lane Craig, "Timelessness and Omnitemporality," in ed. Gregory Ganssle, *God and Time: Four Views* (Downers Grove: InterVarsity Press, 2001).

4. Mullins, "Doing Hard Time: Is God the Prisoner of the Oldest Dimension?" *The Journal of Analytic Theology* 2 (2014).

My Struggle with Uncontrolling Love

Jason Newman

We all want to love and be loved. Most of all, we want to believe that God is Love.

But as I read through Thomas Jay Oord's new book, *The Uncontrolling Love of God*, I found myself struggling. It took me a couple days to figure out why.

Oord's book is engaging. It's well-written, conversational, and non-confrontational. Although I disagree with some of how he builds his case, I found the book thorough and logical.

Here's how I've come to describe my struggle:

The intellectual side of me finds Oord's essential kenosis theory appealing—very appealing. But the emotional part of me struggles. This emotional side wants the injustice that has been done to me and my family to be rectified.

I am a student of history in general, church history in particular. As Oord argued that God could not stop the persecution under Diocletian, Pol Pot, or the Nazis, I wanted to shout, "No! This is *not* how I envision God!"

The world is sometimes ugly. It is "red, tooth and claw," to quote Tennyson.[1] Bad things—horrific things—happen to good people.

So . . . I want a God who 'gets ugly' sometimes. I want a God who responds to injustice with payback, a God who might be cruel or brutal toward those who act unjustly. I want a God who comes in and smashes everything and then sets it right by some standard I find acceptable.

But Oord's theory about the uncontrolling God of essential kenosis is not that God. If Oord is correct, I would have to fundamentally change the way I see God, and I'd also have to change the way I see myself and others.

I once traveled to Mexico as part of a building team. Our general contractor spent almost an hour getting the first corner square. If he measured it once, he measured it 50 times! He not only checked it to be sure it was square; he also checked it against the distance from other buildings, the street, and power lines. He measured everything! Finally, I had enough. I walked up to him and asked why there was a holdup. We were all wasting valuable time, and I wanted to get working.

"The beginning is everything," replied the general contractor.

This applies to how we think about God. If we think of power as logically first in God's nature, then our theology of God will flow from power. Viewing power fits nicely with the smashing and destruction I sometimes think the world needs.

Power-based views of God also allow me to hold onto my grudges. God will settle accounts like I want them settled, right? Power-based views of God allow me to be self-condemning, too. I need to be dutifully punished for the evil I've done—eye for an eye, tooth for a tooth.

When we think love logically comes first in God's nature, a different theology emerges. God-ordained destruction goes out the window, as do my grudges. And I realize that because God's nature is first and foremost love, God *must* love me. As Oord puts it, "God cannot not love."[2]

And if God loves me, I have no excuse for not loving myself!

Part of what open theism and relational/process theology does is remind us that a change in theology means a change in our lives. Theology forms our worldviews. I've found that essential kenosis theology has moved me quickly to an existential crisis.

How can I get past this crisis? First, I must recognize it for what it is. Essential kenosis tries to answer the biggest questions of life: Who is God? What is God like? What does that mean for us?

Answering the big questions is rarely comfortable. Talking about different worldviews—especially varieties within the Christian worldview—can be emotionally charged. After all, we tie salvation to being able to answer the big questions. We think that if even one aspect of salvation is beyond our comprehension, the new idea or worldview must not be Christian.

I also struggle with essential kenosis, because it fits with the biblical text.

Some theories start with defined pre-understandings, predefined suppositions about the Bible. Essential kenosis tries hard not to do that. It takes seriously the all-encompassing statement, "God is love."[3] In essential kenosis I find greater continuity and congruence with scripture than I find with many other systematic theologies or worldviews.

The jury is still out on which side will win in me—the intellectual or the emotional. Past experience tells me that my emotions will eventually come alongside my intellect.

It just takes time. And love.

Jason Newman is a M.Div. student at NNU. For the last six years, he has been the ministry leader for Celebrate Recovery.

Endnotes

1. Tennyson, Lord Alfred. "In Memoriam A.H.H.," in *The Norton Anthology of English Literature*, ed. Stephen Greenblatt (New York: W.W. Norton & Company, 2006), 1994.

2. Thomas Jay Oord, *The Uncontrolling Love of God: An Open and Relational Account of Providence* (Downers Grove: InterVarsity Press, 2016), 161.

3. I John 4:8 (NIV).

What's Prayer Got to Do with It?

Tim Reddish

If we are honest, most of us do not find prayer to be easy. It is, after all, a spiritual discipline, and such practices require effort. We can also be disinclined to pray if we are not entirely sure what good it does.[1] Here are two reasons why this is so, one scientific and one theological.

There is the scientific reason. If, as literal thinkers, we imagine God to be *outside* of an ever-expanding universe, then God is perceived to be ultra-remote and becoming more distant all the time. In addition, if we have subconsciously absorbed into our worldview an image of a mechanistic universe, then this leads us to think of the cosmos as a *closed* system of pure cause-and-effect. For the modern mind, then, a strong emphasis on God's transcendence can lead to the difficulty of relating to a God who is beyond the bounds of a closed and expanding universe. It is no wonder God can seem both silent and distant.

Here is the theological reason. What is the point of bringing our prayer petitions to an omniscient God who knows all that can be known? Even worse, another of God's traditional attributes, impassivity, asserts that God cannot be affected by creation, including being influenced by our prayers. Some theologians respond by saying that although prayer does not sway God or alter the physical world, it changes *our* perspective. Prayer is therefore only for our psychological benefit. This is totally uninspiring! In addition, if we believe the future is already fixed in the mind of God, then prayer cannot modify what God has already decided. If this is the case, in what coherent sense can we honestly say that God 'responds' to our prayers?

We are left praying simply out of obedience, because we believe we should pray. Some even feel guilty for not praying. If we could better understand the process and potency of prayer, then we would be more motivated to pray. This requires us to change our view of both God and creation—and the relationship between the two.

Physicist-theologian John Polkinghorne states that there are two necessary criteria for theological coherence in prayer.[2] The first is that prayer only makes sense *in a certain kind of world*. Prayer is illogical in the rigid framework of a clockwork universe. Although modern physics insists that our world is *not* closed like that, the legacy of that Newtonian paradigm lingers in our consciousness. That mechanistic worldview is officially dead; let us not resurrect it within our *theology* and so inhibit our view of God's capabilities and activities in the world. Instead, let us embrace a world that is open to new and emergent possibilities. Our universe is a mixture of regularity (laws of nature) and randomness (or chance); both elements are necessary to describe God's good creation. Another thing we must remember is that the physical universe is not a self-sufficient system. God has enabled creation to be the 'other' and given it room to become so, but its autonomy is relative to the Creator—who is the ultimate source, sustainer, and goal of all things. "If nature is an open, emergent, and transcendently oriented set of physical systems, there is little reason to exclude the activity of God as a positive causal factor in the ways things go."[3] Second, prayer only makes sense with *a certain kind of God*. God needs to be *relational* and engaged with sequential events as we experience them, rather than purely 'outside' of time. Only from this perspective of openness and relationality will we have the confidence to engage in the discipline of prayer.

Nevertheless, prayer is not magic and cannot change the facts of the present situation—just like the past cannot be altered. Neither can a prayer's effectiveness be proved or disproved logically. Just because a specific request was 'granted' does not mean that the outcome would *not* have been realized had we *not* prayed. We are bound by the arrow of time; we cannot go back and run through the exact same scenario again, this time without prayer, to see if the same result is achieved. We need not, unless we choose to, believe in the causal connection between the prayer and result. The effectiveness of prayer, like the significance of miracles, is a matter of faith. Consequently, prayer is a living expression of our relationship with God and his covenantal commitment to us.

For others, prayer is unnecessary because there is a fatalistic expectation that God will always do what is 'best' anyway. However, there are a myriad of complexities in an open world; this means it is far from likely there is *only one* 'best action' for God. Rather there is a range of creative alternatives open to God. Consequently, what is 'best' if we don't pray might well be different from what is 'best' if we do pray![4]

Returning to the earlier question, why articulate prayer if God already knows what we want and need? Yes, God may know what we want better than we do, but God only knows what we *request* if we actually request it. There is a difference between wishing and asking. We can wish for something without putting any conscious or physical effort into bringing that desire about. In contrast, to request something of God requires us to think of him, rely on his ability, and trust in his character. It is both an act of our will and our faith. This is why it is necessary for us to deliberately articulate our request in prayer, either aloud or silently, and not just hope that God might give us what we desire.[5]

How God will respond to our requests we cannot say, since we do not know the constraints of the whole system or the involvement of others—not forgetting that they too have freewill. Nevertheless, in the complex web of possibilities within an open world, our prayers become part of the causal matrix. Consequently, prayer will *always* make a difference to the world—even if it does not expressly give us the outcome we desire.[6]

Put another way, prayer makes a difference, but so do the necessary regularity of the world and every free choice humans and angels make. We have no way of knowing how the power of prayer intersects with these and other variables. We can pray with confidence, knowing our prayer is heard and makes a difference. But we can't pray with certainty that the difference our prayer makes will have the precise outcome we desire. In this sense we can't be certain our prayer will be answered.[7]

While I—as a scientist—value this logic and find that it encourages me to pray, I can appreciate that for others this rationale may seem cold, perhaps even disturbing! Regardless, as mentioned earlier, we need to have confidence in the power of prayer if we are to practice it. Moreover, the more we engage with God in prayer, the more it will become second nature, i.e., evidence of our dynamic relationship with Him.

Two further thoughts: Matthew tells us that Jesus taught his followers to ask for God's "will to be done on earth, as it is in Heaven."[8] We repeat this phrase all the time in the Lord's Prayer to the point that we have forgotten what the words imply. That statement says that we should continue to pray for God's kingdom to be established because what we see here and now is *not* all that God desires. Moreover, our prayers are, it seems, needed to help bring about God's rule—his kingdom—here on earth. In fact, more than our prayers is needed. We also need to *act*—to be empowered by the Spirit and work to bring about the things God values. Saying "your will be done on earth as it is in heaven" is, then, not merely an expression of eschatological hope—although it is that—but it is an affirmation of our commitment to partner with our Trinitarian God to further God's kingdom. Second, it is quite legitimate to say that the Christian and the Spirit are "co-praying."[9] As Princeton theologian Daniel Migliore says: "Prayer is the fundamental exercise of the new human freedom in *partnership* with the Spirit of God."[10] Since our prayers are in partnership with the Spirit, who is intimately involved in the divine dance with the Father and the Son, this adds significant potency to our prayers and provides a further powerful motivation for the believer to pray.

Tim Reddish (PhD, Physics; M.Div.) moved to Canada from England in 2002, where he was a Professor of Physics at the University of Windsor until 2011, when he resigned to study theology at Knox College, Toronto. See: asamatteroffaith.com.

Endnotes

1. See also, Tim Reddish, *Science and Christianity: Foundations and Frameworks for Moving Forward in Faith* (Eugene: Wipf & Stock, 2016), 138-143; David Wilkinson, *When I Pray What Does God Do?* (Oxford: Monarch, 2015).

2. John Polkinghorne *Science and Providence: God's Interaction with the World* (West Conshohocken: Templeton Foundation Press, 2005), 84.

3. Keith Ward, *Divine Action: Examining God's Role in an Open and Emergent Universe* (West Conshohocken: Templeton Foundation, 2007), 178.

4. Ibid, 161-2.

5. Ibid, 162.

6. Ibid, 163, 169.

7. Gregory A. Boyd, *Is God to Blame? Beyond Pat Answers to the Problem of Suffering* (Downers Grove: InterVarsity, 2003), 134.

8. Matt. 6:10 (NIV).

9. See Rom. 8:26-27

10. Daniel L. Migliore, *Faith Seeking Understanding: An Introduction to Christian Theology*, 2nd ed. (Grand Rapids: Eerdmans, 2004), 242; emphasis mine.

Naming God

Duncan Reyburn

I know it may seem a like an odd thing to ask, but what if having faith is a bit like having aphasia? Aphasia is a condition causing some people to struggle to communicate. It gets in the way of their ability to use and understand words, but it doesn't affect intelligence. They know, but cannot say. People with aphasia will battle to connect with others through conversation or reading or writing, depending on the type of aphasia. With expressive aphasia, for instance, the sufferer will have a good idea of what she wants to say but will find it tricky to get it across. With receptive aphasia, a person can hear or read or write but will lose the message along the way. I know it's a medical condition, and its existence raises all kinds of questions, but it's also an apt metaphor.

Faith, to me at least, seems like something between expressive and receptive aphasia. It lingers as an irrepressible tension between our experience of God and our desire to transfer that experience. In this between, we find communication difficult, if not impossible. Obviously, since the word God is "by its nature a name of mystery," as G. K. Chesterton once noted, it is not all that surprising we have this trouble.[1] How can we speak about what we cannot even properly understand?

It's sometimes said the unnamable is omninamable, but what does that really mean? Does it mean God, the truly unnamable, can be a tree or a piece of moldy cake or anger or the way shadows are cast on Charlie Chaplin's hat and moustache in the movie *City Lights*? Surely some names would be misnomers? In fact, if we are properly to name God, even in our aphasia, we should expect that part of our job would be to denounce and thus also de-name poor ways of understanding God. Perhaps this is why Christianity is split up into different 'denominations?' It seems that different people and people-groups like to name God differently.

Why this matters should be obvious: the way theists name God is going to drastically affect the way they understand and relate to God, and, in turn, is going to affect how they relate to pretty much everything. If our God is named as the patriarchal God of voluntarism, for example, we will believe he can do whatever the hell he wants to. We would also then have to accept that he has the ability to call even the worst evils out there good. If God is named as possessing unadulterated sovereignty, then whatever horrors happen must be OK, and we shouldn't get too mad or sad about them. If God is named as the impotent, weakling God of Philip Pullman's *His Dark Materials* trilogy, I'm sorry to say, we have to believe we're alone here, fending for ourselves with no redemptive hope to which we can cling. If God is named as Nietzsche's dead God, perhaps all of our conceptions of meaning and groundedness are flawed and misguided.

Naming God properly may be impossible, but it still seems unavoidable. Our theological aphasia means that we are always caught in the bind that the great medieval theologian Thomas Aquinas found himself in—always acknowledging the indescribability of God, yet being unable to stop wanting to describe him. In the aftermath of the event of Pure Mystery, we seem to still desperately need linguistic anchors to guide our understanding and our actions; therefore, it would help if those linguistic anchors were at least pointing us in the right direction.

I cannot help but think of the theologian who arguably spent the most time grappling with this problem of naming God: an obscure 5th and 6th century mystical writer who gave himself the pseudonym Dionysius the Areopagite—after the character mentioned in the biblical book of Acts. In his book *The Divine Names*, Dionysius stretches and bends language as far he can, but ultimately—if a ludicrously simplistic summary of his complex work may be allowed—arrives at the conclusion that more or less agrees with where I started this thing: faith really is a lot like aphasia.

It is impossible to name God perfectly or appropriately, or to contain God, or set linguistic limits on the Divine. Perhaps surprisingly, in the process of undoing and being undone by language, Dionysius gives God more than a few names, including "Inexpressible Good," "Inscrutable One," "Mind beyond mind," "Light," "Cause," "Word beyond speech," "Spirit," and a number of others.[2] For someone so reluctant to name God, he comes across as being rather verbose. His is, in a way, a verbosity that wears itself out; it is a wordiness that arrives at wordlessness, awe, wonder, and worship. Perhaps the distance between the indescribable and the describable is not insurmountable.

As Dionysius weaves his way through the strain and struggle of wrapping God up in a net of feeble words, he discovers more than a few ways to discern Divinity. He discovers not the clean lines of the God of voluntarism or unbounded sovereignty, or of the conceptions of God offered by Nietzsche and Pullman. Instead, he finds a mystery within the mystery. It is the mystery of God's providential love.

It is this same mystery that Thomas Jay Oord digs into in his, *The Uncontrolling Love of God*. I almost wrote, "The Uncontrollable Love of God," which I think gets at the same thing.

It's a risky business, trying to explain the unexplainable, but Tom does a fine job of making essential what misguided theologians have made peripheral. He points out if God is love, as he is defined in 1 John 4:8, and if this love is kenotic, then God can't in any way be aligned with evil, which is most manifest in the world as being coercive and controlling. If God truly is love itself rather than just someone who loves occasionally or loves only when that love is needed, then we need to very quickly abandon any theology that makes love out to be an extension of some Nietzschean Will to Power. If God is love, Tom writes, "God cannot not love."[3] His very being is Love, which means that love gets the first and the last word, not control.

Sadly, in far too many instances, language itself comes dangerously close to being an instrument of control rather than love. When we name, we often split and divide reality up and thus risk seeing things in terms of parts rather than in terms of the whole. But love always sees from the whole, and it cannot be vanquished by our hairsplitting or the philosophical incapacities that result from that hairsplitting. It is only love—found, embraced, lived out—that can get beyond language; it is love that draws us towards the Word in which all words and holy-broken-healing selves find their telos.

I mention this because I'm fairly naturally predisposed to theological hairsplitting—a predisposition easily converted into an addiction by my job as an academic. And, to make matters worse, I don't exactly agree with Tom's ontological assumptions. Apart from the fact that this means that some of his conclusions don't sit quite right with me, it also means that I could, given my natural proclivities, spend an awful lot of time and energy annoyingly pointing out how Tom and I might not be exactly on the same page. My theology, for better or worse, is alarmingly Catholic—has my mentioning Chesterton, Aquinas and Dionysius already given me away? And this means, among other things, that I am (I hope you will forgive me) a classical theist—although, for the record, I reject any version of classical theism that conflates divine causality with immanent causality. (How's that for hairsplitting?)

Still, Tom's book—attentive to various finicky details and distinctions as it is—does not force me into a defensive posture, nor does it inspire in me any desire to pit my classical theism against his relational theism. It remains always and ultimately a book about the love of God, and the pastoral spirit that guides its explorations is beyond reproach. I am therefore very fond of Tom's book and the pathways that it carves for thought, reflection, and prayer. In particular, I really like Tom's suggestion that we very seriously consider, in the light of the fact that God's very being is Love, what God cannot do—he cannot deny himself, be unloving, be domineering, or let his power overrule his love. I think it is a suggestion worth pondering endlessly, not so faith becomes a defeatist dance of passivity and negativity, but so it becomes more deeply committed to the positive aspects of existence.

God's providential love becomes something on which to meditate more than it becomes something to solve; it is something that can persuade and lure us to act. Because the primary issue, ultimately, is not what love cannot do—although this is certainly an important aspect of understanding providence. Rather, what is most important is what love will do; what lengths it will go to in order to make goodness a pervasive reality in the world. It will meet us where we are, in our failings and brokenness and suffering. It will even work in and through our aphasia—where we know the excessive self-giving, Trinitarian dance that is God, not just as a concept or as a name, but as the reality through which we live and love and move and have our being.

Duncan Reyburn, PhD, is a professor at the University of Pretoria, South Africa, where he teaches creativity and researches theology. He is the author of Seeing Things as They Are: G. K. Chesterton and the Drama of Meaning (Cascade, 2016).

Endnotes

1. Gilbert Keith Chesterton, *The Everlasting Man* (London: Hodder & Stoughton, 1925), 21.

2. Pseudo-Dionysius, *Pseudo-Dionysius: The Complete Works*, translated by Colm Luibheid (New York: Paulist Press, 1987), 49-50.

3. Thomas Jay Oord, *The Uncontrolling Love of God: An Open and Relational Account of Providence* (Downers Grove: InterVarsity Press, 2016), 71.

Miracle Quotas

Jeff Skinner

Is there a limit to the number of miracles per person? I hope not because we're praying for yet another one! My sister-in-law, Josie, is dying for the fifth time.

Her first brush with death came one Easter Sunday when she collapsed in the shower preparing for church. She had a brain aneurysm rupture. She was rushed to the hospital where she remained in critical condition for over a month. The doctors said it was a miracle, because most people do not survive. While recovering from the aneurysm she contracted MRSA, the flesh-eating bacteria—another bout with death. The doctors were not hopeful that she would recover, but we called the people of God together and prayed, and she did! The doctors proclaimed it miraculous, again. A 'coil' led to brain surgery later in the year, and once more she survived. The doctors were not as quick to give God credit for *that* save.

Several years later, Josie was diagnosed with Metastatic Endometrial Cancer. The doctors treated it with aggressive chemo and radiation. She lost all her hair, but within a couple of years she was cancer free! You can imagine how our family celebrated God's miraculous power, how once more God intervened! And then, almost two years ago, Josie was diagnosed with Papillary Seros Carcinoma—yet another cancer. At this point, we have begun to wonder if it is selfish to ask God for a fifth miracle. Is there a quota?

Miracle. It's not a complicated word in length or even spelling, but it is packed with meaning in terms of what it says about God. Merriam-Webster defines a *miracle* as, "an unusual or wonderful event that is believed to be caused by the power of God."[1] Thomas Jay Oord's definition gives more clarity. He defines a miracle as, "an unexpected *and good* event that occurs through God's special action in relation to creation."[2]

In recent years, I have been hesitant about how I describe miracles, especially regarding how I set expectations for those who are praying for one. It *is* okay to evolve in our theological thinking! The last thing I want to do is give someone the wrong impression of God. I have been guilty of praying, "Lord whether by the miracle of modern medicine or by the miracle of thy hand, please heal 'John' if it is your will."

Perhaps it's time to rethink that prayer for healing. Why would it *not* be God's will to heal *John* or *Josie* for that matter? In Josie's case, it appears to have been 'God's will' the first four times she faced death.

Thomas Jay Oord engages the subject of miracles in a fresh and exciting way with his theological theory, Essential Kenosis (EK). EK seeks to explain more than miracles, essentially saying that God's very nature is love. One might ask why love would ever prevent God from miraculously healing cancer. Common sense might suggest the opposite. EK suggests God's uncontrolling love works *with* creation in the healing/redemptive process. In such an understanding, the role of creatures and created things becomes necessary, because God's very nature limits God's ability to coercively intervene. Coercion and love contradict one another.

If God were to act in any way other than loving, He would cease to be God. Oord says, "Biblical writers frequently say in an explicit way that creatures or creation play a role in the occurrence (or not) of miracles. These accounts strongly support the Essential Kenosis view that miracles happen without divine coercion."[3] Because real love is non-coercive, God needs our permission to act.

Oord asserts that, "Healings are the most prominent examples of miracles involving creaturely contribution, and healings are the most common miracles mentioned in the Bible."[4] There are numerous Biblical examples such as the hemorrhaging woman, the blind beggar, and the ten lepers. In each case, some human participation is required for the miracle to occur. Faith plays a role, to be sure, but faith is not some magic we wield by praying or believing hard enough. Instead, faith compels us to act!

There is also evidence that when God's creatures refuse to cooperate, Jesus is unable to heal. This is apparent when Jesus returns to his hometown and the people refuse to accept him or believe. Mark writes, "Miracles could not be done."[5] Oord comments, "Mark does not say Jesus voluntarily decided not to perform miracles."[6]

But what person would not want to be healed? I know *Josie* wants to be healed. If various capacities of free will exist based upon the complexity of the creature, even cells may have some form of free agency. A cell would have fewer options available for cooperating (or not), because it is less complex, but the possibility exists. Therefore, for Josie to be healed of her cancer her body must cooperate with God's act of healing.

Many people have suffered profound loss and the idea that God allowed the suffering has left them with doubts about a loving God. When pain and doubts are left unrecognized and unreconciled theologically, this often results in angry, rigid people. Richard Rohr says, "When religion cannot find a meaning for human suffering, people far too often become cynical, bitter, negative, and blaming."[7] EK brings some hope and peace regarding God's culpability for suffering.

Perhaps this is a new understanding of God for you. It may seem frightening or produce anxiety to consider that God is not controlling everything from thunderbolts to sunshine or that God is not 'allowing' the pain and suffering for some greater good. Some may think this weakens God or makes God less powerful. Could we be so impatient for our healing that we have decided coercion is the shortcut? The use of force breaks things more often than it heals them. *Love* is the greatest power.

I wonder, which is a more powerful God—one who can control all things, but for reasons known only to God, chooses *not* to intervene? Or one whose very nature is uncontrolling, non-coercive love, which prevents God from forcing God's way upon creation, trusting that very creation to work cooperatively, in love—the kind of love that embodies heart, soul, mind, and strength?

Certainly, there is comfort in the belief that God has everything under control, and we should get out of God's way and let Him do His thing. But if that's the way it is, I sure wish God would hurry up and do whatever it is that God is going to do, because we're dying down here—especially my sister-in-law!

Rev Jeff Skinner is the husband of Dr. Lisa Skinner and father to two adopted children; Blaine (12) and Hayden (9). He grew up in Tuscaloosa, AL. He is a Master Trainer for Dynamic Church Planting International. His Undergraduate degree is from Trevecca Nazarene University, he received a Master of Arts from Northwest Nazarene University, and a Master of Divinity from Nazarene Theological Seminary. He is currently enrolled in Trevecca's Doctoral program for "Leadership and Professional Practice." He

is currently in transition to be The Lead Pastor @ Worthington Church of the Nazarene in Worthington, KY. He has a passion for helping people interpret life in a broken world in light of God's Love.

Endnotes

1. *Merriam-Webster, s.v.* "miracle, "accessed October 7, 2016, https://www.merriam -webster.com/dictionary/miracle.

2. Thomas Jay Oord, *The Uncontrolling Love of God: An Open and Relational Account of Providence* (Downers Grove, IL: InterVarsity, 2015), 196.

3. Oord, 202.

4. Ibid.

5. See Mark 6:5 (NIV).

6. Oord, 203.

7. Richard Rohr, *Things Hidden: Scripture as Spirituality* (Franciscan Media: 2008), 24-25.

Contributing to God's Growing Perfection

Olav Bryant Smith

In the movie, *The Last Samurai*, Katsumoto comes to his family's garden and looks at the cherry trees planted there. "You could spend your whole life," he says, "looking for the perfect blossom."[1]

We experience lots of 'perfect' moments under the specific conditions that exist at a particular time. Let's call that *contingent perfection*. Under the circumstances, that was 'perfect!' The event was as good as we could have hoped for it to be.

Some events in our lives are *really* special—a first kiss, a graduation, an engagement, or the moment when we first hold our newborn child. Moments like these are often captured in photographs. When we look back on them, we might be moved to say that such moments in our lives were 'perfect!'

Some moments are not quite as special as those but still important—when we first learned to ride a bike, when we bought a car, hit a home run, or got an A in a difficult class. We might also be tempted to acclaim these moments as 'perfect.'

A fairly recent phenomenon, as I've gone out to restaurants or talked with someone at a call center, is to hear an enthusiastic voice deem *whatever* I've said as, 'perfect!' Whether it's my choice from the menu or simply the answer to a question like, "What's your address?" my answer is perfect, according to various service providers.

Can all moments be perfect in some aspect? At the end of *The Last Samurai*, Katsumoto's dying words proclaim, "They're all perfect!"[2] In Japan, cherry blossoms represent the fleeting nature of reality—how precious and beautiful things come into being and then so quickly pass away. In Japanese aesthetics, the expression for this bitter-sweet reality is *mono no aware*. Katsumoto grasps that many, if not all, of the moments of his life, like the cherry blossoms, were perfect—even if contingent and fleeting.

In the West, philosophy and theology have inherited a Greek notion of perfection that suggests completeness—something that lacks nothing. The Supreme Being is necessarily and permanently perfect. It's final. But is God ever really *finished*? What if God is the culmination of the entire story of creation? This leads to the idea that there *can* be a fleeting and contingent perfection in addition to the idea of permanent and necessary perfection.

Theological mistakes have been made based on the Greek idea of perfection. Some people think that it would be demeaning to suggest any limits to the divine attributes. For example, the perfect being—in its completeness—would be omniscient in the largest absolute sense of the word by knowing the future as well as the past. It's difficult to reconcile genuine free will with this view. In some sense, the world of absolute omniscience plays out before it even happens, but life doesn't feel that way, and much of the Bible suggests a God waiting to see what we'll decide and then responding accordingly.

In this view, the perfect being would also be omnipotent, having complete power—*all* the power. If God has *all* of the power, however, creatures cannot have any. If I have no power, I cannot choose. I cannot act. The problem of evil arises to challenge a God who has absolute power and goodness but does not intervene in horrible, daily occurrences *or* the great atrocities of history. Our experience shows us that we *do* have power and, again, the Bible suggests that God has, at the very least, granted us the freedom to make decisions.

It has also been suggested that if God is the classically perfect being—lacking nothing—God can never change. God is the necessarily perfect being from the beginning of time to the end of time. Therefore, God completely transcends the temporal world of change. If God changed, it is reasoned, what would there be to change *to*? If God gets better, this would suggest a previous imperfection. If God gets worse, God clearly wouldn't be perfect anymore. God must, therefore, be perfect and stay perfect without changing.

This a false dichotomy. Change, even for God, is not a simple choice between perfection and imperfection. Instead, I suggest that God has a dual nature (eternal and temporal), and there is something we could call the *growing perfection of God* within the temporal domain. This involves a change from perfection to *greater* perfection as God embraces and celebrates our contingent perfections and helps to correct our imperfections.

Our metaphysical compliments paid to God through the ages suggest that God is so perfect that God doesn't have any need to change. Who are we to limit God in this way? Is it really 'perfection' to never be able to grow? Is it really perfection to never be able to experience the contingent and creative perfections of an ever-growing universe, in a new way? Perhaps we need to expand this limited, classical notion of perfection. It seems to me that the greatest perfection of the Supreme Being includes the ability to become more perfect over time in response to the expressions of a universe of creatures striving to participate in establishing their own myriad beautiful creations.

It has been suggested that the classically perfect, eternally complete God is impassive as well. But if God is loving, if God is love, then God is in relationship. To be in genuine relationship with individuals with some degree of free will is to be involved in a process of changing relationship over time. God is in relationship with creatures who have their own power, however limited in comparison with the Supreme Being. Why do we have this power if not to be creative? It could, in fact, be argued that to be creative is what it means to be created in God's image. God has given us the power to create. God has given us the power to create beautiful things. Sometimes we fall short of that beauty, but it is out of the power of personal expression, however flawed, that we have the ability to add something of value to the world. In adding something of value to the world, we are adding something of value to God, thereby adding to God's perfection.

The most perfect moments in life are moments lived in inspiration. They are moments where we live in harmony with *the uncontrolling love of God*. We become inspired vehicles of God's creative love in the world.

Olav Bryant Smith is a lecturer at California State University, Chico and Butte College and author of Myths of the Self: Narrative Identity and Postmodern Metaphysics. *He was the co-owner and managing editor of* Empirical Magazine, *selected as one of ten best new magazines of 2012 by the Library Journal.*

Endnotes

1. Herskovitz, Marshall, John Logan, Edward Zwick. *The Last Samurai*. DVD. Directed by Edward Zwick. Burbank: Warner Brothers, 2003.
2. Ibid.

God Is Not the Jealous Type

Jon Paul Sydnor

You shall not make for yourself an idol, whether in the form of anything that is in heaven above, or that is on the earth beneath, or that is in the water under the earth. You shall not bow down to them or worship them; for I the Lord your God am a jealous God.[1]

The Bible clearly states that God is a jealous God. I don't believe it. Here's why.

In addition to being a college professor and professional theologian, I have also been a pastor, along with my wife, Abby, for fifteen years. During that time, we have counseled people facing a multitude of different challenges. We frequently counsel individuals caught in controlling relationships with jealous partners. Manipulative people seek out manipulatable partners then manipulate them using guilt, shame, anger, fear, silence, and triangulation—anything that gives the manipulator power *over*. Sometimes, when it seems like the controlled partner might leave, a shallow repentance and brief reform occur, but renewed manipulation soon follows.

The pain runs everywhere, and it runs deep. Obsessive jealousy forces friends to take sides. Children develop divided loyalties. The couple is not truly a couple, not two persons joined into one whole by love. Instead, they are separated, one object trying to control another like a puppeteer and puppet. A struggle ensues as the manipulator demands an impossibly perfect control while the manipulated seeks a denied freedom and real relationship.

"He's the jealous type," people say, when someone tends to be suspicious and controlling.

It's not a compliment. Jealous types tend to be obsessive or even delusional.

Out of their irrational distrust, they make things up, causing intense conflict.[2] If your friend is in a relationship with a jealous type, your advice will probably be, "Get out."

Is God the jealous type? In the 21st century, terms like passive-aggressive, dependent, and narcissistic describe various personality disorders that characterize hurtful spouses, partners, boyfriends, girlfriends, et al. When we know people like this, we often suggest therapy, medication, or both. Spiritually, it's not helpful to think of God as a psychiatric patient with torn interpersonal relationships who needs an intervention. It's not helpful to divinize jealousy, which harms the interpersonal relationships for which our loving God made us, of which our Triune God is made.

Divinizing jealousy can hurt interreligious relationships as well as interpersonal relationships. Thinking of God as jealous produces the either/or interpretation of religious identification that characterizes Judaism, Christianity, and Islam. In many parts of the world, religious belonging is not exclusive. Taiwanese can be Confucian and Taoist. Nepalese can be Buddhist and Hindu. But traditionally, you can't be Christian *and* Jewish or Jewish *and* Muslim. At times we worshipers of the one God have summoned murderous rage against each other for worshiping God differently, always in the confidence that our God is the true God—and also jealous.

Some Christians may take offense at my disagreement with the famous and influential biblical passage that defines God as jealous. But Christ often disagrees with Scripture—or at least with individual texts therein. When Scripture demanded that the woman be stoned, he protected her. When Scripture demanded that lepers be shunned, he dined with them. When Scripture demanded no work on the Sabbath, he healed. When Scripture demanded an eye for an eye, he preached turning the other cheek. Jesus re-interpreted Scripture to be more loving and healing. We continue this tradition as present day Christians.[3]

The New Testament fundamentally claims that God is love. A loving Creator desires a flourishing creation, flourishing demands freedom, and freedom is incompatible with jealousy. Generous love forsakes any desire for control. It doesn't trap people in a relationship. Generous love frees people to *enter* into relationship at their choosing and to *leave* relationship at their choosing. That way, when they stay in the relationship it is a sign of their own commitment, not someone else's power. As Paul writes, love is not jealous.[4]

If love desires the flourishing of the beloved, then God wants us to embrace the worldview that promotes our greatest flourishing. This worldview will differ for different people. My dad, a Presbyterian minister, had a friend who was a Southern Baptist minister. Fundamentalism did not suit him well, and he was never able to make peace with Christian claims about Jesus. Over time, he became attracted to the progressive, rational faith of Reform Judaism. This attraction culminated in his conversion. His new faith rejuvenated him—he regained his intellectual integrity, he felt more at home with his fellow congregants, he fell in love with the rituals.

Personally, I experience Jesus as a perfectly transparent window into our God of infinite light. For me, this makes Jesus the Christ. But my dad's friend didn't, or couldn't, believe this. He found a new religious home that blessed him with more faith and peace. I think that his discovery of this home, and the way it helped him thrive, pleased God. I don't think it made God jealous.

Tragically, some churches do preach a God who is jealous, wrathful, and (for example) hates gays. What if someone born gay is reared in a church like that? What does the God of Jesus Christ want for that person?

In seminary, I knew a gay man who realized that he was gay in the fifth grade, in rural Texas, in a family that attended a fundamentalist and homophobic church. One night he was at a sleepover flipping through the Sears catalog with his friends, looking at the women's underwear section, which did nothing for him. Then they strayed onward into the men's underwear section, and he liked it. At that moment, he realized he was gay. Years of culturally induced suffering followed. Somehow, this gay man was able to salvage his faith and go on to become a progressive Christian pastor.

But what if he had been unable to work through his fundamentalist upbringing and reconcile his sexual orientation with his faith? Would God prefer him to be a closeted Christian fundamentalist or a gay Buddhist? God would prefer the latter. In my experience, openly gay Buddhists are happier, more authentic, and more at peace than closeted gay fundamentalists, especially those who are closeted from themselves. If someone finds spiritual solace in Buddhism, then this solace pleases the God of human flourishing.

If God is jealous *for* anything, God is jealous *for love*—the uncontrolling, open love that fosters mutual commitment, meaningful relationship, and spiritual maturity. Such flourishing can occur within many different worldviews, so long as they are freely chosen and serve love.

Jon Paul Sydnor teaches World Religions at Emmanuel College in Boston. He also serves as theologian-in-residence at Grace Community Boston where his wife, Rev. Abigail A. Henrich, is pastor. Jon Paul loves to spend time with his family, especially when that time involves camping, soccer, chess, or Indian food.

Endnotes

1. Exod. 20:4-5a (NRSV).
2. American Psychiatric Association. *Diagnostic and Statistical Manual of Psychiatric Disorder,* 5th Ed. Washington, DC: Author (2013). 90-91, 264.
3. Jon Paul Sydnor, "Christ was not an inerrantist, so Christians should not be either: How Jesus read his Bible," *Open Theology,* Volume 2, Issue 1 (August 2016): 2300-6579, https://doi.org/10.1515/opth-2016-0056 (Accessed January 21, 2017).
4. I Cor. 13:4

Change the Future: Pray!

Luis Torres

Prayer and the Unmoved Mover

Growing up in the Charismatic tradition, I was taught there is power in prayer and it actually makes a difference. There was always an emphasis put on prayer in my household. I was also taught to believe the traditional notion that God is unchanging, unmoved, and completely in control of everything. This means God cannot be changed in any way or be affected by anything we do. If you think about it, viewing God in this way renders prayer utterly meaningless.

We think of prayer as a relational act. Whether it is a prayer of thanksgiving, worship, intercession, or petition; we pray expecting our prayer will have an effect on, or elicit a response from, God. If God is an unchanging, unmoved, all controlling deity; there is no need for prayer, because it will not make a difference to God or the divine blueprint He has laid out.

If God is in control of everything, we are not free in any meaningful sense. The future is 'set in stone.' Whatever occurs is predetermined by God. Your prayers, His answer to your prayers, and the outcome of what you're praying about are all inevitable, *if* God truly is in control in the traditional sense.

Let's imagine for a moment a wife praying for the healing of her husband who is suffering from a terminal illness. Now let's say he succumbs to his illness. In this traditional view of God, He not only determined the husband's death but He also determined the prayers of the wife only for her to be devastated at the outcome of her unanswered prayer.

This is the absurdity with which we are left when viewing God as the all-controlling, unchanging, unmoved mover, but I'd like to suggest a way of understanding the nature of God and the world that makes better sense of prayer and our experiences with it.

Prayer and the Uncontrolling God

Prayer requires a kind of reciprocity in which only a deeply relational God would be able to engage. Genuine relationship is only possible in an open, undetermined world.

To pray a petitionary prayer is to presuppose the future is not set in stone. You're asking God to do something you believe can either come to pass or not. If God knows the future completely as a closed set of facts, petitionary prayer is useless because whatever God knows about the future is what is going to happen. Regardless of how much you pray, it cannot make a difference, because God's knowledge cannot be denied.

If the future is open ended, as we suppose it is when we petition God for something, prayer can make a difference in what comes to pass. In this model of the future God knows it as a realm of possibilities, but which ones will be actualized are not yet knowable to God or creatures.

Revisiting the scenario of the wife praying for her terminally ill husband; in this view of God, He receives her prayer and works in every way He possibly can toward healing. Although God knows the possibilities and the probabilities of what may happen in this situation, He does not know with complete certainty what the outcome will be. This makes praying that much more important, because our prayers *can* affect what comes to pass.

Another distinctive aspect of understanding God in this way is the reformulation of how we understand His power and action in the world. The Bible says God's nature is love. I think most people would agree that love does not control others but requires freedom to be reciprocated; thus, as Thomas Jay Oord puts it in his book, *The Uncontrolling Love of God,* "If love doesn't force the beloved and God is love, God can't force the beloved."[1]

The power of God is better understood in light of His nature of uncontrolling love. Because it simply isn't in God's nature to control others, His power is influential rather than coercive. This too has profound implications for how we view prayer! Since God is always loving, He does not control others as a means of achieving His ends; consequently, it doesn't make sense to pray for God to exercise control over someone or something. It simply does not work that way.

Our prayers should be influential in nature. When we pray, we are not forcing God to do anything or magically making things happen. Rather, our prayers influence others, God, and the world in ways they wouldn't have been, had we not prayed. We add to the possibilities available for God to work with.

God is always doing all He possibly can do to work for the good of creation. Prayer is simply becoming aware of the Divine Presence already active in our lives and the lives of others—aligning ourselves with His good purposes in order to partner with God to achieve His will for creation.

Knowing God is essentially loving and relational means we can be certain God is not deaf to our prayers but receives them and uses them to make a real difference in the world. Although we may not always see the immediate effect of our prayers; it should not discourage us from praying.

The way we think of God has important implications for our prayers.

In the words of the Apostle Paul: "Rejoice always, and pray without ceasing."[2]

Luis Torres is a small business owner in Orlando, Florida. He enjoys spending time with his wife and two beautiful children, fishing, and reading philosophy.

Endnotes

1. Thomas Jay Oord, *The Uncontrolling Love of God: An Open and Relational Account of Providence* (Downers Grove: InterVarsity Press, 2016), 147.

2. I Thess. 5:16-17 (NIV)

God Is Not Great;
God Is Good

Alexis James Waggoner

Police shootings. Environmental disaster. The refugee crisis.

These events all inspire fear and panic—and in many cases they illicit an assurance from Christians that 'God is in control.' For a world plagued by suffering and questions, I don't find this response to be very helpful—and I don't find it to be true.

The classic problem of evil and free will presents two traditional options: 1). God has in some sense orchestrated the events of history, thus our actions, our existence, our story is already determined, or 2). God has given us free will to chart our own course and make our own decisions, though God already knows how the story will turn out. In their own way, each of these options rely on the idea that God is in control.

But neither of these belief systems provides an adequate representation of our experience in the world, and neither provides a framework robust enough for understanding what God is up to.

God is not great, but God is good.

However we combine it with other elements of God's character, I think most Christians agree that God is inherently good. But there is an issue combining goodness and omnipotence (God's ability to exert ultimate power and control). If God *is* the definition of goodness then God's behavior has to be deemed good, regardless of how we feel about it or the pain it causes us. And, when subscribing to a view that God ordains, or controls, or fore-knows all . . . some of this behavior is certainly questionable.

The alternative belief is that suffering is pointless, and we are made miserable at the hands of a God who claims to be goodness and love but has a crazy way of showing it. If God really is 'in control' in the traditional sense, then we have to pick one of these options.

On more than one occasion it sure seems like scripture sets us up for this belief. Given a conventional reading of the Bible, God allows most of creation to die in a flood; God delivers plagues to the Egyptians; God sends God's own people into exile; God casts King Nebuchadnezzar into the wilderness. We can understand these occurrences in a historical-critical context and explain them by looking at the authors of the texts, who they were talking to, and what they were trying to convey. When we do so, we learn that that the authors were speaking from a specific position—clearly not the essential kenosis position!—and with specific motives meant to convey important truths for their time.

But if we reject the position that God is in control, what truths can we glean for *our* time? If we believe that God's word is dynamic, inspired, and speaking today, could these authors be saying something to us, too?

What if suffering is abhorrent and God is love?

Omnipotence, as we typically understand it, is not reflective of God's essential nature of goodness and love. If being all-powerful and all-controlling means that God ordains all events in the world—even those of extreme pain and suffering—then how can we trust that God is seeking the good of the world, which we're told God is also doing? Or, if omnipotence means that God knows humanity will cause pain and suffering, yet we are free to do it anyway—then how can we worship a God that lets evil continue?

I have watched friends walk through life's darkest moments, praising God, because—although they believed God allowed or even caused these events—they know God is inherently good. If God is good, and if these bleak ordeals were ordained by God, then it follows that there is goodness in our suffering.

The belief that God's essential nature is goodness and love provides a way to understand the workings of the world—the randomness, suffering, and evil—*without* baptizing suffering as God's will. It doesn't explain these things away, but it also doesn't make God culpable. It creates room for a God who joins us in our suffering, whose heart breaks at our pain because it runs counter to God's essential nature. It's also the model I think we see Jesus demonstrate through his life, death, and resurrection as fully human, suffering servant, and victor over death.

Love as the final word

It might be disturbing for some to think of a world where God isn't ultimate power, foreseeing every twist and turn, or at least having some general fore-knowledge of events. But for Christians, it shouldn't be surprising that God uses means we might deem counter-intuitive to work toward the kingdom on earth—which we're told is an upside-down, last-shall-be-first, poor-shall-be-blessed kind of place.

If God isn't 'in control' in the way classical theology has explained God to be, it doesn't mean that God is weak, or ineffective—or that something dark and sinister is in control instead. It means that our understanding of power and con-trol and security might need to be re-ordered. It means that our commitment to the Word made flesh, to Love living among us, to the upside-down Kingdom on earth will be tested. This is not something our worldly power structures and hu-man minds understand—and that's exactly the point.

God's essential nature of love *is* God's ultimate power. It's a power that gives itself up so we might be free and sorrows with us when that freedom re-sults in pain. Love is not controlling, therefore God is not 'in control' in the traditional sense; rather, God is working on and in creation with perfect love, asking us to join in the project of renewal that continues to be set in motion.

I believe *this* is the story scripture is telling, the story the world is longing for, and the story we're being called into.

Alexis James Waggoner has a M.Div. from Union Theological Seminary in New York. She is an adjunct professor and a minister of religious education. Her organization, The

Acropolis Project (http://theacropolisproject.com), seeks to raise the bar of theological education in communities of faith.

https://www.facebook.com/theacropolisproject/
@alexisjwaggoner
@acropolisproj

What Kind of God Is This?

Dale V. Wayman

O ne of my favorite theologians, Thomas Jay Oord, continues to write prolif- ically about his conception of who God is and what kind of God He is. Al- though I'm not in complete agreement with his open and process theological concepts, I do regard his depiction of God's character and reputation to be noteworthy.

In fact, Oord's depiction of God as relational is what has endeared me to his writing and to him as a person. I started with Oord's book *Relational Holiness*, then moved to *The Nature of Love*, then *Relational Theology*, and now *The Uncontrolling Love of God*, his latest work.

Being of the same Wesleyan tradition, I appreciate that Oord eschews deter- ministic answers to the problem of evil as he outright rejects Augustine's, "noth- ing in our lives happens haphazardly,"[1] Calvin's, "God's providence, as taught in scripture, is opposed to fortune and fortuitous happenings,"[2] and R.C. Sproul's, "if chance exists in its frailest form, God is finished."[3]

Oord also intensely questions Euthyphro's dilemma as an adequate explana- tion for the problem of evil. The idea that "whatever is initiated and directed by God is moral" or "might makes right" makes one wonder if God actually creates everything.[4] The atheist conception that the objective reality of morality is inde- pendent of God is soundly refuted as well.

I particularly agreed with Oord's

. . . absolute randomness is a myth. But absolute determinism is too. Forces we cannot see regulate all things, animate and inanimate. Chance and law-like regularity characterize our world. If change reigned absolutely, chaos would ensue. If law reigned absolutely, order would eliminate creativity. Both randomness and regularity persist in the universe.[5]

Oord has two basic propositions in his latest work: 1) "God's loving nature requires God to create a world with creatures God cannot control"[6] and 2) His loving nature prevents God from interrupting "law-like regularities" of the natural world.[7]

In other words, Oord is saying God 'cannot' interfere; hence, God is not responsible for evil and suffering.

In practical terms, how do Oord's two basic propositions play out? Does God not interfere in our world? I had to pause for a few days, because as I am writing this, another mass shooting has occurred. A violent act took dozens of people from this earth. Why didn't God stop it?

I have to agree with Hugo, when he says, "Just because one doesn't like the way things are is no reason to be unjust towards God."[8] This seems to be the crux of Oord's position. He seeks to protect God's character by not blaming Him for our world's evil. However, in doing so, God seems milquetoast. If God interferes, does that make Him blameworthy when He does not interfere and controlling when He does?

It seems that God must do something besides being an observer of His creation. Undoubtedly, God feels what we feel and also desires a relationship with us, an intimate friendship. Yet, does God really not interfere?

Practically speaking . . . it is certainly hoped He does interfere. A Being with infinite wisdom and infinite capability surely does interrupt the laws He established in this natural world. When God does so, He performs a miracle. God suspends the natural laws to bring about a desired result. We have examples of where God has not seemingly interfered but we also have numerous examples of miracles as well where God has interfered.

If we believe God does not interfere, then we are left with a form of deism. Surely God is more than a watchmaker, a Creator of a mechanical universe. And as Oord points out, there are random events as well that don't seem to make sense, so the charge of deism doesn't stick because a fine watchmaker would not create opportunity for randomness.

What is important to consider in this discussion is for those of us who have trusted in Jesus for our salvation, we will have an eternity to spend with God. What will we do for all eternity? One supposition is that we will see all the times God interfered and why and also all the times God did not interfere and why. We will see into God's reasoning for his interference and lack of interference.

Another supposition will be that God will spend an eternity showing us where He restrained evil when things could have been much more disastrous. We have evidence of this in our present world. We all have seen times where something evil occurred and were able to see that if the timing had been different or if different people/circumstances had been present, the evil could have been much worse. However, this second supposition does nothing to assuage the victims and those vicariously victimized.

That, I think, is Oord's motivation—helping those who have experienced evil. As I've been reading the progression of his work, Oord, the philosopher/teacher/author, has a pastor's heart. He doesn't want people to turn against the very God who is the answer for our troubles. And it is this motivation that endears me to Oord and to much of his writing.

Dale V. Wayman is a full-time graduate professor of counselor education and supervision with interests in Adlerian theory, Wesleyan theology and cognitive anthropology. In his spare time, he enjoys skeet shooting, tennis, fishing and spending time with his grandchildren.

Endnotes

1. Augustus, *Enchiridion de fide, spe et caritate*, no. 24.
2. Calvin, John, *Institutes of the Christian Religion*, I, XVI, II.
3. RC Sproul, *Not a Chance: God, Science and the Revolt against Reason* (Ada, MI: Baker Books, 2014), 18.
4. Euthyphro Dilemma: http://www.philosophyindex.com/plato/euthyphro/dilemma
5. Thomas Jay Oord, *The Uncontrolling Love of God: An Open and Relational Account of Providence* (Downers Grove: InterVarsity Press, 2016), 49.
6. Oord, 146.
7. Oord, 174.
8. Hugo, Victor. "Les Miserables, Chapter 5." The Literature Network. http://www.online-literature.com/victor_hugo/les_miserables/364

The Relationship Between Good and Evil

Bethanie Young

How can God, who loves by nature, allow or accept genuine evil? This is a question that many people ask, especially in times of tragedy—the hardest question of all. In his book, *The Uncontrolling Love of God*, Oord states, "Theology, science and philosophy explore both the minutiae and the big picture to make sense of reality. Big questions and our attempts to answer them are a big deal."[1] In the Celebrate Recovery ministry that I serve, the big questions come up all the time. Why doesn't my mom love me? Why did God allow that man to rape me? If God is a loving God, then why was I molested day after day, year after year? These are the issues of the world today, and evil seems to be lurking in every corner.

Oord's ideas about randomness and regularities help bring together the importance of God's loving nature and God's inability to change what has been put into motion by creation. This is discussed in the essential kenosis model. When God created humankind, God gave us free will, because God loved us. This free will has created a path for the world that God is not able to move or change without jeopardizing that freedom. I found this hard to grab hold of and run with at first, but freedom to love and seek relationship *is* what creation is all about. This is where, "the right combination of randomness and regularities makes the universe capable of existing, evolving, and developing novel forms of life," starts to make sense, especially in an open and relational theology.[2] "Believers are wise to say that God creates in and with the randomness and regularities of existence."[3]

It is important for us to understand that both evil and good are present in the world, interrelated by the choices we make. I have been stretched, and I have grown, as I consider this in light of the response to evil and its role in my life. Sometimes, I forget to think about the blessings, focusing entirely on negativity that has flowed in and around me. But, goodness cannot just happen. People have a responsibility to make good choices.

Celebrate Recovery can sometimes be overwhelming. As a leadership team, we took a huge hit when one of our most loved servants turned out to be a five-time child molester and rapist. He had been lying to us for eight years. It was a big shock to all—especially those closest to him. "To make sense of life, we need to account for both evil and good."[4] As leaders, we had to focus on the good that this man had brought to our lives and the lives that had been saved because of the work that God has done through him. The evil is present though, so we also have to respond to the hurt, loss, and pain of all who are affected by this situation. Essential kenosis gives us the ability to understand that these acts were not from God, nor allowed by God, but carried out through the choices of a created being. God is sorrowful for all who are involved. God's heart—perhaps even God's Spirit—is broken due to this loss and hurt.

However, God forgives because of the nature of love, and we are called to forgive as well. Oord's description of uncontrolling love is very intriguing and makes sense. There is no other way to make sense of this kind of senseless evil, just like there is no way to make sense out of the stories in the first chapter of Oord's book. The victims will never be the same. The world is a very scary place. In all of these stories, God was not able to act outside of divine love. "Divine love is uncontrolling, which means God cannot coerce."[5] No matter how evil or terrible the experience may be, God can *persuade*, but God cannot *force* someone or something to alter the path they are choosing.

The world is so full of negative actions that it can be difficult to see the good. This is where miracles play a role in our relationship with God. Oord defines what a miracle is in the last chapter of his book, and I believe that we need to grasp how simple a miracle can be, helping others to experience miracles anew. "Miracles may fill us with awe or astonishment. We may tremble in worship or shout ecstatically with joy. We may bow in silent reverence. Whatever our response, miracles indicate something unusual occurred."[6] This reminds me of the story of Elijah in I Kings. Elijah heard God in the whisper, not in the earthquake, the fire, or the loud noises all around him. I wonder how many times people seek God in the loud, obvious places instead of looking for the miracle where it is least expected.

The Uncontrolling Love of God has opened my eyes and mind to a new approach to evil and God's role in evil. I believe that evil occurs because of the choices of creation. I also agree that God is unable to change the course of creation without going against God's own nature of love and the freedom of choice that God gave humankind at the beginning. There are still many questions and Oord does admit, "Theology doesn't have all of the answers."[7] This, however, does help in all that I do with Celebrate Recovery. And, it reminds me that no matter how you answer the hard questions, there will always be more that may not have answers, yet.

Bethanie Young is the Connectional Ministries Pastor at Longview Church of the Nazarene. She has a Master's Degree in Project Management and Masters of Divinity and Spiritual Formation. Bethanie is a wife, mother of six, and foster mom to many. Her passion is discovering new ways to share Jesus with others and finding ways that she can love those that seem to be hard to love. Bethanie shares, "God has blessed me with many lessons in my life, and I hope that the future holds new adventures and new lessons everywhere I go."

Endnotes

1. Thomas Jay Oord, *The Uncontrolling Love of God: An Open and Relational Account of Providence* (Downers Grove: InterVarsity Press, 2016), 15.

2. Oord, 43.

3. Ibid.

4. Oord, 69.

5. Oord, 183.

6. Oord, 197.

7. Oord, 15.

∾ SECTION TWO ∾

Introduction:
How God Acts

Thomas Jay Oord

As I said earlier, the topics of this book's sections overlap. Most essays could have been placed in any of the three sections. But that's the nature of big ideas: we can't contain them in tidy categories!

The essays here pertain, in one way or another, to how God acts. I offer a few thoughts on divine action to set the stage for reading them. I'm not implying that every author agrees with what I write. But offering my thoughts about divine action, in general, might be a touchstone for reflection on this section's essays.

God Acts

I think God acts. That belief may seem obvious and uncontroversial to most people. But it's rare among theologians. It's rare, at least, if by 'act' we mean God acts in some way analogous to how creatures act. Relatively few theologians believe God acts similar to how we do.

It's common for theologians who accept classical theologies and the philosophies that inform them to say either that God is one pure act or that God's actions are entirely different from our actions. Come to think of it, saying God is 'one pure act' *is* really just saying God's action is entirely different!

Rarely mentioned as the driving force behind this absolute difference between divine and creaturely action, is classical theology's view of God and time. Most theologians have thought God to be essentially timeless. A timeless God does not engage in a series of actions. The most a timeless God can do is one

timeless act. But a timeless act is absolutely different from creaturely acts, because creaturely acts are time-oriented. So it makes little sense when these theologians say, "God acts."

By contrast, I believe God acts moment by moment. God's acts were pre-
ceded by other divine acts. And God will act in future moments. God's actions are
timefull in a way analogous to timefull creaturely actions. (By the way, I coined
'timefull' as a contrast for 'timeless' to emphasize the time-oriented nature of
activity.)

I also think God acts upon creation, and creation responds by acting upon
God (and others). In other words, God engages in a real, give-and-receive relationship with creatures. I can't imagine what divine love would mean if God
didn't act to relate with creatures. As I see it, love requires relationship.

Many major theologians in history—e.g., Augustine, Aquinas, and Calvin—
think God does not act in timefull, give-and-receive relationships. For that reason,
their theologies cannot effectively present God as a loving being who acts moment-by-moment in relation to creation.[1] Schubert Ogden expresses this well:

"Faith's testimony to God's love has been all but completely obscured by
[classical metaphysics]. Consequently, the deep reason for a theological rejection
of classical metaphysics . . . is that such a metaphysics never has allowed, and, in
principle, never could allow an appropriate theological explication of the central
theme of [the] evangelical witness that God is love."[2]

Amen, Schubert!

God's Action Cannot Be Perceived by Our Five Senses

I have been active in science-and-religion discussions over the last few decades. I
like that these discussions often explore divine action. Some of the scholars involved worry that science squeezes out any belief that God acts in the world.
Because I'm a big believer in science and also that God acts all the time and everywhere, I participate in science and religion research, give lectures, and publish my
thoughts on various subjects.

Two views often go unmentioned in science-and-religion discussions of
God's action. The first is a view common among theologians. It says God is a
bodiless spirit who cannot be perceived by our five senses. Some people talk
about the 'unseen God' or God as the 'soul of the universe.'

We can't look out our windows and see God biking down the street, for instance. We can't smell God after a good rain or taste God during dinner. Even claims about hearing God's voice don't require properly functioning ears. The typical word for God's spiritual composition, which our five senses cannot perceive, is 'incorporeal.' God does not have a divine body.

The second view—often unmentioned in science-and-religion discussions—is the common view among believers that God is omnipresent. Most believers think God is present to all creaturely things and pervades all creation, all the time. This means, for instance, that we cannot do scientific experiments to isolate parts of reality in which God is present from those in which God is not. God cannot be the subject of an experiment requiring a control group devoid of divine influence.

Similarly, it's impossible to make a movie visually depicting a day in the life of God. God cannot be seen, and God is present to all existence. For all of their interesting ideas, movies like *Oh God!*, *Bruce Almighty*, or *The Shack* cannot depict an omnipresent God imperceptible to movie camera lenses.

Saying God acts as an omnipresent, bodiless spirit helps us with the problem of evil, however. While creatures sometimes use their localized bodies to prevent evil, God has no localized divine body for such use. Humans may snatch children from oncoming traffic, for instance. But God doesn't have divine hands or body for such rescue. God can call upon embodied creatures to use their bodies for rescuing. But creatures must choose to cooperate.

God's Action as Uncontrolling Love

I believe it's impossible to act in isolation. I don't know this with certainty. But everything about existence points to this statement as true. When we talk about action, it's always in relation to something else. Action is causal; it influences others.

I think God's action is causal and done in relation to creation. As an everlasting and loving Spirit, God exerts causal influence upon all creation, all the time. But as I have said, I don't think God ever controls others. God causally provides the power for freedom, agency, and/or existence to creatures. God self-gives and other-empowers.

When God acts in each moment, God acts for the good. We use a variety of words to describe God's loving action, words like redeeming, healing, exalting, saving, creating, revealing, restoring, calling, judging, guiding, commanding, advising, rescuing, and convicting. All of these are acts of love. And God never controls others when doing them.

I believe God acts lovingly all the time. When creatures respond well to God's loving action, positive things happen. Such love promotes overall well-being, or what Christians call blessedness, *shalom*, abundant life, or salvation. God's uncontrolling love does good!

When it comes to God's loving action, I could write page after page. My writing muscles get pumped up! In fact, I've written several books on the subject. But I'd better stop here. As the title suggests, this section's essays explore God's action. I hope the preceding provides a framework for thinking about them. Happy reading!

Endnotes

1. I argue this at length in my book, *The Nature of God: A Theology* (St. Louis, Mo.: Chalice, 2010), see especially chapter 3 on Augustine's theology of love.
2. Schubert Ogden, "Love Unbounded: The Doctrine of God," *The Perkins School of Theology Journal*, 19, no. 3 (Spring 1996): 16.

Coming Out:
An Act of Non-Coercive Power

Anthony Austin

D uring my final year at a Canadian evangelical college, my roommate opened up to the school community and shared that he was gay. While I don't know the details of what happened from an administrative point of view, the end result was that he no longer was welcome to pursue his theological education at that institution, and his hopes of being a pastor ended. At the time, I saw him as a victim of circumstance—someone who was at the mercy of the college and its community. What I doubt he realized, and what I certainly didn't understand, was his coming out (something I initially perceived as a powerless act) would later become a defining moment in my life, and I suspect in the lives of many others.

For an LGBTQ individual, revealing one's sexual orientation often begins within the immediate circle of loved ones—those with whom deep relationships are already formed. If my roommate and I had not already built bonds of friendship, I doubt his coming out would have had any lasting impact on my life. At that time, I did not know anyone who was openly gay or lesbian, and he instantly became the personal connection to a previously detached stance on this issue. Prejudice and discrimination can no longer be expressed in an ideological/ moral vacuum when someone we know and love is impacted and hurt by these views. My personal relationships with LGBTQ persons are why I care so deeply about this issue. It is through our relationships that real change occurs.

When gay men and women, and transgendered and bisexual people, ultimately accept who they are and reveal their orientation to friends and family, commonly labeled 'coming out,' it becomes surprisingly symbolic of Oord's view that God's power is expressed as uncontrolling love rather than as an uncaring, coercive power.

Isn't this how God's power works? Its effectiveness to transform and influence the world is dependent upon the relationship God has with creation. Because real change requires the co-operation of and response from creation, God cannot unilaterally change the world. It's relational. The very fact that God is not detached from the goings-on in the world is why Oord and others believe God can be deeply wounded by the things we do and the things that are done to us. Controlling power requires no connection; it is most effective when there is little to no resistance.

It is precisely because of these relationships that the act of 'coming out' exposes one to significant vulnerability, since those we love have the greatest capacity to hurt us. 'Coming out' is not risk-free. It is, at best, a calculated risk as LGBTQ individuals have little control over the reactions of others. There is no guarantee things will be all right in the end. Parents have disowned their children, friends have broken off ties, and Christian students have been kicked out of school.

I'm pretty certain my roommate's life has not been easy. He wanted to serve in a church, and that was taken away from him. Mutual friends of ours still post pejorative articles about the sins of same-sex relations or how traditional marriage is under attack. The threat of violence and discrimination is an ever-present reality. I doubt my roommate, or any LGBTQ person, wants to be a martyr for this cause, but any person who 'comes out' knows this is one of the many risks involved. In spite of this, people are still 'coming out.' There is power here . . .

Jesus didn't walk into Jerusalem simply to be crucified. Jesus entered Jerusalem as a form of protest against the coercive power of Rome. Knowing full well the risks involved, Jesus nevertheless entered the city. God's love doesn't give up on the world because the world may reject the divine calling. God's love shares in our pain because that's what loves does. Love is not real love if it is not vulnerable, if it does not involve risk.

When parents stand up in support of their LGBTQ children, and when friends become activists in solidarity with this community, acts of 'coming out' move from the private realm and become a political act, a social movement. Together they challenge the power structures of the status quo by seeking to expose as unjust the dominant narrative claiming heterosexual as the one 'normal' orientation. 'Coming out' is a public petition for justice, a call for laws that provide and protect civil equality for the LGBTQ community. While these measures are important, they cannot change hearts; only love can.

The temptation when reading Oord's book is to confuse God's uncontrolling love with a love that is undemanding. Although God cannot force a just world into being, God's love is more than simply a suggestion for justice. It is a demand for it. The potentiality of divine love as true power is only realized when that love transforms and empowers us to act. Coercive power can do neither of these.

One of the most amazing things about my former college roommate is his ability to be graceful and respectful to those who disagree with his so-called 'lifestyle.' He has maintained relationships with people who, in the name of religion, hold views I know are hurtful. He is able to challenge these views without personally attacking the ones who hold them, to patiently wait and trust people can change. His love and kindness toward them can be transformative.

A well-known quote, often attributed to Martin Luther King, Jr. says, "Let us realize the arc of the moral universe is long, but it bends toward justice."[1] This serves to illuminate the difference between coercive and non-coercive power. With coercive power, the arc may be much shorter, easier, and less risky, but it inevitably bends toward injustice. The uncontrolling love of God, wherever it finds expression, is our hope for a more just world.

Anthony lives Summerside PEI, Canada. He has a Bachelor of Arts degree from Canadian Nazarene College and a Masters of Theological Studies from the Atlantic School of Theology. In addition to being a full-time parent, he is the director of "The Abbey" worship community, which focuses on contemplative prayer, creativity in worship, and has adapted process theology as the primary lens through which to view God and the world."

Endnotes

1. Martin Luther King Jr., "How Long, Not Long" (delivered on the steps of the State Capitol in Montgomery, Alabama, March 25, 1965).

When God's Plan Falls Apart

Catherine Beals

S ince I was 12 years old, I believed the first spiritual law that said God loved me and had a wonderful plan for my life. I believed this in a very literal way and thought that 'God's Plan' was very specific. I thought God orchestrated events in my life to lead to the place He wanted us to live, the church He wanted us to attend, and the job He wanted me to have. I believed that God closed doors He didn't want me to go through and opened the ones He did. I never felt that I was controlled by God. I had a choice whether or not to go through the doors He opened. But when I didn't get a job, I would rationalize it by saying, "it must not have been God's will."

This way of believing worked for my husband and me for many years. It brought us happiness and fulfillment. We have been very blessed by what we see as God's provision in our lives. We enjoyed giving back to others all that God had given to us through ministry at our church and at the Christian university where I worked. During my 25 year career in education, I had always believed it was God's plan for my life to go back and work at this Christian university from which I had graduated. I believed it was my calling to teach future teachers. I had worked many years to earn the degrees I needed to be qualified to work in higher education. During my first few years working there, I felt I was living not just my calling but my lifelong dream. I believed I was following God's plan for my life. Then it began to fall apart.

It is hard to adequately describe the perfect storm of events that occurred in my life all at once. Our university went through a very public conflict over the firing of Oord. I believed that his firing was unethical on the part of university leadership and was dismayed at how he was treated by the administration and

Board of Trustees. It deeply affected me to watch what some call 'the machine' of organized religion in action. I saw behaviors on a Christian campus that were devastating to me and caused me to question my faith. It seemed religion was about denominational control, image, exclusion, conformity, power, money, and numbers. I saw arrogance and hate, not compassion and tolerance for diversity. I was completely disillusioned with the church.

In addition to all of the other controversy on campus, my department had been greatly downsized. I was working for all new leaders who had not hired me because the team I was originally hired to be a part of had all retired. I was not fitting in well with the new team. They made it clear to me and others that they didn't see value in my contribution to the team. Some suggested I look for another job. It was demoralizing to be treated in a disrespectful way, especially in what was supposed to be a Christian environment. My colleagues had a very different vision for the future of our department than what I believed about preparing good teachers. I ended up being assigned a role in my department that I had never applied for and didn't want. I didn't see any way my role would change for the next several years. I felt called to lead but didn't see any way to fulfill that calling at the university. I was incredibly confused. I was so sure that working at this university was God's plan for my life, yet I was very unhappy and professionally unfulfilled. There were also events going on in my personal life that made dealing with the conflicts at work very difficult. I just didn't know what to do.

I felt that my only option to find the freedom to be the person and the leader I believed God created me to be was to leave this university that I loved. That broke my heart. I had spent my whole life devoted to this dream—one that I wholeheartedly believed was God's plan for my life. My entire life was built around my work and ministry at the university. I couldn't picture what life could be like outside of it. I was scared, confused, and hurt, but I was also angry at the church. I felt the church had betrayed me. I was wondering if I even believed in Christianity anymore. Well-meaning people suggested perhaps it was 'God's Plan' for me to leave, but that went against everything I believed in my heart. God's plan was not making any sense to me. Then, in the words of a Toby Mac song, "love broke through."

Through reading *The Uncontrolling Love of God* and hearing Oord speak, I have come to understand that 'God's plan' for my life is a much larger concept than I previously understood. I now believe that 'God's Plan' is simply to live a life of love. It isn't a specific script or planned path for my life. I can follow 'God's

Plan' in a variety of ways. It is not bound by denominational, cultural, organizational or geographical boundaries. Oord says, "God relentlessly expresses love in the quest to promote overall well-being."[1] I realized that God loved me as His unique creation. The Spirit's plan for me was not to stay in an environment that was not healthy for me. God's Plan for me was to follow love. Oord says, "God providentially calls all creation toward love and beauty."[2]

I now have a new job that I love outside of the university. My leadership role in public education allows me to promote the wellbeing of teachers and students every day. I am still living the calling I felt on my heart 20 years ago to teach teachers. I am finding joy in what I call 'God's Plan B.' I have rebuilt my life, guided by love for my family, love for my work in the world, and love for God. I work with loving people from a variety of religious affiliations who bring out the best in me. Oord says, "We can be God's partners and co-conspirators by following the Spirit's lead. God's collaborative love seeks all who want to work for well-being, which is God's purpose (Rom 8:28)."[3] By following love and the Spirit's lead, I was able to find my way through this very painful season of my life.

Dr. Catherine Beals is the Administrator of Curriculum, Instruction and Assessment for the Kuna School District in Kuna, Idaho. She is an alumnus of Northwest Nazarene University and holds advanced degrees from Boise State University and University of Idaho. She is a busy mom of two teen-agers and has been married to her best friend for almost 29 years. She enjoys spending time in the outdoors with her family, especially at the beach.

Endnotes

1. Thomas Jay Oord, *The Uncontrolling Love of God: An Open and Relational Account of Providence* (Downers Grove, IL: InterVarsity, 2015), 161.
2. Oord, 94.
3. Oord, 165.

What Use Is God?

Robert D. Cornwall

What use is God if God can't or won't prevent evil from occurring? That's a question people have been asking for millennia. Theologians and philosophers have done their best to offer answers defending God (the term for this is theodicy), but the question keeps arising. It would be easier if Christian theology allowed for the existence of two equally powerful gods, one good and the other evil (dualism). Then evil could be blamed on the evil god, leaving the God of love untainted (it's an idea that Marcion, for one, embraced). While Marcion's vision is still with us in many ways, if we are to remain true to a monotheistic vision in which God has no ultimate rival, then we'll need to look elsewhere for answers to the question of why evil exists.

A seventeenth-century theologian suggested this is "the best possible world,"[1] and so we should accept things as they are. This solution, however, fell short of expectations and ultimately failed to gain full support. Either God is capable of keeping evil at bay (omnipotent) and fails to do so, or God is too weak to address evil. If either is true, then why bother with God?

There might be another option, one offered by Thomas Jay Oord. As an advocate of open/relational theology, Oord both affirms God's full ability to act and God's inability to prevent evil. It's not a question of divine power; it's a question of what takes precedence—power or love. Oord chooses love, declaring that love precludes God from acting coercively. If this is true, then a loving God cannot coerce creation into achieving a satisfactory outcome. Even if God cannot act coercively, this does not mean God does not act in creation. According to Oord, divine agency is marked by God's partnership with creation itself to achieve healing. This is why the cross stands at the center of the Christian faith.

The cross is the means by which God overcomes evil and brings healing or shalom to creation. As a relational theologian, Oord suggests God works in creation at a deeper level than we usually presume. Indeed, God goes down to the subatomic level to pursue change. At that level of existence, God is busy encouraging the very elements of the universe to work together for the common good.

Oord's proposal presents a challenge to us. We humans often want God to act directly and visibly in bringing about a desired outcome (overcoming evil). What we want, it seems, is Superman. The God we encounter in Jesus, however, doesn't appear to work that way. That is troubling! Jesus chooses not to take on the guise of Superman. Instead, as he tells Pilate, his kingdom is not of this world. In overcoming evil, Jesus isn't going to make use of traditional tools. Could we say that he will engage in spiritual warfare using a different set of tools than we might normally expect?

In developing his theodicy, Tom turns to what he calls "essential kenosis." In this mode, he envisions God in terms of the "self-giving, others-empowering nature of love."[2] Because of this radical love "God cannot withdraw, override or fail to provide the freedom, agency, self-organizing and law like regularity."[3] In other words, God provides the opportunity to partner in the work of shalom, but because love defines God, God cannot override this freedom. Despite claims to value freedom on the part of many denizens of this world (especially in places like the United States), I would venture to guess most Christians (and those who might be attracted to the faith) wouldn't mind a bit of intervention once in a while just to rescue us from our own stupidity! Why else do we so dislike our governing leaders?

As we ponder these questions, especially considering such horrific expressions of evil as demonstrated by the Holocaust or the horrors of Aleppo, how might the biblical story of the cross provide us with answers? How does the cross overcome evil? We could point to the resurrection, of course, which affirms evil doesn't have the last word, but with all due respect to God's love, why must we reject divine coercive intervention as contrary to love? If God has the power to keep evil at bay, why not use it? Wouldn't that be the loving thing to do?

I must admit I'm both attracted to and unsure about this proposal. I affirm the primacy of love. It is a principle that informs nonviolent responses to injustice. At the same time, part of me wants God to intervene directly and set things right. I'm not quite as confident as Oord appears to be that we will respond appropriately to God's invitation. Part of me wonders whether Tom is taking the presence of evil as seriously as perhaps he should. Even if I don't embrace a dual-istic theology, it does seem that there is a spiritual power at work in the world that seeks to disrupt the work of God. Thus, I'm attracted to the premise es-poused by Richard Beck in his book, *Reviving Old Scratch,* which invites the 'doubters and disenchanted' to reconsider the idea of the devil/Satan. Beck rec-ognizes that the idea of spiritual warfare can be dangerous in the hands of human beings, so we're attracted to the idea of keeping "our focus on the love, mercy and grace of God."[4] That is a worthy goal, but considering our realities, Beck believes we need more than simply a commitment to social justice. We may need to en-gage in spiritual warfare. The good news is that Beck's vision of spiritual warfare fits well with Tom's emphasis on God's love. Beck's vision is rooted in his belief in the "One Love" idea, where there is no conflict between loving God and loving creation. Beck suggests that in his mind, spiritual warfare involves a "choice be-tween the cross and all that is tempting us away from the cross."[5] By satanic, he means "all that is *opposed* or *adversarial* to love, all that is opposed to the cross."[6] Thus, his vision of love is cruciform. Again, I think that this vision fits well with Tom's vision of love. I might suggest that these two proposals be read in tandem.

Tom's proposal is attractive, in part because it offers us a vision of how God might work without foreknowledge of the future. It's one thing to prevent some-thing bad from happening if you have foreknowledge and could do something about it ahead of time. If you know your product will cause cancer, then you likely will be held liable in a court of law. So, if God knows that bad things are bound to happen, shouldn't God be held liable for the consequences? On the other hand, if future acts of evil remain unknown to God until they occur, then it would seem to hold that God can't be held liable for not preventing them from occurring. The question then becomes: how will God respond. Will it be an act of violent resis-tance or an act of love, and what does this love look like?

Open Theism, such as Oord embraces, allows for an open future, while in-sisting that God is always at work and will not give up on achieving shalom. Therefore, we can take confidence in God's determination to work in willing partnership with creation to achieve shalom. Love will always serve as the guide to this work of God. That the future remains open and unknown, even to God, is also true. The future contains unknown risks.

The good news is, in Oord's words, God is an 'omnipresent spirit.' Therefore, as Paul declared: "If God is for us, who is against us?"[7] I take Paul's word to mean, in light of Oord's musings, that God is persistent in pursuing the common good for all creation. Therefore, even in the face of evil, there is reason for God! Indeed, there is reason to be in relationship with this God who seeks to be in relationship with us! If we are to engage with God in spiritual warfare, as Richard Beck lays out, then what will this look like in light of the cross? Beck also speaks in terms of kenosis and love, suggesting that "spiritual warfare is the tactical interruption of the world with love," and, furthermore, "love subverts and sabotages the pattern of the world playfully, innovatively, theatrically, extemporaneously, spontaneously, opportunistically, and artistically."[8] As I ponder Tom's vision of God acting noncoercively in love, but acting nonetheless, I'm wondering how this might express itself in terms of Beck's vision of spiritual warfare. It's an important question considering the current realities we face in our world, where love seems to be disadvantaged by a vision of fear and anger.

Robert D. Cornwall is pastor of Central Woodward Christian Church (Disciples of Christ), Troy, Michigan. He is the author of thirteen books, his latest being Marriage in Interesting Times, (Energion Publications), and he blogs regularly at bobcornwall.com.

Endnotes

1. Gottfried Wilhelm Leibniz, *The Monadology*, Robert Latta, trans. (South Australia: University of Adelaide, 2014), https://ebooks.adelaide.edu.au/l/leibniz/gottfried /l525m/ (accessed January 23, 2017).

2. Thomas Jay Oord, *The Uncontrolling Love of God: An Open and Relational Account of Providence* (Downers Grove, IL: InterVarsity, 2015), 169.

3. Ibid.

4. Richard Beck, *Reviving Old Scratch: Demons and the Devil for Doubters and the Disenchanted,* (Minneapolis: Fortress, Press, 2016), pp. xvi-xvii.

5. Beck, 92.

6. Ibid.

7. Rom. 8:31 (NRSV).

8. Beck, 179.

Natural Evil and Why Our Hope Is Secure

John Culp

O ord's Uncontrolling Love's treatment of natural evil points toward a more secure basis for hope in the defeat of natural evil and the role of humans in responding to evil of all types. Natural evil, as experienced in earthquakes or lung cancer in someone who has never smoked or lived in an area with polluted air, raises some of the most difficult challenges to understanding how God loves our world. While human freedom causes much of the destruction in the world, it seems as though human actions would not interfere with God's love for the natural world, and love would be effective in deterring destruction. And yet, natural destruction such as earthquakes and cancer in children occurs and challenges claims that God's love is present.

Oord helps us understand the occurrence of natural evil by pointing out the importance of regularity for moral responsibility. If we don't know that sharp edges cut human flesh, we can't be held responsible for hurting someone because we don't know what will result from certain actions. The regularities of nature tell us that sharp knives cut people, but Oord recognizes randomness occurs in the natural world as well. Furthermore, randomness opens up an opportunity for a world capable of developing in creative ways. However, accepting randomness as part of our reality appears to indicate God is not in control of at least some events. While God, acting out of love, may have created a world of regularity resulting in hurricanes; God creating a world in which random events occur appears to mean there are aspects God does not cause or control.

Oord's acceptance of randomness is one reason why some people have criticized his emphasis upon God's uncontrolling love as leading to a concept of God as limited. A limited God cannot overcome destruction that has no purpose—evil. If God is limited, God is unable to love the world adequately by removing evil from God's world. Such a God is unworthy of worship, because we cannot trust that God to save us from evil.

However, understanding God as characterized by uncontrolling love shifts the emphasis from God's power to God's love as the primary characteristic of God. God, out of love, creates a world with both regularity and randomness rather than a world completely determined by God's specific actions. Emphasizing God's love rather than God's omnipotence provides a better way of understanding God's actions in the world. Stressing God's love does not result in an unreliable God who cannot be worshipped. In fact, love offers a more adequate basis for God's reliability than power. We can trust God to care for us, because love is who God is; but if God is first characterized by power, God's power could be used to bring about destruction rather than love. God's love directing God's power can be trusted to bring about good rather than destruction and even to bring good out of destruction. Power alone might respond to destruction by destroying what has caused that evil. Instead, God's love for God's creation leads to God working with every aspect of creation in continuing creativity.

One of the implications of the priority of love, in understanding God, is God involving the creation in God's activity. Humans, and all creation, share in creating. Our activity can contribute to God's purposes. Our involvement in bringing about God's purposes may even surprise and please God. We too may be startled by how God enables us to respond to situations threatening to overwhelm us. The person who lifts a car off a person pinned under the car is astounded at what they were able to do. God working with us to bring good out of evil is more loving than God guaranteeing our safety by direct action without our action. Working with us demonstrates God values us, and our contributions, even though we frequently limit God's care for the world by choosing against God's love.

The priority of God's uncontrolling love also has important implications for our understanding of humans as created in God's image. If God's uncontrolling love has priority over God's power, then as creatures in God's image we also should demonstrate love rather than power. Our abilities to do and to create should be used for the care of others rather than for the control of others. Bringing aid to those who have suffered destruction from a hurricane is a way of caring for those who suffer rather than a way of demonstrating our superior abilities.

Sacrifice, as part of God's love, then becomes important for us. Sacrifice values other created realities by working to bring good out of evil in cooperation with God as uncontrolling love. We respond in love to the victims of the hurricane in Haiti and to the person who never smoked and suffers from lung cancer. The priority of divine love over power leads to an understanding of natural evil that challenges human creativity and sacrifice, in imitation of God, creating hope by working to bring good out of evil.

John E. Culp's studies at Greenville College, Asbury Theological Seminary, Butler University, and Claremont Graduate School prepared him to teach at Bethel College (IN), Olivet Nazarene College, and Azusa Pacific University. His work in philosophy of religion has been challenged and inspired by teachers he has had, students in classes, and numerous colleagues all of whom he is grateful to. Playing and coaching soccer led to being a Manchester United fan.

Is Time of Death Preordained?

John W. Dally

W hat is God waiting for?"
"What have I done to deserve this?"
"She will die when it is her time."
"It must have been his time."
"It was not her time."
"God had his hand on him."
"I guess God was not ready to receive her yet."

These statements reveal the belief that someone's time of death is some-how dependent upon God's action or will. Is time of death preordained, unchangeable?

To begin with, let us look at death caused by others. We have all heard of people dying of tainted food that was not processed properly. People have died of Listeria, E. coli, Salmonella, Staph Bacteria, and Hepatitis A. Each of these comes from either processing problems or the criminal neglect of producers cutting corners. If God is using these situations to meet his predetermined time of death, then the people involved are not culpable. And why risk the expo-sure of an entire population to reach the specific individuals whose time had come to die?

Another cause of death is automobile accidents. Such accidents are responsi-ble for over 30,000 deaths in the US every year. The causes of these accidents can be the result of negligence, poor road conditions, refusal of the driver or passen-gers to use seatbelts, or driving under the influence. In each case some die, some do not. It is unreasonable to assign the blame for these deaths to God. Why would

God use something like a 'chain reaction accident' to get to the few whose lives he intends to end?

Lately we have read of too many instances of a person going into a public place and shooting up a crowd, be it at a theater, a mall, or a school. From Columbine to Sandy Hook, some died and some did not. It does not make sense that God would use scattering bullets to kill only those God has preordained to die while missing those whose time is not up. To assign the blame to God, one would have to accept that God instilled in the mind of these mass murderers the need to kill innocent men, women, and children. This makes such murderers instruments of God, so God's timing can be fulfilled. It makes God the murderer. Add to this other human acts like abortion, genocide, and war, and we have to wonder: is God directing these actions to meet a timetable?

Before we come to any conclusions, we need to look at the other side of the coin—surviving.

Joan was under hospice care because she had three fistulas. A fistula is a passage from an internal organ to the outside surface of the skin. She had to have ostomy bags attached over the fistulas to catch the fluid leaking from her intestine. The leaking was so bad that, without the aid of saline infusions, she would dehydrate and suffer excruciating pain in her joints and limbs. She asked me what God was waiting for. I asked her what would have happened if she had not had that first surgery.

"I would have died."

It was the same for the second and third blockages. As opposed to an act of God, her choices have kept her alive. During our next visit, she told me she had set a date, after Christmas, when she would discontinue the infusions and 'let things run their course.' The last time I saw her; there was a joy in her I had not seen before. She made the choice, this time, to let death come.

In October of 2005, I woke up with pain in my chest. My wife saw that I was awake and asked what was wrong.

I said, "I don't feel well."

She turned on the light and what she saw was her husband, ashen in color and sweating profusely. She called 911 and paramedics came, stabilized me, and got to me to the hospital where they placed two stents in my left anterior descending artery. This event is referred to as 'The Widow Maker,' because when the LAD is fully occluded, as mine was, it will cause a massive heart attack and probably death. If not for the paramedics, who did not exist until after 1970, and stents, mine had been available for only three years before my event; I would most likely be dead or severely debilitated.

In both these cases, lives were extended by medical technology and human choice—not by a timetable. Human intervention changed the outcomes.

We also find examples of human intervention affecting time of death, in Scripture.

Abraham bartered with the Angel of the Lord over the destruction of Sodom and Gomorrah.[1] Moses changed God's mind about destroying the Israelites at Mt. Sinai.[2] Hezekiah was given fifteen more years to live.[3] Jonah was disappointed that God changed his mind about destroying Nineveh, because the people repented.[4] While in the Hebrew Scriptures God was responsible for the flood, plagues, and wars; they were not preordained times of death for individuals. They were acts that God took after disobedience to God's will. Even the destruction of Israel and Judah were not preordained. Prophets warned the people that their disobedience would lead to destruction *if* they did not change their ways. Here is the irony of Jonah. He told Nineveh they would be destroyed. However, they repented and changed God's plan.[5]

The above examples from life and Scripture are illustrations of Kenotic Theology. As Jesus emptied himself, God the Father does the same to allow free will.[6] This makes our interaction with God based on a loving relationship without coercion. While this has its downside, as with the deaths cited above and the suffering of living longer with medical intervention, it also has a big benefit. We are in a loving relationship with God, and God will not forcefully intervene to meet his predetermined design, even if it means we will suffer.

This also leads to another important observation. If humans can affect their actual time of death, this results in unlimited possibilities for the future (What if Hitler had died in WWI?). While God knows all possibilities, the future is uncertain until humans make their choices. This is the basis of Open Theology—the future is not determined, because both humans and God have free will. Since God is not a God of coercion, human free will—and even the nonhuman, that is, the whole of the cosmos—determine the future. Every element of the cosmos is free to follow its own nature. Therefore, a meteor can strike the earth causing the final blow to the dinosaur, or a seed can blow on the wind and land anywhere.

From this overview of time of death we can conclude:

1. Time of death is not preordained but is determined by an interaction, based in God's love, between the person and God.
2. God is a loving God and does not preordain; but through the concept of Kenosis, God allows humanity to determine its fate.
3. The future is open, because humanity can make decisions that can shorten or extend life, which has far reaching implications.

The conclusion that I have arrived at is that our time of death is not pre-ordained. Our lives can be shortened at the hands of people or extended by the use of modern medicine. In either case, our time of death is subject to the free will of others or our free will actions. Even the Bible attests to this give and take.

John Dally is an ordained elder in the church of the Nazarene. He has pastured and taught bible and theology for the Nazarene Bible college extension in Pasadena and for their online program. He has been serving as a hospice chaplain for the past nine years. His interests are history, science, and theology.

Endnotes

1. Gen. 18:22-23 (NIV).
2. Exod. 32:11-14
3. Isa. 38:5
4. Jon. 3:10
5. Ibid.
6. Phil. 2:3-13

Does the Bible Really Tell Me So?

Craig Drurey

I am one of those people! Yes, I enjoy reality T.V. shows—not all, but many. One in particular that I like is *"Little People."* In case you have never had the pleasure of watching, this show has followed the Roloff family. The Roloff family consists of two parents who happen to be little people, three regular size children, and one son who is also a little person.

Those of us who have followed the Roloff family have witnessed the children growing up, going to college, and getting married. The family has experienced bumps along the way as well as many joyful and memorable experiences. As is typical of reality T.V., each person shares his or her perspective as these good and difficult experiences unfold. Each person has a unique, yet truthful, way of seeing a particular situation. If this show included, let's say, only the father's perspective; important depth and a full picture of the love this family shares would be missing from the story. Only as each person is heard, can this reality be shared in its full light.

I have been considering for some time the full meaning of incarnation. Incarnation, in its simplest conception, describes how God took on flesh. Jesus became human. Orthodox Christianity describes this tension as being fully God and fully human. In God's desire to demonstrate God's love for creation, God came and lived with us. God desired to experience creation from the perspective of one of God's created—as a person.

Thomas Jay Oord's recent book, *The Uncontrolling Love of God*, has caused me to consider further what this incarnation reveals about how God works with creation. It seems to me that this is how God takes on most, if not all, activity—in cooperation with creation. Jesus—fully God and fully human. The Church—fully God and fully human. Even in our individual faith journey, we like to say that God lives in us and with us. Why would the Bible be any different? If God always acts in cooperation with creation, then could we not say the same about the Bible? I assert that scripture was written, canonized, and even now is read through a process of being fully God and fully human.

Going back to the example of the Roloffs, we could not see the depth of love and interaction if only the father dictated his perspective to the camera. Indeed, we could understand to some extent, but I would suggest that we would not be able to fully connect with the family. God understands this dimension in God's desire to unpack the reality of *our* family.

As the church, we have often described the Bible as God's story. Indeed, it does reveal God's interaction with creation. However, I think we leave out an important segment that God values when we describe scripture in this way. A more helpful way would be to describe scripture as not only God's story, but our story—the story of how humanity has interacted with God.

In this view, God would never authoritatively dictate the words to be written, the books to be canonized, or our interpretation as we read today. Absolutely, God was, is, and will continue to be fully involved in the process of scripture. However, just like the Roloff family, God invites and desires full human interaction with scripture. The uncontrolling love of God makes for a much more beautiful view of scripture—a view where scripture is not only fully God but fully human. Scripture takes on the sometimes flawed humanity but still reveals a loving God perfectly.

How does this view change our interaction with scripture? We no longer have to argue the discrepancies, contradictions, and flawed views people have espoused over time. Tremendous amounts of time do not have to be consumed in an effort to force the Bible to become a history or science textbook. No longer can other biblical view camps claim that we throw out certain portions of the Bible. For in this view, we embrace the fully human parts along with the revelation of God and God's desire to redeem all things.

With this perspective, we see just how beautiful the uncontrolling love of God really is. Just as Jesus took on human flesh and then took on all the sin, hatred, and violence we could throw at Him through the cross, God has done the same in scripture. Any flaw, discrepancy, or contradiction does not make the

Bible less believable but more beautiful. God so loves creation that God is not threatened by human involvement. Instead, God actually cherishes, desires, and welcomes it. For the Bible tells me so!

Craig Drurey is a lifelong resident of Northeastern Ohio. He earned a Bachelor in Business Administration from Mount Vernon Nazarene University. Wanting to deepen his walk with God, Craig then went on to earn a Master of Divinity from Northwest Nazarene University. He is currently in the dissertation phase for a Doctor of Ministry in Wesleyan Practices from Ashland Theological Seminary. He currently serves as the Director of Discipleship for Green Valley United Methodist Church. Craig is also an adjunct professor for multiple Christian Universities. He teaches spiritual formation and discipleship courses, helping students to understand and engage transformation in Christ.

Why, God, Can't You Control this Madness?

Mike Edwards

S ome may question why so much evil exists if God truly loves. If God is powerful enough to create, surely God could stop at least some evils. Some sufferings lead to good. A surgeon may have to break open your chest to save your life. But, what purpose is served when a child is raped or when a dictator tortures and kills millions? Why doesn't God, like any good parent, prevent such evils if possible? How we respond to this question can determine whether we believe in God or whether, in the midst of suffering, we feel abandoned by God.

Some appeal to mystery when their explanation to this question suggests God's ways are not always moral—humanly speaking. God cannot participate in evil actions but claim not to be evil. God's communication through words in the Bible then becomes nonsensical. If God calls favoritism evil but plays favorites, this plain and simply makes a supposedly loving God evil. The Old Testament does not suggest God's ways are mysterious to the human mind: *". . . my thoughts are not your thoughts, neither are your ways my ways . . ."* (Isa. 55:8). The context exhorts readers to forsake their wicked thoughts and ways and turn to God's more moral thoughts and ways.

For this time in my life, Thomas Jay Oord in his book, *The Uncontrolling Love of God,* offers the best answer to this age old question. Freedom is the only path that brings the most joy to authentic relationships. There is no greater feeling than knowing partners, children, and friends love you because they want to love, not because they feel obligated to love. Human beings know 'controlling love' is an oxymoron and not love at all. God, like parents, had a choice—to not create or to create knowing suffering was a possibility in the process of attaining intimacy.

It is impossible for God to create without freedom or to create and control. God's nature, instead, is love that never controls. Since God's love is uncontrolling, God cannot stop the evil that results in so much suffering. What God's love can do is prevent evil through the free decisions of others to change or intervene in the lives of those around them. God can influence in all the appropriate ways, but divine love limits divine power. We ask why God did not take Hitler out of this world, but Hitler was enabled and chosen by many who could have stopped him.

God doesn't seek obligatory love any more than parents wish their children to feel manipulated to love them. God may have surmised over time that God's overpowering presence in our lives could cause consuming guilt or obligation to obey. Obligatory choices don't always lead to lasting change. God's lack of interference and visibility may allow the independence needed to become more the person we want to be in the long-run. God's invisibility may come out of uncontrolling love rather than cruelness. God's constant interference and presence might prevent a superior world from emerging as a result of limiting the moral development and improvement of free creatures to make loving, independent choices.

The uncontrolling love of God is also a better explanation than God 'allows.' When we say God allows, it gives the impression God stands by when God could stop evil. No one admires those who stand by in the name of freedom while individual rights are being violated. How can we justify God doing nothing if God could control evil in the first place? An explanation is that God cannot stop evil, thus act controlling, except through influence without violating one's freedom. God can no more control others than God can choose not to love them perfectly.

But, if God is capable of miracles, God obviously is able to intervene and limit power, sometimes. Miracles are not the norm, but I must admit that why God intervenes sometimes and not others may be beyond our capacity to understand. God may be able to perform miracles and answer prayers while balancing the gift of freedom and uncontrolling love. The 'butterfly effect' suggests that the flap of a butterfly wing in one part of the world can influence weather in another part of the world at some time in the future. We can't know all the factors involved that God can see and know. What we do know is that God never wants us to suffer undeservingly, and God always wants to answer prayer, but God has constraints because of freedom. When God doesn't perform a miracle or when God's doesn't answer our prayers, there are factors involved for why God acts the way God does.

This explanation of God's uncontrolling love may make it seem like God is less powerful unless it is compared with the love of parents who do not control their children, thus demonstrating a greater degree of love. God's love is self-sacrificing rather than controlling. God came down to earth in the person of Jesus and faced tremendous undeserved suffering to convince us of God's incredible love in hopes we might be inspired to allow God to empower us to reflect God's love to others. God's love can always prevent evil through the free decisions of others to change or intervene in the lives of others. The answer to, "Why God," may ultimately come down to trust. Does God prevent all the evil possible without controlling one's freedom? Is God's love arbitrary and coercive or is God's love all-encompassing and uncontrolling?

Mike Edwards blogs at: http://mikeedwards123.wordpress.com. In his spare time, Mike loves to play tennis, read, and spend time with his family.

Prayer to the Uncontrolling God

Rodney A. Ellis

L ord, teach us to pray, as John taught his disciples."[1]
As far as we know, John had offered no secret handshake or genuine decoder ring, but he had instructed his disciples in ways of prayer. Jesus' disciples wanted him to do the same. So he taught them, offering those famous words that have been recited for two millennia, "Our Father, who art in heaven."[2]

He provided a prayer, spoken faithfully and dissected theologically over the centuries. It was a prayer to the uncontrolling God.

What does it mean to our prayer lives that God is uncontrolling? How does that differ from praying to a God of coercion? The implications are doubtless many. Among them are: we speak to a God who persuades us, we speak to a God we may persuade, we may know better what we may expect of our God, and we may know better how to watch for our God's answers to prayer.

Prayer to the God who Persuades Us

The way we see God matters, for many reasons. One of those is the way we relate to God in prayer. If we pray to a controlling God, we pray to the ultimate domination system—a model of rule consistent with that of Caesar. If we pray to an uncontrolling God whose core essence is love, we speak to the Father who longs for us to come willingly, uncompelled, and to see his kingdom spread in a cooperative, non-coercive manner.

How does God persuade us? The uncontrolling God isn't waiting with an ethereal paddle to wallop us into submission. I suppose a wallop might be efficient, but it would be pretty severe. It seems to me the loving, uncontrolling God would prefer gentle coaxing to wallops. Therefore, seeing God's true nature can help us approach him with more of the love he desires and less of the fear a domination system imparts.

Prayer to the God we May Persuade

God's loving, uncontrolling nature also shows us he can be persuaded. We can influence God to change his mind. The Scriptures offer several examples of this, providing evidence that the future is not fixed by the unmovable will of the Almighty. (Remember Abraham's prayer for Sodom and Gomorrah and Jesus' prayer in the Garden that the cup might pass from him?) Rather, the witness of Scripture suggests we are collaborative partners with God, influencing him and being empowered by him in the work of establishing the kingdom on earth.

The idea that we are collaborative partners with God has a significant impact on our prayer lives. In essence, we go to God not only trying to discern his will, but also suggesting solutions ourselves. We are wise, of course, to leave the ultimate decision up to the Almighty. Where, after all, were we when he laid the foundations of the world? Still we are free to argue, debate, and recommend. By joining in this kind of interaction we are better able to understand God's reasoning and participate more fully and intentionally in God's vision.

Knowing Better what We can Expect of God

How can we expect God to react to our prayers? We go to him to praise, to confess our sins, to give thanks, and to make requests. We can expect him to receive our prayers taking our mutual well-being to heart. We cannot expect God to intervene in everything or blame him when we are faced with tragedy. Rather, in recognizing his nature we can see he simply cannot coerce outcomes in certain situations. We can, however, trust him to gently influence the direction and decisions of both creatures and nature.

I just returned from a trip to Haiti, the poorest nation in the Western Hemisphere. Ravaged by a couple of centuries of leadership issues and ill-advised international aid, most of its people live in absolute poverty, often uncertain as to where they will find tomorrow's food and shelter. Why does God not simply wave his magic wand and change things for the Haitians? I believe there are two answers. One is he cannot; he is forbidden by his loving nature to violate the free will of those who would be affected by such a decision. The second answer, in my opinion, is that God wants to work collaboratively with us to solve the problem. Understanding how God works can motivate us not only to trust his enticing power, but also to be more active in righting the wrongs in the world.

Knowing How to Watch for God's Answers to Prayer

Confession time: I have been known to pray the occasional 'smite prayer' asking God to strike down my enemies. After all, I have rationalized; if it was good enough for David it is good enough for me. The problem with the smite prayer, of course, is that it's pretty out of line with God's loving nature. It's also out of line with the uncontrolling way he works in the world. A God who is love is not eager to smite. Rather, he is eager to work alongside us as co-laborers bringing about his will. This is a single example of the way our expectations of how prayers are answered change when we see God as he is. Prayer to the loving, uncontrolling God means looking for opportunities to influence rather than dominate. It means being alert for the gentle breath of the Spirit rather than constantly looking for hurricane blasts.

Conclusion

"Teach us to pray," the disciples asked, and Jesus did.[3] Yet prayer is about much more than knowing the right words to say. It is also about knowing the God to whom we pray. Our God is love, and therefore cannot be controlling. Let us go to him nestled in the tender embrace of his love and persuasion.

Rodney A. Ellis (Rod) is former a lot of things. Most recently he is a former mental health practitioner and soon to be former Associate Professor of Social Work at The University of Tennessee. He plans to move to Haiti following his retirement in December, 2016 to continue the work he and a small but amazing team have begun establishing—mindfulness programs in the schools and orphanages of that country. His major focus will be supporting the work of a school established by the American Haitian Foundation. He is also the proud pappy of an 18-year-old son, Cody.

Endnotes

1. Luke 11:1 (ESV).
2. Matthew 6:9 (ASV).
3. Luke 11:1 (ESV).

Transcending Fear Itself:
A Journey from the Personal
To the Political

Patricia Adams Farmer

"The only thing we have to fear is fear itself."[1]
—Franklin Delano Roosevelt

When I was young seminarian in the 1970s, I suffered from anorexia nervosa. I learned to starve myself for the sake of unnatural thinness—and this was before eating disorders became a contagion on campuses around the world. As a 'pioneer in the field,' my absolutist-oriented anorexic mind was of the opinion that if you ate one cookie, it was like the "Domino Theory" during Vietnam, which goes something like: If Vietnam falls, so goes all of Southeast Asia! Letting my guard down for even one cookie meant my whole world could fall into utter chaos, overrun by barbaric hoards.

Of course, anorexia is not so much about food and thinness; it's really about fear and control. What did I fear? I feared being fat, yes, but that was just the surface. What I really feared was not being liked, not being loved, not being good enough—that deep, dark, basic human predicament that sociologist Brené Brown calls 'shame.' Only if I exercised rigid control over my food could I trick myself into feeling worthy—even special. Starving myself gave me a false sense of superiority, characteristic of rigid people.

I felt imprisoned in a tiny cell. Of course I wanted to be free—I could see happy people through the bars of my window—but I was too afraid to open the door and walk out into the wideness and sunshine. What if I lost control? Worse, what if I discovered that I was only mediocre, nothing special? Fear was starving me, body and soul. And it affected everyone around me like an invisible poison infecting the air.

When fear takes on a life of its own, it becomes a contagion. And when there is a contagion of fear, there is the danger of a full-blown famine of the collective soul. You could say that anorexia is analogous to what's happening in our world today—a form of social anorexia: rigid ideologies, soul-shriveling theology, us-vs-them worldviews, all issuing from that dark place called 'fear itself.'

Fear itself is fear that has taken on a life of its own, disconnected from reality. Fear of the Other, fear of scarcity, fear of change, fear of not being good enough— all this excess fear starves and shames the soul, resulting in a xenophobic contagion of rigid ideology, religious fundamentalism, and scapegoating that stirs up racism, misogyny, homophobia, and Islamophobia.

But how can fear do all this damage? Fear lives in a landscape of distorted perceptions. There is no debating a person held hostage by fear. We wonder why facts roll off the backs of the rabid extremists, why they seem immune to reason. But starving souls perceive things in a garbled, confused way, like an anorexic. They simply can't see straight.

I remember standing in front of a full-length mirror and declaring myself hopelessly overweight, when in fact I was skin and bones. My mother said I looked like a victim of a death camp, while I saw a fat person. I simply could not see—or face—reality.

But if I was in seminary, studying the Bible and theology, how could such a disease of the mind take over? Where was God? To be honest, God was only making things worse. At the time, I was studying at an institution that was falling headlong into the tragic black hole of Christian fundamentalism. The theology I studied focused on an all-controlling view of God: a God to be feared. This made perfect sense to my anorexic, absolutist mindset. I needed a 'strongman' sort of God to take care of things, to take care of me.

But when I got well—when my vision cleared and I could see reality—only then could I begin to question the 'strongman' view of God. I fell, for a time, into a rather freeing agnosticism, allowing me space to study broadly and inquire courageously and imagine wildly—this time with a healthy mind.

I discovered the key to health was to face my fears with acceptance, love, and courage: to dare to be vulnerable. I also discovered, with a great deal of help, that I was a mere mortal surrounded by a host of other mere mortals who were all struggling like me to make sense out of life. By coming down the lonely mountain of self-righteous superiority and daring vulnerability, my judgmental attitude fell away, replaced by a deep compassion for others as well as for myself.

And when it came to God, I knew I did not need a God of fear and control. Rather, I needed a God of love, a God of vulnerability, a God who—if I opened the door to my little cell—would meet me, not with judgment, but with open arms.

The courage to re-think everything, even theology, is part of the work. My friend Thomas Jay Oord recently wrote a remarkable and controversial book called *The Uncontrolling Love of God*. Challenging the status quo is risky and sometimes comes at a great price. To me, he is a hero, one who dares to become vulnerable for the sake of love.

By embracing the uncontrolling love of God—modeled by Jesus himself—I learned to let the dominoes fall, to eat a cookie when I want one, and to exhilarate in the beautiful world outside the prison of absolute control.

Those of us who choose to widen out in love rather than shrink back in fear not only bring health to the individual soul, but also to the wider world where the threat of a 'strongman' to solve our problems is always a temptation. But this is a delusion. For the truth is, fear tempts us into thin, rigid, and judgmental worldviews, while love lures us to go wide with compassion, courage, and imagination. Along with Thomas Jay Oord, I choose to stand—at all costs—on the side of love, vulnerable love, empowering love: uncontrolling love.

Patricia Adams Farmer (patriciaadamsfarmer.com) is an ordained minister in the Christian Church (Disciples of Christ) and the author of several books, including Embracing a Beautiful God and Fat Soul: A Philosophy of S-I-Z-E. With advanced degrees in theology, philosophy, and education, her special focus is process theology, aesthetics, and storytelling. She is a featured writer for Jesus, Jazz, and Buddhism (edited by Jay McDaniel), and works with Process and Faith. After five years of living, exploring, and writing in the beautiful country of Ecuador, she currently resides with her husband, Ron Farmer, in Albuquerque, New Mexico.

Endnotes

1. Franklin D. Roosevelt, Inaugural Address, March 4, 1933

God Is Not All-Powerful, and the Bible Tells Us So

Christopher Fisher

C hariots of Iron.

In the beginning chapter of Judges, God is with the people of Israel, wishing to give them the Promised Land. God helps Judah defeat many enemies, but when they finally reach the plains, cutting-edge military technology is encountered:

"And the LORD was with Judah, and he took possession of the hill country, but he could not drive out the inhabitants of the plain because they had chariots of iron."[1]

Judah was not able to defeat an army of chariots. Where was God? Did God suddenly withdraw protection? Can God be defeated by chariots?

This isn't an isolated instance. In 2 Kings, there is an interesting section where God promises Israel victory over the Moabites, saying it will be an easy win. Things do not turn out that way:

"This is a light thing in the sight of the Lord. He will also give the Moabites into your hand . . ."[2]

"When the king of Moab saw that the battle was going against him . . . he took his oldest son who was to reign in his place and offered him for a burnt offering on the wall. And there came great wrath against Israel. And they withdrew from him and returned to their own land."[3]

What is going on in these passages? Was God unable to instantly kill the attacking army? Why does God promise to easily give Moab to Israel, yet they fail so dramatically? Isn't God omnipotent?

God, it is said, has the ability to do anything possible. God has 'all power.' Admittedly, there are innumerable texts describing God's potency, yet this has been challenged by critics of Christianity. They often point to these curious passages throughout the Bible describing God's defeats. The claim is then made that Yahweh was historically a local cult god, rather than the omnipotent God of the universe. Is there an alternative way to understand this?

In his book, *The Uncontrolling Love of God*, Thomas Jay Oord proposes a system known as essential kenosis, where God's power is limited by His non-coercive goodness. While Oord might take issue with combat illustrations being used to discuss essential kenosis (a system rooted in love), this article is merely interested in examining the contingent quality of essential kenosis, which might offer a better way to understand existing Biblical narratives.

Oord asserts God gives free will and does not revoke it: "First, this model of providence says God necessarily gives freedom to all creatures complex enough to receive and express it. Giving freedom is part of God's steadfast love. This means God cannot withdraw, override or fail to provide the freedom a perpetrator of evil expresses. God must give freedom, even to those who use it wrongly."[4]

Oord elsewhere describes God working synergistically with human beings: "God can be the mightiest without controlling others. God can exert power upon all creation without unilaterally determining any. God can be the ultimate source of power—empowering and enabling others—without dominating any creature or situation entirely. Almighty is not coercive."[5]

From Oord's perspective, God neither forces events to happen nor interferes to ensure they occur. This certainly would explain why God would promise one thing (an easy victory over Moab), but another thing entirely takes place (a retreat of Israel). This would also clarify other odd passages of the Bible.

In 1 Kings, the prophet Micaiah describes a scene in God's courtroom. The angels gather around God, who is wondering how to convince the evil king Ahab to go to war. He invites the angels to give suggestions. Each angel presents a plan, until God endorses one He prefers. It is not God who will accomplish this plan; God empowers the angel to take the lead: "You are to entice him, and you shall succeed; go out and do so."[6]

The courtroom scene is paralleled in Job, when God engages in speculation with an angel (traditionally identified as 'Satan'). This angel likewise becomes the empowered creature in the text. This agent is again seen in texts like 1 Chronicles

21:1 (contrasted with 2 Samuel 24:1) and in Numbers 22:23 (the incident of Balaam in which 'Satan' intervenes on God's behalf). God is operating through an intermediary. This seems to be standard practice in the Bible.

The question becomes: what happens when an intermediary fails? What happens when Israel decides to retreat although God promised to empower them? What happens when God prophesies against Tyre and Egypt, and then his emissary is unsuccessful (see Ezekiel 26:7 and 29:20)? God does not seem to follow up and right the failures of others, at least not as recorded in the Biblical text. Perhaps a better way to understand God, as posited by *The Uncontrolling Love of God*, is God working *through* people not *in spite of* them.

In the Biblical text, God invites dialogue, as with Abimelech in Genesis 20. God invites and often takes council as happens in the discussion of Sodom in Genesis 18. God then uses creaturely agents to execute that council. Angels are common emissaries, although God empowers individuals like Moses or King David, as well. God even uses pagan nations to do His will (Ezekiel 23:22-23).

In any case, it is readily apparent the God of the Bible is not a micromanager, hoarding power for Himself. God's first act toward humans, after all, was empowering them to name the animals—a curious, hopeful, and loving action. God is hurt when people choose to do wrong (Gen 6:6). God continues working through free will creatures, even though sometimes they fail. When this happens, God does not abandon His desire to work through them. Perhaps God's nature of love leads to valuing collaboration at the risk of a failed outcome.

Christopher Fisher the author of God is Open: Examining the Open Theism of the Biblical Authors. He is a blogger at RealityisNotOptional.com and the lead editor of GodisOpen.com. He graduated from the University of South Dakota in 2006, Cum Laude with both Computer Science and Political Science majors and both Mathematics and Economics minors. His honor's thesis was on Platonic influences in the early Christian Church: "The Hellenization of Christianity: A Defense of Open Theism."

Endnotes

1. Judg. 1:19 (ESV).
2. 2 Kings 3:18

3. 2 Kings 3:26-27

4. Thomas Jay Oord, *The Uncontrolling Love of God: An Open and Relational Account of Providence* (Downers Grove, IL: InterVarsity, 2015), 170.

5. Oord, 190.

6. 1 Kings 22:22

Creative Love

Scott Nelson Foster

I recall sitting in high school art class agonizing over a watercolor. It is like being eaten by a shark: there's only one way to go, and it's darker.

Of my painting, I asked, "Why won't you be beautiful?!"

Considering my frustration, another student wondered why I was even in the class. The question proceeded from the assumption that art making—being at best a marginally useful endeavor—should at least provide entertainment value.

Nothing worth doing is free of frustrations. What I've come to know is the process of creation, as experienced by artists, is often drudgery. In the struggle to give form to something that exists only as a concept, a wide gamut of emotions ebb and flow through the artist. We see the contrast between what is and what might be. The greatest pain is in the knowledge that there is no straight road between the two. What roads exist obey no Cartesian logic. On this path, digging a hole is no less likely to land me on top of that mountain than is a trek up the nearest trail. Often the best artwork coalesces around the heap of which I had despaired.

Artist Ted Seth Jacobs once said that the greatest teacher is the white page.[1] Every mark is right or wrong based on its relationship to the previous and subsequent marks. It is hardly a straightforward way of artmaking to weigh each jot and gesture, to modify and adjust, yet real creation happens in concert and in collaboration, in response and in relationship. An artist works by embracing uncertainty and indeterminacy and by giving up some control. An artist who paints by rote and by number will end up with an effigy, not artwork. Free will and random chance are necessary components of human creativity for this reason.

That is the great truth of all art making, beauty from chaos, life from death. It is a truth we also see played out in Scripture, and a truth that encompasses God's providential interaction with creation: God bringing forth creation and redeeming it with his love. In his recent book, Thomas Jay Oord lays out a case for an uncontrolling model of divine providence, predicated on *kenotic* love. This love is essentially self-giving and other empowering.[2] It is a model that allows for the free will of created beings as well as the apparent randomness resultant from the interaction of so many free wills. It is a responsive model in which both God and creation respond to, and influence, each other. Responsivity is also a hallmark of creativity, and I believe that the human impulse toward creativity offers insight into the uncontrolling love of God.

What does it mean to be creative? It is more than the conventional image of the artist, working at two o'clock in the morning and slinging paint around at random. Regardless of their individual methods, what artists have in common is a process of thinking based on finding connections between disparate subjects, developing a rhythm between diligent work and free exploration, and identifying strengths and weaknesses to be preserved or adjusted. The creative process consists of observation, execution, and reflection. It is an open-ended and responsive process. By open-ended, I mean that creativity is cyclical. The critique of an artist's work leads to new insight; those insights lead to new work, or might prompt a revision of one's initial observations.

Working responsively means the active scrutiny of one's activity and openness to alternatives. By attending to one's subject, materials, and creation; new insights are gained. I can buy five or six different kinds of black watercolor paint. Lamp black is light and powdery. In a wash it recedes, creating the illusion of depth. Mars black has metaphorical and literal gravity. The weight of iron oxide literally pulls the pigment out of suspension. This creates a texture that commands focus in the foreground of a painting. These two blacks are of exactly the same hue—in fact, if I'm not careful, I easily confuse the two—but I would never consciously substitute one for the other. No one taught me this in school; it was something I learned from the paint itself.

While I value my paint, our relationship does not perfectly analogize God's relationship with creation, but this responsive aspect of the creative process is something that we see reflected in God's actions. If one could sum up the entire Bible in a phrase, it might be that it is a story of God's relationship with humanity. A responsive God is attentive to Moses' plea for the Israelites following their infidelity in the desert.[3] Similarly, although Jesus is disinclined to heal the daughter of the Syrophoenician woman, he is won over by her insistence.[4] In these situations, and in others, people call out to God from their suffering, and God is there. There is no straight path along which this history unfolds. Rather, with many turns and doublings, a story unfolds as people respond to God's call to love, or fail to do so. As with all creative endeavors, the artist struggles to resolve the work. Out of the paint, forms are both materialized and obscured by each stroke. It is rare that hand and brush move in perfect concert and fluidity.

Indeed, the beauty of the world is marred by much anguish and distress. Oord addresses the problem of evil not by saying God has a pedagogical goal, or that good will come out of it. Rather, Oord sees evil as the product of random chance and free will. This does not mean that God is flying blind, or that God is impotent. God's relational identity, God's very self-giving love itself, precludes coercive action. While in communion with people, animals, and even microbes; God is providentially active in the world. It is when we respond to God's call to love that God's will is done.[5] Amid the apparent random chaos of life—the suicide bombings, broken relationships, fires and floods—God is marshalling all creation to action. It is my prayer that we all respond to that call. Genuine evil may be the product of free will and random chance, but so too is authentic life.

Scott Nelson Foster received his first instruction in drawing and painting from his uncle, Roland Giampaoli, and from his grandfather, Will Nelson, while growing up in Boise, Idaho. Mr. Foster has worked in a variety of two dimensional media, including wax, glue and egg temperas, watercolor, oil, and serigraphy. His interest in esoteric and unusual artistic practices has allowed him opportunities to work with iconographers, fresco painters, performance artists, and alchemists. Scott's paintings have been featured in solo and juried exhibitions on the east and west coasts, including the upcoming Artists of the Mohawk Hudson Region exhibition at the Hyde Collection in Glens Falls, NY. He has completed portraits commissioned by the St. Kateri Tekakwitha Parish and the Musician of Ma'alwyck. He is represented by the Carrie Haddad Gallery of Hudson, NY. Mr. Foster received a B.A. in Fine Art from Northwest Nazarene University, and an M.F.A. in Painting and Drawing from Utah State University. Scott is an Associate Professor of Creative Arts at Siena College. He and his wife Katria currently live in upstate New York.

Endnotes

1. Ted Seth Jacobs, *Drawing with an Open Mind: Reflections from a Drawing Teacher* (New York: Watson-Guptill Publications, 1991), 39-40.

2. Thomas Jay Oord, *The Uncontrolling Love of God: An Open and Relational Account of Providence* (Downers Grove: InterVarsity Press, 2016), 94-95.

3. See Exod. 32

4. See Matt.5:21-28

5. Oord, 178.

God's Unprivileged Love

Paolo Gamberini

While the great Doctor of the Church, Augustine of Hippo, was working on his book about the Holy Trinity, he walked along the seashore. As he walked, he contemplated the mystery of the Holy Trinity. Augustine saw a boy run back and forth from the water to a small hole on the seashore. The boy used a seashell to carry ocean water to that spot in the sand. Augustine approached and asked, "What are you doing?"

"I am trying to put the whole ocean into this hole," the boy replied.

"But that is impossible, my dear child," said Augustine. "The hole cannot contain all the water."

The boy paused in his work, stood up, and looked into Augustine's eyes. "It is no more impossible than what you are trying to do," he replied. "You are trying to comprehend the immensity of the mystery of the Holy Trinity with your small intelligence."[1]

This story reminds us of the limits of human understanding before the incomprehensibility and infinity of God. And yet we must do our best, knowing our limits, to speak of God. Theologians often begin with God's infinity and absolute perfection. God's Name is, "I am who I am."[2]

Many theologians continue by adding to this basic view of perfection. Thomas Aquinas, for instance, said God was 'Pure Act.' Bonaventure said God's 'self-diffusive love,' by contrast, identified God not as remote or static but rather with an eternal actuality. God is intrinsically related to Pure Creative Act of being.

I've come to believe that God's being is essentially and eternally related to creation. Being essentially related to creation does not mean that God depends on creation in order to be God. It means God is 'open' and embraces—eternally and internally—creaturely 'otherness.' "[God] truly wants to have the other as his own, he constitutes it in its genuine reality. God goes out of himself, he as the self-giving fullness. Because he can do this, because this is his free and primary possibility, for this reason he is defined in scripture as love." Karl Rahner clearly states: "When God wants to be what is not God, man comes to be."[3] God's internal relation to creation can be defined as love. Love so generously moves God's being that He does not want to be God without creation.

Unlike God, creatures are finite, limited and imperfect, pluriform and differentiated, with degrees and multiplicity, with more and less, and defined by time and change. God's self-communication is one whole and perfect loving act (*interminabilis vitae tota simul et perfecta possession*) and unfolds itself in the created temporal distinctions of past, present and future.[4] This self-communication is God's eternal generation.

From God's point of view, the generation of the Word is an eternal revelation, but *from the human point of view,* the eternal revelation occurs and is realized when it is received within the individual subjectivity of existence and it is objectified in social realizations (religions). God's self-communication can only take place and be realized according to the capacity of the human spirit to accept or reject it (*quidquid recipitur ad modum recipientis recipitur*).[5] God speaks His one Word only once from eternity. But the reception of this one Word happens, throughout time and space, in many forms and occurrences. Such reception by faith is the event of God's personal revelation, which allows God's one and only Word to become incarnate.

By saying that God has made Himself 'gradually' known to His people, the adverb 'gradually' must be ascribed to the human perception and reception of the One Word of God. From God's point of view, revelation is always given and by itself is always effective, because it is the generation of the Word. From the human point of view, God's eternal self-communication (*generatio Verbi*) becomes effective and therefore embodied when someone becomes aware of it and accepts it (*incarnatio Verbi*). Jesus has been the definitive revelation because he has *fully* realized and became *fully* aware of God's self-communication. Therefore, whenever and wherever there is the *full* and *final* acceptance of this Word, God has been finally revealed. "In the past, God spoke through the prophets to our ancestors in many times and many ways. In these final days, though, He spoke to us through a Son."[6]

Any differentiation and graduality, therefore, are not the outcome of a divine 'preference' for someone, or the result of special divine actions. God's love is a unique, undifferentiated, eternal, creative act of self-communication, and every becoming, finiteness, graduality and differentiation is to be ascribed to creature-liness and not to the divine being.

St. Thomas offers the "principle of predilection." This principle affirms, he says, that "nothing would be greater if God did not will it more good." In my view, this principle must surrender to "the principle of differentiated createdness."[7] Something or someone is not better solely because of God's will or preference. Instead, God loves all people equally and without discrimination. God's love is the cause of the goodness in all things.

According to the principle of predilection, the reason why God chooses some to be saved and others to be damned must be sought in God's inscrutable decision. The reason why God elects some and rejects others depends finally on God.[8] But if God's grace is not discriminating, since any distinction and differentiation is caused by createdness, then it is up to human freedom to determine in which way – more or less – to receive and accept God's grace, and even to repudiate it. There is neither predestination nor divine election in God. God does not prefer someone more than others or some people to other peoples.

I believe that free humans must decide whether to receive or reject God's grace. God does not prefer one person, or group of people, over another. There is no election on God's side, only the particular reception and discovery of the universal love of God.[9]

Initially, the people of Israel experienced and interpreted their relation to God as a special 'call' and 'election.' "For you are a holy people to the Lord your God; the Lord your God has chosen you to be a people for Himself, a special treasure above all the peoples on the face of the earth."[10] Later, their religious perception became more universal. God neither predestines nor elects one group or another. "'Are you Israelites more important to me than the Ethiopians?' asks the Lord. 'I brought Israel out of Egypt, but I also brought the Philistines from Crete and led the Arameans out of Kir.'"[11]

The principle of created differentiation allows us to say that God's love is both unique and universal, both the same and different. God's love is the same, simultaneous and universal. But our human perception of divine love is unique for each individual, temporally diffused and expanded. God's love in itself is not pluriform, but it is the way God's love is received and assumed by each creature, in each instant, the reason why we talk about multiple expressions of God's love.[12]

Creatures experience God's love unfolding in a crescendo in time. This unfolding does not depend on God's special and progressive interventions or on God's discriminating choices.

This view of God's creative love has important consequences for the question of evil. God does not 'intervene' or 'thwart' human freedom (and the whole nature in its lawfulness and randomness), because God's nature is kenotic love. God shares power and lets something else be other than Godself. God's creative love is the act of defining, of making something definite and distinct from God. Consequently, createdness may be thought of as God's self-definition.

Søren Kierkegaard argues that divine omnipotence is an act of withdrawing Godself on behalf of another. "All finite power makes [a being] dependent; only omnipotence can make [a being] independent, can form from nothing something that has its continuity in itself through the continual withdrawing of omnipotence."[13] God's sovereignty and the presence of evil must be considered within this concept of divine omnipotence. God's omnipotence is His goodness, for goodness is to give oneself away completely.

All finite power makes creatures dependent; only omnipotence can make creatures independent. The possibility of evil is, therefore, a consequence of both kenotic love and God's act of creating an autonomous being. Anything that is 'non-God' is imperfect and therefore risks potential failure. The alternative would have been not to create anything at all. The more creatures depend upon God's love, the more they experience autonomy and freedom.

Paolo Gamberini S.J., is a Jesuit, born in Ravenna (Italy), and author of books and articles on Systematic Theology. He has been teaching in Italy and Jesuit Institutions in the US. He is Associate Professor of Theology at the University of San Francisco.

Endnotes

1. Story taken and adapted from: Jacobus de Voragine, *The Golden Legend or Lives of the Saints*, as English by William Caxton, volume 5 (J.M. Dent and Co. Aldine House: Edinburgh 1900), 66.
2. Exod. 3:14 (NIV).

3. Karl Rahner, *Foundations of Christian Faith: An Introduction to the Idea of Christianity* (New York: Crossroads, 1991) 222-223.

4. Severinus Boethius, *De Consolatione Philosophiae*, book 5, chap. 6.

5. Rahner, 154.

6. Heb. 1:1 (CEB).

7. ST, I, q. 20, art. 2.

8. ST, I, q. 25, art. 5.

9. Andres Torres Queiruga, *Repensar la revelación. La revelación divina en la realización humana* (Madrid: Editorial Trotta, 2008) 336-344.

10. Deut. 7:6-8 (NKJV).

11. Amos 9:7 (NLT).

12. Thomas Jay Oord, *The Uncontrolling Love of God: An Open and Relational Account of Providence* (Downers Grove, IL: InterVarsity, 2015), 165-166.

13. Søren Kierkegaard, *Journals and Papers*, trans. Howard and Edna Hong (Indiana Univ. Press, 1970): vol. 2, entry 1251 from 1846 (VII1 A 181 in Danish edition).

Dancing Robots and Engaging Love

Roland Hearn

Many years ago, my family made plans to go to the beach for the day. We looked forward to enjoying the wonder represented in a clear blue sky, golden sands, a gentle breeze, and cool waves breaking on the shore. As the day approached, we discovered an unexpected event would make it impossible for our oldest daughter to come, and she was deeply disappointed. My wife and I decided we would grant one of those rare opportunities for a break from school by rescheduling the trip to a school day. A couple of days before the rescheduled trip, we discovered our oldest son was now unable to come. He had committed to an after-class robotics club on that day. He felt he needed to keep that commitment and decided to skip the trip to the beach.

The afternoon we returned, we were met by a very discouraged, upset and somewhat angry boy. His day had been a disaster. He and his partner had created a dancing robot and were getting ready to display it when they met a major problem. Another group of boys had accessed their computer and accidentally deleted all the programming they had been working on for months.

As a parent, I want my children learn to deal with disappointment in appropriate ways. I saw a teaching moment. I started to talk about the best ways to deal with his situation: my son became increasingly agitated. As he communicated his frustration, I felt my own level of annoyance increasing. In that moment it seemed more important to me for him to gain an understanding of bigger issues than to keep rehearsing his pain and disappointment.

Across the years, I have learned, when talking with people who are distressed, to first try to listen to their struggles before I attempt to fix them or offer advice. As we talked, I discovered, even more disappointing to him than the robot failure was the decision we had made to go to the beach without him. That revelation significantly increased my own level of irritation—we had given him plenty of opportunity to communicate earlier his true feelings. Now I had another teaching moment: the importance of honest communication as well as accepting responsibility for choices.

I began the teaching exercise, but at the same time I did some honest introspective processing. I discovered my own level of displeasure was not about his missing the lessons I was trying to teach. It was much more about my feelings of inadequacy. Like most parents, I want to be a father who makes it possible for my children to live happy lives. As he talked I felt culpable in his sadness. At a deep level I felt I had failed him in this fundamental task. I felt bad about myself, because my son was experiencing pain. I wanted to fix the situation, and getting him to accept my lesson would relieve my pain. I stopped immediately and told him I understood how disappointing his day was and how the world looked unfair and devaluing from his perspective given those circumstances. I told him I was sorry. Without hesitation he smiled and his demeanor transformed.

Recently, I recounted that story to him. He had no memory of it. However, he did say that while he didn't remember the incident he remembered the environment and how much it had shaped him into being a person who tries to listen to others' struggles and not react from his own. Huh, turns out I'm not such a bad parent after all.

My response in that situation was built on years of processing an important truth: Love seeks not to control but to engage. Love's confidence is not in its capacity to make circumstances right but in developing love soaked relationships in the midst of circumstances, both good and ill. The best of life is not built on resolved struggles but on the pervasiveness of love. Love draws toward the goal of creating more loving people. It does not arbitrarily prioritize other goals, even admirable ones, and then drive toward them. It certainly does not seek to fix situations and circumstances without regard to developing relationships into mutually valuing ones.

As I have wrestled with the truth of engaging love in my own life and in my leadership opportunities, I have come to understand how powerful a principle it is. I am far from adequately able to represent this truth, but it has become my unshakeable goal to live and love in this way. A key idea that has helped me discern the difference between love and control is that love is experienced as worth. When God created out of love, he called it good—creation is innately valuable. The trajectory of scripture is God communicating love by revealing the worth of his beloved. This is best seen in the incarnation. If I desire to communicate love to another, I must first communicate their value to them. Control does not communicate worth, because it implies that the one being controlled is of inferior worth. If I desire another to move toward a certain goal, I must engage with them and cooperatively seek that end. If I coerce, manipulate, push, or use authority; I may achieve the goal but I will damage the relationship by reducing the perceived worth of the other.

As a human being, I can choose my means of goal achievement. I can choose to make my goals higher priorities than my relationships, but that would not be love. God, who is love, cannot do that. He cannot choose to act as less than love. He cannot communicate with us in a way that dishonors our worth. It is not that He will not control; he cannot. His nature forbids it. God cannot control. God expresses love through engagement.

Roland Hearn is the District Superintendent on the Australian North and West District of the Church of the Nazarene and has been a pastor for more than 30 years. He is married to Emmy and has four adult children. Roland continues to research in the area of the impact on practical theology of a Wesleyan development of a theology of shame.

Believe It or Not,
God Has Faith in You

Wm. Curtis Holtzen

When my daughter was 15 years old we began a routine that all parents dread—driving lessons. We would go to the business park on Sunday afternoons and drive through the parking lot, since it was mostly empty. Every now and then I had to grab the steering wheel to keep her from hitting a light post or exclaim, "brake, brake, brake!" with increasing volume and intensity as we approached a wall. With each lesson my apparent felt need to take control decreased as my trust in her increased. Still, the day she first drove off alone was tough. My love for her meant that I wanted to be by her side to take control should the need arise. But that same love led to an even stronger impulse—a desire to trust that she was ready and to show that I believed in her.

At the risk of being overly simplistic, 'love' involves, at least, the desire to act for the betterment of the beloved. It genuinely seeks the greatest good for the other. Sometimes love leads us to action: the good may mean taking the wheel (and no, I have never heard that song). As a husband, parent, and friend I can think of dozens of examples of love being active. Love calls us to lift up, patch up, and clean up those we can. Yet sometimes love also calls us to refrain from acting. It calls us to give others the freedom to live, to learn, and to make mistakes. Love led me to be hands-off and sit quietly while my daughter made turns that I would not have made. The difficulty comes in having the wisdom to know when to be active and when to be passive—when to take control and when to be uncontrolling.

The relationship between love and control is a curious one. Paul seems to note the tension between the two when he writes that love both "always protects" and "always trusts."[1] Protection seems to suggest that a lover takes some kind of control—often by sheltering and shielding. Trust, however, means a lover gives up control, giving the loved one freedom and privacy. Trust requires that we give up power over the other, give them the control. Yet both of these impulses, to protect and to trust, can most certainly be born out of love. In fact, trust is the key factor in the act of relinquishing control. Faith is a hallmark of an uncontrolling love.

Think about the times in which you had a strong impulse to control a situation. Whether you loved the persons involved or not, I bet your desire to control was because you did not trust those around to handle what might happen. Perhaps you were worried that the eventual outcome would not be best for all parties involved. While the desire to take or give up control could obviously, and tragically, be set in selfishness; it is often motivated by love. Yet the decision to actually *give up* any or all control naturally comes when we trust those around us to do what we believe is right. Healthy love wants to empower the other, to let him or her grow and flourish. I contend that God's love is uncontrolling because love calls God to trust. God has faith in this creation. God has faith in the Church. God has faith in the people of this world.

I understand Thomas Jay Oord's reasons for concluding that God does not 'give up' control; namely because God's loving nature never allowed God to have control in the first place. I grant there is a lot to be said for this approach. However, what I am emphasizing is that God's love might be uncontrolling in another way—not because love never controls, but rather because love leads God to seek out ways to trust. Love may sometimes cause one to seek to control situations, but real love would not want control to be the norm. The stronger impulse of love, what love looks for long term, is to trust and to have faith.

The Bible tells us that God is seeking those whom God can trust. Not only are we called to faith and faithfulness; we are also called to be trustworthy. The Hebrew Scriptures highlight God's covenants with both individuals and Israel. Covenants, by their nature, require trust by both parties. Job is a story depicting God as a deity who bets on the faithfulness of his servant. God has faith that Job will be true. The New Testament also offers examples of uncontrolling trust. Most of us are familiar with the parable of the talents, but have we heard sermons on how God has *entrusted* us with these "talents?" The parable suggests that God gives us what God believes we can be entrusted with. The entire arc of scripture can, I suggest, be read in this way: acting in love, God has faith in this creation, has entrusted us, the Church, with the Gospel, and is asking for that same love and faith in return.

As a relational theist, I believe that God desires and has created us for relationship. It is, of course, possible to trust those for whom we might not feel a sense of emotional love. I am thinking of my auto mechanic. It is also possible to feel a strong love for those whom we do not trust. Addiction is a problem in my family, and I honestly love my siblings who battle with these addictions, but I do not trust them. However, love ultimately moves us to trust those whom we love. Love pushes us to find ways to have faith in those whom we love and with whom we desire relationship. Relationships of love are good: relationships of loving faith are better.

Along with trust, God has hope for us—has hope in us. God has not only entrusted us with many goods but has hope we will use them and our freedom wisely, that we will partner with God in bringing about the reconciliation of all creation. To love but not trust is painful, but to love and not hope is to despair. God is not in despair but is patient like a hopeful father watching and waiting for his son's return. God celebrates, as does all of heaven, when God's hopes are realized.

Perhaps there is more to God's uncontrolling nature than love alone. Maybe, along with love, God has hope and faith. Or said another way, to love is to hope and trust. Perhaps, only when all three are present, can we then understand God as truly relational.

Wm. Curtis Holtzen D. Th. is professor of Philosophy and Theology at Hope International University. He is the co-editor of "By Faith and Reason: The Essential Keith Ward" and "In Spirit and In Truth: Philosophical Reflections on Liturgy and Worship." Curtis fancies himself as a foodie and lover of all things Simpsons and Beatles.

Endnotes

1. I Cor. 13:7 (NIV).

The Suffering of Love

Hannah Howard

N ow I rejoice in my sufferings for your sake, and in my flesh I complete what is lacking in Christ's afflictions for the sake of his body, that is, the church."[1]

Generally, when people ask, "Why do bad things happen?" they are really asking, "Why do people suffer and die?"

A piercing awareness of human frailty comes about when one has an encounter with true suffering or is faced with the reality of human mortality. The deep pain and anguish that arise from such experiences can leave a person convinced that suffering, death, and even life itself, are meaningless. What if, however, they are not? Perhaps, through his atonement, Christ somehow radically redefined the very nature of suffering and death, imbuing them with supernatural meaning and dignity as has never before been seen in the world? To understand this radical redefinition, one must first understand why suffering and death first entered the world.

The story of humanity's first disobedience can be found in Genesis, and with it, the origin of suffering and death. God presents a divine law: "You may freely eat of every tree of the garden; but of the tree of the knowledge of good and evil you shall not eat . . ."[2] In the same breath, God warns Adam and Eve of the consequence of disobeying this divine law: "[F]or in the day you eat of it you shall die."[3] It should be noted that the very presence of law implies free-will; a creature lacking free-will could not *choose* to obey or disobey a law. The death of which Adam and Eve were warned was not simply a physical death—the separation of body and soul, but also a spiritual death—the eternal separation of humans from God. Adam and Eve freely chose to disobey the divine law of God, thus death entered the world. By sinning, Adam and Eve not only committed an offense against God but also an offense against themselves. By disobeying God, Adam and Eve severed themselves from what was proper to their being—union with God. What is against God is necessarily against self. Thus Adam and Eve acted against God, and consequently against themselves, and death entered the world. It is a mistake to assume that simply because one does not understand *why* sin brings death into the world, that God is somehow unfair.

Both suffering and sin are experiences of evil. Humans passively *experience* evil when they suffers, but they can also actively *cause* and *experience* it when they sin. While it is often tempting to view evil as an entity in itself, it must not be viewed as such. When viewed properly, evil is understood as the absence of goodness. This is true for both suffering and sin. In the case of suffering, a sick person, for example, is understood to suffer from the absence of health. Similarly, a sinner suffers from the absence of a properly ordered will. When humans sin, they goes against reason and against the will of God. This is sin: placing one's own will above the will of God. In both cases, evil is the experience of lacking a good that is proper to oneself (health and union with God).

As long as there is sin in the world, suffering and death are inescapable. However, Christ, through his suffering, death, and resurrection made a way for humankind to escape the eternal death caused by sin: "For as in Adam all die, so also in Christ shall all be made alive."[4] God has not suddenly changed his mind concerning divine justice; the divine law of God cannot be repealed and death is still the consequence for sin, but Christ, through his own self-gift, overcomes death and offers a new way for humans to return again to his presence. Christ has linked suffering and love, making suffering in union with the body of Christ a means of achieving salvation, and death the very road by which we enter eternal life. Christ declares, "Greater love hath no one than this, that he lay down his life for his friends."[5] Thus, for the followers of Christ, suffering and even death need not be meaningless. The Christian can suffer and die out of love and for the sake of love. St. John tells us, "God is love."[6] Thus Christians, as members of the body of Christ, have an opportunity to unify their sufferings with the sufferings of Christ in an act of love. Furthermore, all people may join in this unity by becoming members of Christ's Body, the church: "[S]o we, though many, are one body in Christ."[7]

Humanity, as contained in Adam, is ultimately responsible for death entering the world; yet Christ, out of his love—expressed though his passion, death, and resurrection—makes a way for humans to return again to eternal life. Humans are no longer doomed to perish but is now redeemed through Christ's sacrifice: "You know that you were ransomed from the futile ways inherited from your fathers, not with perishable things such as silver or gold, but with the precious blood of Christ . . ."[8] Christ's sacrifice radically overcomes any absence resulting from the fall; his gift of redemption may be freely chosen by all. John 3:16 beautifully summarizes the reality of Christ becoming incarnate in the fallen world, and the redemption He offers to 'whoever believes': "For God so loved the world that he gave his only begotten Son, that whoever believes in him should not perish but have eternal life."[9]

Christ's mysterious sacrifice offers humans redemption from eternal death, and while it is important to explore how divine providence and evil relate to one another; it is equally important to acknowledge the reality of the mystery of the incarnation. Both the mystery of Christ's own incarnation, and the mysterious way by which the Christian unites his sufferings with the sufferings of Christ, through participation is his body, must be acknowledged. As Christians we ought to embrace the good of the intellect without neglecting the reality of mystery; we ought to embrace a life of both faith *and* reason, understanding what things can be known to us and what things remain mysterious. Can we know *why* it is that God decrees "[I]n the day you eat of it you shall die"?[10] Can we know *why* disobedience leads to death? These are the sort of inquiries that are at the root of the question of suffering: Why do we suffer when we go against God, and of necessity, against ourselves? If we look at God and accuse him of injustice for not preventing an evil that results from humanity's free choice, then we judge God. We must not fall into the trap of the sin of our first parents, who desired knowledge to "be like God."[11] The human who would assert the necessity of intellectual consent to the workings of divine providence makes a devil of God, and a god of himself.

We may never fully understand why things happen the way they do in this life. We ought never to forget, however, that as Christians we live as members of the Body of Christ and unite our sufferings to his. As Christians we live in the promise that "in everything God works for good with those who love him."[12] No matter the magnitude of the suffering, we have been promised that good can come from any circumstance, and that God will never disappoint us: "[W]e rejoice in our sufferings, knowing that suffering produces endurance, and endurance produces character, and character produces hope, and hope does not disappoint us, because God's love has been poured into our hearts through the Holy Spirit who has been given to us.

Hannah holds a BA in Liberal Arts from Thomas More College of Liberal Arts, and is currently pursuing an MS in Bioethics. She loves theology, philosophy, and spending time with family.

Endnotes

1. Col. 1:24 (RSV).
2. Gen. 2:16-17
3. Ibid.
4. I Cor. 15:22
5. John 15:13
6. I John 4:8
7. Rom. 12:5
8. I Pet. 1:18-19
9. John 3:16
10. Gen. 2:17
11. Gen. 3:5
12. Rom. 8:28

The Kenotic Creation:
A Universe of Moral Choice

F. Jerry Josties

The excessive abstraction in physics/science that began with Galileo, measurement, and the primary-secondary quality distinction, was explicitly intended to separate science and theology. This essay is an adventure in poetic theological metaphysics that hopefully will inspire others to achieve a deeply beautiful reconciliation between science and theology by interpreting scientific abstraction in terms of fully meaningful moral choice in a world view that can be called panentheistic panpsychism.

I've been thinking about how the creation story should be told if God's creative Love is truly uncontrolling. If I were telling this story, here's what I might say . . .

In the beginning, God, as Infinite Love, gave of Himself (kenosis) so completely that the creation experienced infinite freedom. This freedom is so complete that potential identities could choose whether or not to come into existence as egos partially separate from God. These creatures would be only partially separate from God, because they exist entirely within Infinite Love. How could particles that do not yet exist make a choice? In order to tell a creation story, it is necessary to have a prior, deeper understanding of time. In this story both space and time are the result of free moral choice.

Those who chose to exist became the smallest elementary particles. Those who chose to remain with God became the elements of empty space—identities that might have been.

The deep underlying meaning of the space of the initial particles is the initial kenosis of God. And subsequent kenosis of particles gives additional space/free-dom to other particles. Space is due to kenosis, or the choice for other. The ex-pansion of the universe is then seen as the contraction of ego, correlating with the emergence of higher levels of identity (see below).

The deep underlying meaning of what we call the 'flow of time' is also due to free choice, the choice for ego/self. This is because these choices in general can-not be anticipated, so that the resulting events can only be considered and expe-rienced in an essential sequence, which is the meaning of 'time.' The choice for other may be considered the default anticipation, and then might not contribute to 'time.'

So the kenosis of God is the origin of moral choice. Such choices were re-quired in every subsequent encounter, so all events/encounters had outcomes dependent on a double binary choice. That double binary choice was between self and other and made by both identities in the encounter.

The creaturely choice for the other is a kenotic choice. In this, creatures mimic the choice made by God in creating. The kenotic choice brings one back at least to a partial reunion with God. In acting like God, we merge or reconnect with Him. This is why the moral choice for other 'feels good.' It is in itself a degree of existential completion.

All motions by selves/egos and all assertions of freedom (choices *for* self/ego) require empty space. They depend on the initial choice by many potential identi-ties to remain with God. This means that empty space is an immediate reminder of the ubiquitous presence of the kenotic God. To illustrate this practically, we can walk across the room only because of the presence of God.

This creation story also helps us tell the underlying story of physics. 'Expla-nations' in physics are only nominal because they always terminate on the 'laws of physics,' which are only abstract (albeit, beautifully integrated) descriptions of our observations. They are not ultimate explanations. Explanation is a psycho-logical process that consists in the reduction to the familiar, and ultimate expla-nation consists in the reduction to the ultimately familiar—oneself and one's most intimately ultimate feelings—feelings of love for others and for God. Ulti-mate explanation can therefore be possible only in a panpsychic world, in which all identities are conscious like oneself and capable of love and moral choice, and is then effected by psychological identification with the identities active in the process to be explained.

We can interpret physics (and mathematics) as consonant with the theological vision I've described. This interpretation replaces the scientific categories of abstract description with theological categories of explanation—love, freedom, and moral choice. The entirety of physics reduces, without ontological remainder, to 'fermions' and 'bosons' (or particles and fields, respectively) and their behavior in space and time. Fermions are defined by identity distinction, via the Pauli Exclusion Principle; whereas, bosons are characterized by superposition or merging, or absence of identity distinction. But identity distinction or its absence is quite precisely what is determined by moral choice: the choice for self/ego is exactly what distinguishes an identity from others, and the choice for other effectively merges our identity with other and with God. It should now be clear from these remarks—even though the detailed story will need to be elaborated by others—that ours is a universe of moral choice.

When both identities in an encounter make the kenotic choice for the other, a higher level identity is the result. The degree of mutual deference, or the amount of freedom given up by the original identities, determines the coherence of the new identity and the amount of freedom that it can now exercise. This process is often called 'emergence,' and accounts for the hierarchy of 'physical' identity. Lower levels are further evolved morally than higher levels, because they have had many more interactions. As a result, they have discovered the beauty and lure of kenotic love and, therefore, much more commonly choose to defer to other or to God.

The laws of physics, which apply to lower levels of the hierarchy, are due to a global deference to God by particles, that then choose to behave entirely in accordance with the anticipations of God. What we call 'determinism' is thus entirely due to free moral choice and applies to the lowest levels of the hierarchy, but not to the same extent to the higher levels like ourselves. We have inherited a considerable amount of freedom from our constituent identities who are largely in a state of deference to us.

The complex identities that emerge in this way continue to have internal choice interactions among their constituent identities, as in our 'brains.' These mediate our experience of the external world, but they also produce, or rather, constitute, what we call 'logic' and 'mathematics.'

The creation story I'm telling helps not only with explaining the being of creation (ontology). It also helps to explain how we arrive at truth or knowledge of creation (epistemology).

The knowledge we have of the world, or truth, is the feeling of rapport with ultimacy of some kind. Understood in this way, truth can characterize not only science but also poetic feeling, music, art, and love. All forms of truth are indirect forms of theological truth, which is union with God/Infinite Love. Beauty, for example, can be thought of as Infinite Love shining through the many expressions of freedom.

We arrive at truth by some form of communication. In fact, conversation between people is paradigmatic of all forms of communication. There can be great joy and deep meaningfulness in conversation (with anyone). Indeed, together we can be close to God.

The kenosis story of creation says that sacred communication comes through a process of mutual kenosis/deference. Parties give themselves to the other. Creatures defer to each other, engaging gently with each other.

Because all parties at least partially defer, they are partially merged with God. They imitate God, who defers when creating. When we communicate as agents of love, we work together in mutual deference to elicit a stronger presence of God in our 'midst.'[1] And in doing so, we have greater access to truth.

This creation story tells us that all of reality, and even our method of knowing reality, derives from kenosis. It tells us that kenosis in the present reenacts God's kenosis in the beginning. I believe that a reasonable criterion for the validity of any creation story is that every event be interpretable as a reenactment of the creation moment. In our story, that moment is kenotic choice.

The creation story I've offered is, of course, open to revision. No story can tell us all truth. But the kenotic creation story is for me—and I hope it can be for you—a story that makes sense of life.

It's a story to live by.

Acknowledgements: I am of course indebted to all my conversation partners over the years, to God to the extent that the story is correct and not just an expression of my own ego, and to my wife, Esther, and family. But I especially want to acknowledge: my mother, Susie L. Baker Josties, who taught me philosophy and how to think independently; my father, Frederick O. Josties, and Alfred North Whitehead, who both taught me that feelings are more important than abstractions; Thomas S. Kuhn, who taught me that paradigm change is a normal aspect of scientific progress so that thinking 'outside the box' is to be encouraged; Martin Buber, who helped me to understand communication as mutual deference; James W. Christy, a colleague of mine in astronomy, whose very intuitive mind gave to me innumerable insights in developing a panpsychic interpretation of science over the last 45 years; Thomas Jay Oord, for his wonderful concept of Essential Kenosis and very helpful editorial assistance.

Jerry Josties is a retired astronomer with a life-long interest in the deepest possible understanding of philosophy, science, and theology.

Endnotes

1. See Matt. 18:20 (NIV).

Rethinking the Phrase "God Allowed"

Mark Karris

Aman came into my office to speak with me about difficulties he was having with concentration. He was also struggling with anxiety and suffering from insomnia. After a brief conversation, I asked him if he took any solace in faith or spirituality.

His demeanor changed instantly. His face started to flush. With an angry voice, he said, "Screw God! God allowed my wife to die in a car accident. I am left with three kids, barely having enough money to pay my bills, and I am at my wits' end. I am tired of people telling me, 'God has a plan. God allowed your suffering to happen for a reason.' As far as I am concerned, I want nothing to do with God."

As a pastor and therapist, my heart sank. I felt sad. This precious man, who was broken and grieving, could not turn to a loving, compassionate God for comfort. One of the main reasons for his inability to find comfort in God was because of his view of God, especially as it related to his wife's passing.

Two words stuck out to me in this man's view of God. I heard them all the time from people who experienced trauma and who were angry at God. They were the words: "God allowed."

The way we talk about God matters. I have recently concluded that saying "God allowed," in regard to evil and suffering, is a terrible theological phrase. While it has the potential to ease some anxious Christian hearts; for others, it often erodes trust in a profoundly loving and trustworthy God.

Deconstructing "God Allowed"

Saying "God allowed," in reference to evil or tragic events, such as the man's wife dying in a car accident, is a poisonous phrase to the sensitive, God-seeking, and traumatized soul. It distorts the beautiful and loving character of God by making God out to be the One who is responsible for evil and tragedy.

The phrase also presents God as one who shows favorites and is cold and monstrous. It makes Him out to be a voyeur who occasionally jumps into time, willfully intervening in some people's lives to save them from harm, and choosing not to intervene in others. Where God doesn't intervene, the phrase suggests He is intentionally consenting to and permitting each individual horrific or tragic event to occur.

Imagine, for example, what it must be like for God to watch a psychopath begin to rape a helpless woman. The God most people believe in must say, "I planned this before the foundation of the world. I know I could stop this, but I am going to allow it to happen." Although all-powerful, this God just watches and does nothing to stop the rape.

In another moment, God watches another psychopath begin to rape another helpless woman. But this time, God says, "I also planned this before the foundation of the world. But in this case, I will intervene and stop this man." Perhaps God intervened by causing a neighbor to stop by the victim's house. The perpetrator heard the neighbor, became startled, and darted out the door.

I am among many people who are aghast at the God who allows some instances of evil but prevents others. The God most people believe in, which is illustrated in the rape event, 1) is in control of everything that happens in the world, 2) is powerful enough to stop any evil act from happening but often doesn't (which is unthinkable), and 3) preordains these evils as part of some master plan.

Is this the kind of God and God-story we want to tell people when they are suffering? Is the kind of God who has the power to stop evil from occurring, but chooses not to, really a loving, gracious, compassionate God?

Let's return to the rape example. If God 'allowed' the rape, He must have also been able to take His big metaphysical index finger and flick the rapist away. Or God could have acted like Quicksilver in *X-Men: Days of Future Past* by manipulating objects or people at the speed of light to keep the rape victim from harm.[1] God could have but chose not to.

But God doesn't flex his metaphysical muscles in this way often enough. It is not because He has the power to do so but intentionally permits and consents to the traumatic or evil act to occur. It is not as if He could have done otherwise but willfully decided not to. God doesn't unilaterally intervene, stopping every evil or traumatic event from occurring, because He is uncontrolling love.

God Is Not In Control

Contrary to popular belief, God cannot do some things. God cannot lie,[2] He cannot be tempted,[3] He can't be prejudiced,[4] He cannot sin,[5] He cannot get tired,[6] and He cannot unilaterally control people and events.

In his book, *The Uncontrolling Love of God,* Thomas Jay Oord offers this comparison: "Mermaids cannot run marathons because a mermaid's nature includes leglessness. [Analogously], God cannot create controllable creatures because God's nature is uncontrolling love."[7]

While it is true that mermaids do not exist; the idea here is that God cannot unilaterally control events, because His loving nature is uncontrolling. God cannot control people and events in the world, and His agency competes with other variables, such as randomness, creaturely agency, and law-like regularities.

In regard to the man's wife's sudden passing due to a car accident, it is not that God did not want to stop the accident from occurring. I believe God would have wanted the woman to live and be in good health. But God simply could not unilaterally control the people and law-like regularities involved in that horrific event, thus being unable to stop it from occurring.

The point is this: If God's love is uncontrolling; we should not say God allows evil or horrific events to occur. Instead, we should say it is impossible for God to control people and events. And this uncontrolling influence enables free creatures, randomness, and law-like regularities (e.g. gravity, weather systems, etc.) that sometimes run amok.

Simply, evil and traumatic events occur precisely because a loving and uncontrolling God does not control all things.

God Is Controlling (Just Not Like We Think)

Just because God is not in unilateral control does not mean He is passive. According to *The Oxford English Dictionary*, the word "control" can mean "the power to influence or direct people's behavior or the course of events."[8]

I suggest that God can lovingly influence us by inviting, empowering, inspiring, filling, convicting, leading, comforting, healing, and challenging us toward ever-increasing experiences of shalom. God exerts this kind of 'control.'

God is a Spirit, and God is love. He always does the most loving acts possible in every moment, in every nook and cranny of existence. Furthermore, God can be one-hundred percent trusted, because He would never purposely or maliciously harm any person, especially for some grand Machiavellian purpose.

What I'm suggesting may seem a grand revelation. But it becomes believable without the cognitive dissonance-producing phrase 'God allowed,' so typical of Christian responses to evil.

A Few Words for Moving Forward

Permit me to make a request to my fellow Christians.

Would you please stop saying things like, "God allowed your husband to die in that car accident"?

Could you stop attempting to cheer up traumatized parents by saying, "God allowed your baby to die as part of a plan?"

I propose that we stop using the phrase 'God allowed.' If we did, I suspect fewer people would be confused, or worse, blame God for the horrific events that occur. Eliminating 'God allowed' could remove an unnecessary obstacle that prevents many from having a loving connection with their Creator. Sit with them, listen to them, weep with them, but get rid of that distancing and dusty old phrase.

Permit me also to say a word to spiritual seekers.

I get it. I also wouldn't want to love a God who allows some evils and prevents others. But I hope my comments in this essay will prompt you to rethink what God does.

When you think about the abuse, pain, suffering, or flat out evil in your life; you don't have to believe God allowed or caused it. Often, other people with free will cause evil. Sometimes, evil occurs as an unfortunate random event. Other times, we suffer because of our own unwise choices.

After some reflection, I hope you will come to believe in a freedom-giving, uncontrolling God. God would never will evil and trauma in your life. This loving God seeks only what is good for you to grow, flourish, and live to your fullest potential.

Mark Karris is an ordained pastor, licensed marriage and family therapist, musician and all around biophilic. He is the author of Season of Heartbreak: Healing for the Heart, Brain, and Soul (2017). MarkGregoryKarris.com

Endnotes

1. Goldman, Jane, Simon Kinberg, Stan Lee, Hutch Parker, Lauren Shuler-Donner, Matthew Vaughn, et al. *X-Men, Days of Future Past*. DVD. Directed by Bryan Singer. Los Angeles: Fox, 2014.
2. Heb. 6:18 (NIV).
3. James 1:13
4. Acts 10:34-35
5. Deut. 32:4
6. Isa. 40:28
7. Thomas Jay Oord, *The Uncontrolling Love of God: An Open and Relational Account of Providence* (Downers Grove, IL: InterVarsity, 2015), 148.
8. Angus Stevenson, ed. Oxford Dictionary of English, 3rd ed. (Oxford: Oxford University Press, 2010), 379.

Is Everything the Will of God?

Richard Kidd

I remember it clearly. I was working at a radio station as an announcer. I was not on the air but in the 'Radio Jock Lounge' as we called it.

One of the other DJs who *was* on the air at the time, came running into the lounge screaming, "We have been attacked! The World Trade Center was hit by passenger jets! It's a terrorist attack!"

The Jets were still coming and the buildings were falling. It was surreal. We were all in a state of shock.

Afterwards, everyone had an opinion of why this happened and, yes, eventually the questions came, too.

"Why did God let this happen?"

"Was it God's will?"

"What kind of God would cause this tragedy?"

Of course, all the usual TV preachers were saying it was because of abortion, or the gays, or because they removed prayer from the schools. It was judgment, and it was the will of God. This was their mantra. Every time a tragedy happened it was the will of God.

This is the reason people talk about theodicy—why do bad things happen to good people or why is there evil and suffering? Some refuse to believe in God because of theodicy, but others accept it as something God simply allows.

The idea of God's will hit me like a boulder when my wife lost our child to a miscarriage in the fall of 2000. It affected her worse, because she not only lost our child but also an older brother at the young age of 48 due to heart issues and diabetes. A few years prior to that, she lost her dad to cancer and a 19-year-old nephew in a car wreck. I could not see trying to tell her this was all God's will and perfect plan for her. It was God's will to allow all these tragedies to happen within such a short timeframe?

Many people lose their faith over such theology. Would you tell a person who lost their child to cancer it was God's will? Is God in complete control of everything? Is God's will over our wills in every instance and every event happening around us? Thomas Jay Oord says, "No," and this is bad and dangerous theology.

Oord believes in the uncontrolling love of God, not the controlling will of God. We are not puppets. Oord shows us the different models of God's providence. They are: God is the omnicause; God empowers and overpowers; God is voluntarily self-limited; God is essentially Kenotic; God sustains as impersonal force; God is initial creator and current observer; and finally, God's ways are not your ways.

The first model is a common view in the Reformed Calvinist tradition, that believes God is in control of all things and causes all things. In other words, God's will is everything that happens—even awful tragedies in the world. The last view of providence (God's ways are not our ways) is a true statement; however, it is like saying it might be God's will but I will throw out the mystery card to play it safe.

Oord does not play it safe. Instead, he hits the problem of theodicy head on by not only critiquing the other models of God's providence but by giving us an alternative with the kenotic model. Oord believes, "God's eternal nature is uncontrolling love. Because of love, God necessarily provides freedom/agency to creatures, and God works by empowering and inspiring creation toward well-being."[1] This also means, "God upholds the regularities that derive from God's nature of love. Randomness in the world and creaturely free will are genuine, and God is not a dictator mysteriously pulling all the strings. God never control others."[2]

This does not mean God never intervenes by miracles, but He intervenes in noncoercive ways. God is already present in all of creation without being a part of creation; therefore, God is working with, in, and under to bring about change out of love and not by force. God is relational and works in a process with free creatures, and the future is open to a number of possibilities. God knows all of them. God's promises are true, but they are not actualized until they are acted upon. God, out of love, takes risks to relate to humans instead of control and domination. God's uncontrollable love is one of giving and receiving love and also willing to be rejected by the beloved.

Love does come first. We see it in the person of Jesus Christ who took the form of a servant by humbling himself and giving himself up on the cross. This is the cruciform love of God that is self-giving and others empowering. Instead of saying everything that happens is God's will—especially tragedies, deaths, natural disasters, diseases, and yes, even miscarriages—then we must say no! If God's love comes first and God's nature is uncontrolling love, then God cannot unilaterally prevent genuine evil. There are limits to God's power. God cannot do what is illogical. Contradictions do not exist, especially in God. God cannot change the past and or act contrary to God's own nature. God cannot deny God's self.

Thomas Jay Oord says, "God must give freedom, even to those who use it wrongly. This is the cause of evil besides randomness in the world, not God."[3] Oord continues to explain preventing evils caused by random events would require God to foreknow and control these events occurring at whatever level of complexity we find them. Controlling randomness would require God to withhold the simple power to become and exist with stable regularity. God creates and interacts, sets limits, and offers possibilities through uncontrolling love. We as humans, by faith, cooperate with God. God is not a bully and does not act violently or with force or controls. Instead, God empowers and enables with uncontrolling love.

This message is a comfort to those who have lost a loved one, witnessed a tragedy, or are suffering from a threatening disease. God is not willing that anyone would perish. God's will is good, but the problem is sometimes God's will does not happen in every situation. This is the price for having freedom. There are consequences of another's freedom with the randomness and regularities of nature. The uncontrolling love of God is much better than a God who is not love but a dictator. We see this God fully in the person of Christ. Jesus shows us the Triune God who acts out of uncontrolling love. Death, tragedy, and evil are not God's will, nor do they have the last word. God's love does.

Richard Kidd is an Evangelical Lutheran Church in America (ELCA) pastor in Boardman, Ohio. He loves books, music, and is a member of the Society of Holy Trinity.

Endnotes

1. Thomas Jay Oord, *The Uncontrolling Love of God: An Open and Relational Account of Providence* (Downers Grove: InterVarsity Press, 2016), 94.
2. Ibid.
3. Oord, 170.

The Power of
Non-Coercive Miracles

Sarah Lancaster

O ne of the 'sticking points' for many people in thinking about an uncontrolling God is the possibility of miracles. In his book *The Uncontrolling Love
of God*, Oord rightly points out that the definition of a miracle is at the heart of
this problem. Two Greek words, frequently translated as 'miracle,' belong in different semantic fields. Those words are *dunamis* and *sēmeion*. *Dunamis* refers to
power or ability, while *sēmeion* refers to a sign. It seems to me that these two
words point to distinct dimensions of what a miracle is.

Most of the questions people have about miracles regard the *dunamis* dimension of a miracle. Does God have the power or ability to act miraculously in our
lives? This question has been especially highlighted since David Hume defined
miracles as violations of the laws of nature.[1] Oord addresses Hume's misleading
definition and offers an account of an uncontrolling God's power to do surprising things to promote well-being.

I would like to address the other, often neglected, dimension of a miracle,
namely as sign. I think that the idea of an uncontrolling God has the advantage of
drawing our attention to the *full scope* of the miraculous—signs of God's love and
care for us. To illustrate what I mean, I draw from my own experience of what I
consider miraculous healing.

In 2008, I had a stroke caused by violent vomiting brought on by a stress-
induced headache. The vomiting produced so much pressure in my throat that
my carotid artery dissected. The bleeding from that injury formed a clot that

went to my brain and paralyzed and blinded me on my left side. Fortunately, my husband was home, and he found me and acted quickly to get me medical attention. I was able to receive cutting edge treatment to remove the clot, and I recovered quickly and fully. Even the doctors called me a 'success story.' Everything about this incident could be explained by the ordinary regularities of the world—the doctor used a method of treatment developed to meet the needs of human body functions. But there was nothing 'ordinary' to me about my recovery. I was blind, and now I could see: I was paralyzed, and now I could walk. This experience turned me toward God in overwhelming gratitude. I was grateful, of course, for regained abilities, but I was also grateful for the minds that developed the treatment, for the hands that carried it out, and for my husband's wisdom and quick action. Most of all, I was grateful for the ways God had worked consistently and regularly through all the things that were involved in my healing.

Although the speed and extent of my healing was surprising to most people, a focus on power alone might cause one to miss the miracle I experienced. One advantage of thinking about God as uncontrolling is that it allows and impels us to look for God in the regular events in our lives. Even when surprising events take place, they should not distract us from noticing the regular ways God provides for us every day. In fact, something miraculous, sign *as well as* power, will focus our attention on God in such a way that we are able to see God's involvement in more ways than we usually do.

When new parents talk about the 'miracle' of birth, they are talking about the way an ordinary life process means so much more than an operation of what bodies do naturally. It is a sign of hope and love and, for those with the eyes of faith, of God's blessing. An uncontrolling God is active in ways we often fail to see, and a miracle, whether surprising or not, serves to draw our eyes to see what we otherwise would likely miss. This, too, is a kind of power.

Sarah Heaner Lancaster is professor of theology at Methodist Theological School in Ohio. She has authored several books, including, Romans, a theological commentary in the Belief Series, as well as many articles and chapters in books.

Endnotes

1. Hume, David. *An Enquiry Concerning Human Understanding.* Vol. XXXVII, Part 3. The Harvard Classics. New York: P.F. Collier & Son, 1909–14; Bartleby.com, 2001. www.bartleby.com/37/3/

Life in the Spirit:
Out of Control

Bob Luhn

Recently, the church where I am serving as interim pastor completed a video Bible study series, "When the Spirit Moves," by Jim Cymbala, senior pastor of the dynamic Brooklyn Tabernacle. Lesson 5 entitled, "Who's In Control?" contained Rev. Cymbala's teaching on being filled with the Holy Spirit.[1] He began this segment by talking about David Berkowitz, a serial killer who terrorized New York City for many months beginning in the summer of 1976 and ending with his arrest in August of 1977. He said he had joined a satanic cult and felt he was controlled by Satan through a dog that belonged to his neighbor, Sam. He took the name Son of Sam when he spoke or wrote of himself. Since his arrest and imprisonment, he has confessed faith in Christ and become involved in prison ministries. He said it was easy having once surrendered control of his life to Satan to now renounce that and surrender control to the Holy Spirit. The implication is that control by the Holy Spirit is only different in degree from being controlled, dominated, or manipulated by evil spirits. It is control either way; one is controlled by an evil force or one is controlled by a good force, i.e., the Holy Spirit.

Cymbala then asked the question, "What does it mean to be filled with the Spirit?"[2] He answers in this way: "Filled doesn't mean filled like a glass . . . it means to be controlled by the Holy Spirit."[3] Cymbala goes on to say that Christians are to "not only walk in the Spirit but be controlled by the Holy Spirit."[4]

Cymbala consistently uses the language of control to describe the Spirit-filled life. He even mentions demonic possession as a counterfeit of genuine Spirit control.

What a contrast Thomas Jay Oord provides in *The Uncontrolling Love of God*. His basic premise is summarized well in these words,

Because of love, God necessarily provides freedom/agency to creatures, and God works by empowering and inspiring creation toward well-being. God also upholds the regularities of the universe because those regularities derive from God's eternal nature of love. . . . God is not a dictator mysteriously pulling strings. God never controls others, but sometimes acts miraculously, in non-coercive ways.[5]

Throughout his book, Oord consistently uses terms like influencing, empowering, inspiring, wooing, non-coercive, guiding, and calling. All of these terms emphasize his basic concept that the God who is love, "never controls others."[6] Love, by nature, doesn't control, dominate, manipulate, or rob people of freedom in any way. In fact, it is the non-coercive, others-empowering love of God that sets a person free to be fully human—capable of loving God with one's whole being and loving one's neighbor as one's self.

Let's look at one well-known passage of Scripture: Galatians 5:22-23. Nine virtues known as the "Fruit of the Spirit," or the character qualities that form within the life of the Spirit-led person, are listed here. The last one is self-control. It is not Holy Spirit control but self-control. It is not Holy Spirit domination; it is not being consumed by the Spirit or losing one's identity in the Spirit. It is not being overwhelmed and swept away by the Spirit. What *is* emphasized is individual persons being given control of their own lives, after previously being under the sway of the flesh.[7] Increased freedom from sin, decreased selfishness, and control of one's lower impulses are provided by the working of the Spirit in a Christian's life. The Holy Spirit, as an indwelling presence, is constantly influencing the person in the direction of free and holy love.

I see this fruit of the uncontrolling Spirit in my own life. Prior to committing my life to Christ and being filled with His Spirit, I was not free to love or to want anything but my own selfish way. After the Spirit moved in, I felt strength, motivation, and encouragement to love others as I loved myself. I was not being controlled, but for the first time I felt like someone was cheering me on as well as supplying energy to make loving choices in every situation. Sadly, sometimes I have used my freedom poorly and have not made the loving choice. In these moments of failure I am very aware that the Spirit has granted me self-control. I am not forced, dominated, or manipulated by the Spirit. I am granted power to love and freedom to make a loving or unloving choice. It is always my hope to make the loving choice.

I believe Oord's understanding best provides a way of understanding Scriptures that refer to the Spirit-filled life. The Third Person of the Trinity shares the essential characteristic of God: uncontrolling love.

Bob Luhn has served as a pastor in the Church of the Nazarene since 1973. Currently retired, he works as an interim pastor and he and his wife Kathy are catching up on visiting their three daughters, sons-in-law, and seven grandkids.

Endnotes

1. Cymbala, Jim. *When God's Spirit Moves, Lesson 5.* DVD. Grand Rapids, MI: Zondervan, 2011.

2. Ibid.

3. Ibid.

4. Ibid.

5. Oord, 94.

6. Ibid.

7. See Galatians 5:19-21 (NIV).

The Weakness of God

Lon Marshall

Malcolm Gladwell has a podcast called *Revisionist History*. I recently listened to episode 7, entitled "Hallelujah."[1] In this episode, he talks about artistic genius and how it works. Sometimes it is seen in Bob Dylan, who writes songs that practically write themselves. Other times it is like Cézanne, who has been called an experimental innovator. He experiments, doesn't like it, changes it, and (after many iterations) comes up with a painting he likes. The episode spends a good deal of time talking about Leonard Cohen's song "Hallelujah."[2] This song is in the consciousness of most contemporary music lovers, but it almost never came to be. Its history includes several years, several record labels, and several artists taking it up and rewriting it. It took a number of people, a lot of luck, and unique circumstances to give us the song we have today.

That is kind of what happened to this essay. I've turned in four different 'final drafts.' I probably should not have been so eager to submit each one. Each time it did not convey what I originally hoped to say. It's a bit embarrassing. Tom and his editors have been very gracious. Friends have offered their input, and I have had experiences that have helped me reflect on what to write. I'm not trying to say I am a creative genius, just that my brain seems to work like these experimental innovators, and the collaboration of others combined with time, experiences, and contemporary circumstances have all worked together to create this essay.

When I imagine God anew with the theological lens of open and relational providence presented in *The Uncontrolling Love of God*, many possibilities become available in how to interpret scripture and think about God with an eye for Shalom. Becoming aware of my assumptions reforms something lower and more foundational than beliefs or doctrines. Knowing I am created in God's image, I am reminded this is what God is like, with an open mind to the future and the audacity to cooperate with humanity and creation as an experimental innovator.

God is like Jesus

I'm not sure where I picked up the idea, but my default assumption used to be that Jesus was somehow less than God. Without ever saying it out loud, I assumed that Jesus was not the complete package. The powerful, violent God of the Old Testament was being subtracted *from* in the revelation of Jesus. Some Bible scholars like to interpret the Apostle Paul's letter to the Philippians to say he 'emptied himself' in this way. But recently, theologians are thinking about this differently. Instead of talking about how God diminished God's self in the incarnation, some are saying the revelation of God in Jesus is a more complete revelation of God's true nature.[3]

This means God's full nature can be seen in how Jesus lived, taught, and acted. It was radical then, and it still is today. We need look no further than Jesus to see what God is like. And it is clear that Jesus was love personified. He lived and died a self-sacrificial life. His weakness was his superpower. He overcame violence and death by nonviolence. He told Pilate his followers would not fight. His kingdom is different.[4] "He is the image of the invisible God."[5] Tom says, "God's power is essentially persuasive and vulnerable, not overpowering and aloof. We especially see God's non-coercive power revealed in the cross . . . which suggests that God's power is cruciform . . . other-oriented love."[6] In my opinion, Tom even goes as far as to suggest Jesus was an experimental innovator. He describes Jesus as seeking people to cooperate with him in miracles of healing. Jesus does no healing where the people do not believe, rather he often says, "Your faith has healed you."[7]

If we keep separate the God of the Old Testament from Jesus and read all scripture as equal, we may extrapolate *"sword" instead* of a cross.[8] It matters *"what lens we are using."*[9] As those following an uncontrolling God, we examine the scriptures with new eyes—the eyes of Jesus.

God is looking for partners in the new creation project. God is looking for vulnerable, other-oriented people like you and me, who are willing to love at great risk to ourselves and to influence the dynamic cosmos for good. God is looking for partners who understand the gospel of peace and how to live it in a cruciform fashion. God is looking for partners who use mercy and restorative justice as their weapons, who stand with the rejected, who long for the reconciliation of all things, and who will do no harm (no matter how right it may seem).

Thomas Jay Oord's, *The Uncontrolling Love of God*, is advocating that God's transformative quality is love, not power.[10] From a certain perspective, this may seem like a weakness. We, in our humanness, tend to like the certainty of guarantees through a coercive, forceful God. The God revealed in Jesus imagines a new world of mercy, peace, and enemy love that brings a new hope for everyone. This is the God of uncontrolling love.

Lon Marshall is a licensed Marriage and Family Therapist. He spent most of his life in the Church of the Nazarene. Lon is an alumnus of MNU and UMKC, with an MA in Counseling Psychology. He now attends a rural Mennonite MCUSA church and lives in Kalona, Iowa. He's been married to Julie for 27 years and has 3 daughters, 22, 18, and 13. Lon blogs at http://lonmarshall.blogspot.com/

Endnotes

1. Gladwell, Malcolm. "Hallelujah". *Revisionist History*. Podcast audio. Episode 07 (2016). http://revisionisthistory.com/

2. L Clement, "Hallelujah Rufus Wainwright". YouTube video. 04:06. Posted [Sep 8 2007]. https://www.youtube.com/watch?v=xR0DKOGco_o&feature=youtu.be

3. Thomas Jay Oord, *The Uncontrolling Love of God: An Open and Relational Account of Providence* (Downers Grove: InterVarsity Press, 2016), 153-160.

4. John 18:36 (NASB).

5. Col. 1:15

6. Oord, 155.

7. Oord, 199-204.

8. Bailey, Sarah Pulliam. "Jerry Falwell Jr.: 'If more good people had concealed-carry permits, then we could end those' Islamist terrorists". Washington Post. December 5, 2015. https://www.washingtonpost.com/news/acts-of-faith/wp/2015/12/05/liberty -university-president-if-more-good-people-had-concealed-guns-we-could-end -those-muslims/

9. Hoag, Zach J. "We're never going to survive unless we get a lot more Jesus-Centered".

Christian Week. August August 24, 2016. "www.christianweek.org/never-going
-survive-unless-get-lot-jesus-centered/

10. Thomas Jay Oord. "The Uncontrolling Love of God: An Open and Relational Account of Providence". Filmed [Nov 2016]. YouTube video. 04:48. Posted [Nov 2 2016].
https://www.youtube.com/watch?v=Sp3GVIqhYQk&feature=youtube

The God of Chance

Bradford McCall

In his book, *The Uncontrolling Love of God*, Thomas Jay Oord says randomness and chance are real occurrences in the natural environment.[1] I agree. I find the notion of randomness and chance, as operative in nature, consonant with my view of a God who lures creation to higher levels of complexity through the processes of biological evolution.

As I see it, God does not determine the outcome of random events, but God does constrain randomness by setting broad boundaries. God empowers particles, systems, and organisms to interact according to natural laws within these set boundaries, and this produces a wide range of beautiful results.

Various sciences suggest randomness shapes the world, but there is debate about how much of reality is random. In his magnum opus, *The Structure of Evolutionary Theory*, Stephen Jay Gould emphasizes the importance of recognizing both the reality of structural constraint and the historical origin of structures.[2] Life's pathway includes many features predictable from the laws of nature, but these aspects are too broad and general to explain evolution's particular results—such as cats, horses, lilies, and people . . .

According to Gould, the history of life is not necessarily progressive, and it is certainly not predictable. The earth's living systems have evolved through a series of unexpected and unplanned accidents.

Humans, for example, arose as a contingent outcome of thousands of linked events. Any one of those events could have occurred differently, thereby leading evolutionary history on a pathway making consciousness impossible.

There are many examples of massive randomness in evolution. For instance:

- Had Pikaia not been among the survivors of the initial flourishing of multi-cellular animal life in the Cambrian explosion some 520 million years ago, it is unlikely vertebrates would have inhabited the earth at all.
- Had a small group of lobe-finned fish not evolved with a radically different limb skeleton capable of bearing weight on land, vertebrates possibly would never have become land-dwelling.
- Had a meteorite not struck the earth about 65 million years ago, dinosaurs would probably still be dominant today. Other animals would still be small creatures living within the dinosaurs' world.
- Had a small lineage of primates (i.e. monkeys, baboons, gibbons, apes) not evolved the ability to walk upright just two million years ago, human ancestry might have wound up as a line of ecologically marginal apes.

Simon Conway Morris offers perhaps the most sustained critique of Gould's radical randomness argument. Conway Morris argues that similar patterns regularly appear in widely divergent groups and calls this "convergence."[3] We find many examples of convergence in life. These multiple patterns and repeated histories suggest, despite some randomness, evolution is more predictable than Gould envisioned.

However, Conway Morris argues the likelihood of the same cognitive creatures evolving again—with five fingers on each hand, a blind spot in each eye, thirty-two teeth, and so on—is remote, even if, somehow, the Cambrian explosion could be recreated.

Convergence operates at all levels of biological organization. Humans are one of the best examples of the power of convergence. We are not entirely the products of a cosmic accident, but we are also not the result of a meticulously ordained plan.

Evolutionary convergence notes the repeated tendency of biological organization to arrive at the same 'solution' to a particular 'need.' What we regard as complex is usually fundamental in simpler systems, thus the real novelty in evolution is how things are put together. The number of evolutionary end-points is limited, which means not everything is possible. What is possible has usually been arrived at multiple times. However, this evolution of likened forms takes billions of years to become increasingly inevitable.

In sum, convergence tells us evolutionary trends are real. Adaptation is not some occasional component in the machine, but it is central to the explanation of the emergence of life.

So what does this brief analysis of Gould's and Conway Morris' writings mean for those of us who insist on God's uncontrolling love? I suggest two things.

First, there is genuine randomness in nature. God does not control even non-human creatures and entities. God uses this randomness in order to achieve the filling of creation by maintaining dynamic stability in complex systems.

Second, this genuine randomness does not exclude the expression of similar form, even among widely different evolutionary lines. Randomness isn't the same as absolute chaos. Continuities emerge over time. In fact, constraints are part of the evolutionary process. Even considering elementary forms of life, the pattern of convergence dominates.

All of this suggests, even though God's love is uncontrolling, that God still acts with purpose. God woos and lures creation forward toward greater complexity.

Bradford McCall is an adjunct professor of theology at various universities. He has multiple degrees, including ones in biology and theology. He enjoys writing about theology & science issues.

Endnotes

1. Thomas Jay Oord, *The Uncontrolling Love of God: An Open and Relational Account of Providence* (Downers Grove: InterVarsity Press, 2016).

2. Stephen Jay Gould, *The Structure of Evolutionary Theory* (Cambridge, MA: Belknap of Harvard UP, 2002).

3. Simon Conway Morris, *Life's Solution: Inevitable Humans in a Lonely Universe* (Cambridge: Cambridge University Press, 2003).

When God Is Not in Control

Janyne McConnaughey

I don't have choices."

The words hung in the air. My therapist and I had been struggling with this for almost two years. It was a deep-seated belief for which we could find no source. My story of repressed childhood sexual abuse (from the age of three) would have predicted anything but success, and yet I had a Ph.D., professional career, and 38-year marriage. I obviously made choices—good ones. Yet, I said I did not have choices—again. Where was this buried? Then, as a result of a car accident on a Los Angeles freeway, the memory of skidding out on a mountain road surfaced.

"I didn't die, I didn't die."

I screamed this as I ran from the car, not knowing where I was running. I was looking for the cliff I had run to 40 years earlier—the cliff where I tried to end my life after a betrayal so deep I never recovered. As my car skidded and I ran to stand on the edge of the cliff, a man stopped to help me. Obviously skilled, he convinced me to turn and step back; but the dirt crumbled beneath my feet and I slid off the cliff and clung to a tree root until he rescued me.

As I lay on the dirt, I believed God had stopped me from ending my life. I believed the choice was taken from me. I had been taught God was always in control and the only way I could make sense of my life was to believe God allowed the abuse *and* stopped me from stepping off the cliff. Why would he stop me but not all the others who succeeded in ending their lives? Did he love me more? Was he trying to build character through the trauma I had experienced? Did he have some great purpose I had not yet fulfilled?

Every morning for forty years, as I emerged from sleep, I re-enacted the fall from the cliff in a symbolic feeling of dread. My hands never relaxed and on the dark days when I said, "I feel like I am falling off a cliff," I was trying to express the reality I had repressed.

Buried with the repressed memory was the reason I believed I did not have choices—it was all about theology.

After I was coaxed back to my car, the man sat beside me and asked, "Do you believe in God?"

Oddly enough, I said, "I believe God loves me."

The broken child in me never doubted God's love, but it was almost impossible to reconcile with the truth I now knew about the life I had lived. During two years of intensive therapy, the pain had exploded out of my soul. I was three . . . I was six . . . I was nine . . . I was twelve . . . I was fourteen. Finally, I was a young adult and I knew God loved me, didn't protect me when he could have, and made me live when I wanted to die. It was difficult to make sense of it all.

"What is your anchor, Janyne?"

In my mind, I was in a lake of pain about to be sucked into a whirlpool.

"I know I am supposed to say God. I know you want me to say God. But no, God is not my anchor."

The words spoken from a couple dozen fractured parts of me hung between us. If God could prevent pain why didn't he?

It would be months before I understood I did have choices. I finally realized I could not accept I had choices, because I could not accept the fact that those who hurt me *also* had choices. It was all about freewill. If I could choose, then they could choose, and God really was not in control. If God wasn't in control, then he did not save me from stepping off the cliff, and there was not some great purpose I needed to fulfill . . . and I wasn't sure I wanted to live. This was something my theology would never allow me process.

I drove down the mountain by following the taillights of the man God had sent to keep me alive. I was like George in the movie *"It's a Wonderful Life."* God had chosen for me to live, and I needed to live a life worthy of his choosing. I let others make choices for me, I believed what they wanted me to believe; I became a theological chameleon and buried my pain so deeply it didn't erupt until I turned 61. I did live a wonderful life, but I was never able to truly worship the God who chose to make me live but did not protect me.

The day I realized I had choices was the day I understood God was not a controlling God. He did not control me on the cliff; I chose to turn and live. I chose, but so did all those who hurt me. We *all* had freewill. I didn't need to say nonsensical things such as, "God allowed my abuse to build character."

He felt sorrow, he comforted me, and he prompted me to seek help, but I made the choices.

She asked me again, "Janyne, do you believe you have choices?"

"Yes, I do believe I have choices because I believe God loves me and as a result he has given me freewill. He has given everyone freewill and he will not stop human choices, be they for good or for evil. Everyone makes their own choices."

Outside of an understanding of an uncontrolling God there is no potential for truly transcending the human experience of trauma, living life abundantly, and worshipping freely. The God who controls could not be my anchor, but the God who loves me, comforts me, brings me support by prompting the actions of others, and guides my choices most certainly can!

Dr. Janyne McConnaughey retired in 2015 after 40 years in education. Prior to her 33 years in higher education as a teacher educator, she taught in and directed early childhood programs. She and her husband, Scott, are enjoying living full-time in their 5th wheel at a park just outside of Garden of the Gods in Colorado. She enjoys spending her days writing, walking, and connecting with friends and family. She especially enjoys every minute she is able share with her children and grandchildren in the Seattle area.

Maybe God Does Not Have a Plan for My Life

Angela Monroe

"D on't worry, God is in control."

I've heard it over and over. It's the phrase that is supposed to bring me comfort. I know people mean well. I know they say it to make me feel better. Somehow, though, it doesn't.

I am young. At 23 years old, I have no idea what I'm doing. In my life, my career, my calling, and my marriage; the possibilities are endless and overwhelming. I could be *anywhere* in just a year's time. Life seems to be limitless but also sometimes feels directionless. Plans change daily as doors open and shut, and it can be stressful and confusing. I think many people my age experience the same thing. We're all just trying to figure it out. It's the universal feeling of being lost. There are a million places we could go, but the path . . . to anywhere . . . isn't clearly marked. Yet, pictures on social media, devotionals, and council . . . *all* avenues . . . tell me that God has a plan for my life, and that he is in control.

Sometimes it doesn't feel as if this is true. It feels like the opposite. Sometimes I ask God to *take* control of my life, but he doesn't. He doesn't answer me one way or the other. He is silent. Sometimes, bad things happen. When there is seemingly endless pain and suffering around me, how I am supposed to believe that God is in control? It's not the easiest thing to do, and it certainly doesn't bring me comfort when I think about the purposeless pain that, if God were really in control, he could have prevented.

This phrase seems easy to say in times of hardship. It seems like it should be comforting to someone like me, someone who doesn't feel a clear sense of direction for her life. It ties a nice little bow around our problems and lets us know that whatever we do, God is going to take over, and it won't really matter in the end.

It may be my youth, or it may just be my stubbornness, but I want to have a part in what goes on in my life. I want to be in control . . . at least a little bit. I want the choices I make to matter. I want my life to make a difference in the world. But if God is truly in control, then it doesn't seem to matter what I do.

A few years ago, I had the privilege of taking a class with Thomas Jay Oord. For other students, taking difficult classes means lots of homework and late nights studying. For theology students, it means completely rethinking your worldview and idea of God. This is exactly what Tom's class challenged me to do. Tom challenged my beliefs with questions that are addressed in *The Uncontrolling Love of God.* If God is really all powerful, can he be all loving? And, if we say God is love, how could he be in control? I wrestled with these questions over and over throughout the class and have yet to come to a solid conclusion. However, after reading through Tom's latest book, I find comfort in some of the possible answers.

In Oord's view of essential kenosis, God does not have the ability to control anything. Rather, his love allows for randomness in the world as well as human responsibility. In this view, God's uncontrolling love gives humans the ability to control their own lives. Although God walks alongside, loving and wooing people toward him; humans ultimately make their own decisions that, in turn, affect their lives and the lives of others. Maybe God's love really is all-encompassing. Maybe, *because* God is love, he is not completely in control.

This idea of essential kenosis is comforting to me. It accounts for the random tragedies that occur as well as the random luck that we experience on a regular basis. It also makes space for an understanding of God's character as relational love as opposed to power.

In this viewpoint, God does not have a plan for my life. Although that may sound heretical to some, it is comforting to me. God is not sitting above me planning every detail of my life before I even have the chance to make a decision. Rather, he is walking alongside me, wooing and guiding as I take each next step. His love for me is so great, so deep, that I get to participate in it. I get to be in relationship with the all-loving, uncontrolling God, and in that I find comfort.

～

Angela is a recent graduate of Northwest Nazarene University with degrees in Music Theory and Composition and Christian Ministry. She has stayed on campus, working full time in the Admissions office. Angela has been married to her high school sweetheart Todd for just over 2 years. Todd is continuing his education as a Mass Communications major and will graduate in May 2017. In their free time, they love to go on walks, drink vanilla lattes, and watch reruns of The Office.

Stuff Happens!

Dyton L. Owen

My wife, Tammy, and I have had countless conversations revolving around a statement we have often heard, most frequently after some tragedy has befallen a community or a family. Usually it is spoken by well-meaning people—often Christian people—who feel as though they must say something in the face of another person's pain or grief rather than remain silent.

"Everything happens for a reason," or the variation, "this must have been God's will," both imply God causes—or wills—everything that happens.

At first blush, this statement seems encouraging. Think about it. You or your family has just endured the news of the loss of a loved one. Word quickly spreads to your friends, community, church and neighbors. As any good person would do, many flock to your side to shower you and your family with love and support. During the rush of people coming and going, offering to help in whatever way they can—perhaps by providing meals, watching your children, taking care of household things—someone sits next to you on your couch, puts an arm around your shoulders and, as you weep trying to take in all you have just heard, says, "Everything happens for a reason. It's all a part of God's plan. You may not know what the plan is, but God never does anything without a purpose."

The person means well. He or she is trying to offer comfort in what is the most painful time of your life. The individual may honestly believe everything does happen for some reason we may not be able to see or understand in the moment—some reason that will become clearer as time passes. Such a sentiment is often offered as comfort; however, the truth is, it often comforts the one saying it more than the one receiving it. In other words, it is spoken so the one saying it is comforted because he or she was able to 'say something.'

It would be better to say nothing at all. Such an idea portrays God as uncaring, distant, and aloof. It implies God willfully brings about tragedy. It is as if God's hand is literally guiding a person toward misfortune.

When I was nine years old, my family moved to Tulsa where my father would serve as the senior pastor of an up-and-coming church. Three days after we moved in—boxes still unpacked—Dad walked in the front door and called for my mother who was in the kitchen making a grilled cheese sandwich lunch for my brother and me. He announced their oldest son—our brother—had been killed in an accident while serving in the Army. At that moment the world stopped. I was too young to comprehend what dad had just told us. My mother collapsed on the floor; Dad sat next to her. My older brother and I just stood there, not knowing what to do or say.

Somehow, word had gotten out in the church. Within minutes, leaders of the church were at our door. They had come to express their sorrow and offer any help they could. One of them was a physician. He had come to offer his condolences and, thankfully, administer a mild sedative to my mother. As my brother and I stood there, trying to take it all in, not knowing a single person who came into our house, I saw one of those people sit on the couch next to my mother and heard her say, "You may never know what God's will is in all this. . . ."

It was the first time I remember thinking to myself, "Did God really cause my brother's death? Was the accident really not an accident, but something planned . . . by God?"

In his book, *The Uncontrolling Love of God,* Thomas Jay Oord helps clarify why this is poor theology. In the chapter entitled, "Randomness and Regularities of Life," Oord addresses the misguided and harmful notion that God's hand guides every incident of every day in every person's life. In other words, the chapter suggests it is erroneous to believe there are no accidents, only 'incidents in God's plan;' and to reject randomness, therefore, to presume 'everything happens for a reason.' At the same time, Oord reminds us there are regularities we cannot deny. If the regularities of nature were dominant, nothing new would ever appear. On the other hand, if randomness ruled creation, chaos would ensue.[1]

Oord's idea that God is 'essentially kenotic,' opens a wide door and allows a fresh wind of understanding to blow on how God acts in relation to creation. If God's nature is uncontrolling love—i.e., because God is love, God provides creatures freedom to do as they choose—then God cannot control every action of God's creation. Controlling love is *not* love. Oord goes on to show, because God is essentially love, all the regularities of creation stem from God's loving nature. Because of God's essential love, God never controls creatures or creation. Randomness happens; however, God is always calling creation on to love, beauty, and health even in the midst of tragedy. The accidents we experience in life—such as the accident that took my brother's life—are just that: random events. Because of God's uncontrolling nature of love, God could not intervene to prevent it.

It was not part of God's plan. It was not a case of 'everything happens for a reason.' It was not God's will. It just happened.

There is more to it, as Oord reminds us. Simply because a random tragic event occurs—as devastating as it may be—does not mean good cannot come from it. The death of my brother serves as an example. Because of his death, my family was better able to minister to families who have found themselves in similar situations. We know what it is like to lose a loved one to random events with tragic endings. God's uncontrolling love means God does not will everything that happens; but in everything that happens, God wills good to come from it. When tragedy strikes, perhaps knowing this will move us closer to the love, beauty, and wholeness toward which God is constantly calling us.

Dr. Dyton L. Owen is a United Methodist pastor, author, church consultant and clergy coach. He is also a family system theorist that he utilizes in his ministry.

Endnotes

1. Thomas Jay Oord, *The Uncontrolling Love of God: An Open and Relational Account of Providence* (Downers Grove, IL: InterVarsity, 2015), See 43.

Suffering Underneath the Uncontrolling Love of God

Jesse Thorson

An individual's first experience of suffering or deep pain often leads to an intense questioning of reality and a loosening of once tightly held convictions. For followers of Jesus, these seasons sometimes serve to pull a loose thread from our perfectly knit, neat understanding of God's goodness and power. A single, loose thread in the fabric of our systematic theology can threaten the efficacy of the entire tapestry, sometimes completely unraveling our understandings of God's love and sovereignty.

In his book, *Lament for a Son*, Christian philosopher Nicholas Wolterstorff pens a guttural lamentation in response to the death of his 25-year old son Eric in a mountain-climbing accident. He wrestles with the widely-held view that, for God, death is a tool used to send us all to the heavens of the next world at one time or another, a seemingly arbitrary moment when 'our time is up' and God decides to 'take us home.' Attempting to piece together the role of death and God's goodness in the great puzzle of reality, Wolterstorff ultimately concludes, "I cannot fit it all together by saying, 'He did it,' but neither can I do so by saying, 'There was nothing he could do about it.' I cannot fit it together at all. I can only, with Job, endure. I do not know why God did not prevent Eric's death. To live without the answer is precarious. It's hard to keep on going."[1]

Thomas Jay Oord, in his work, *The Uncontrolling Love of God,* goes as far as to offer an answer to this predicament so poignantly problematized by Wolterstorff. Although I must admit that I am one-part skeptical and one-part excited when I hear that a theologian has stepped forth to solve the problem of evil, I am very compelled by Oord's proposed account of theodicy—the *essential kenosis* model of providence. Most importantly, Oord maintains that "uncontrolling love is the logically preeminent attribute of God's nature" and that because that is the case, "God's power is essentially persuasive and vulnerable, not overpowering and aloof."[2] Oord understands that insofar as God inevitably and necessarily loves his creation, which he does, God necessarily does not exercise coercive, unilateral power over and against this creation. Here, the answer to the problem posed by Wolterstorff is that God did not cause Eric's death but instead, perhaps surprisingly, did everything within his power to bring flourishing and goodness out of the accident, because the nature of God is uncontrolling love. Because "God *cannot* unilaterally prevent genuine evil," genuine evil exists in the world *even though God does not wish this to be so.*[3]

In what has been my first true season of suffering, I have likewise questioned the extent to which I can claim that the agency of God is responsible for all that transpires, not only within *my* experience of the world but also throughout reality at large. Confronted by a mixture of life-goods blurred together with deep pain, I often find myself in a similar situation as Wolterstorff—puzzled and unable to make sense out of any notion of God's sovereignty.

I am quick to thank God for the blessings of friendship and support during this season, because I can easily recognize these gifts as flowing out of the loving, others-oriented nature of God as demonstrated in the person of Jesus Christ. But now that suffering has entered my life in a new and intense way, the often-whispered superficial promise that, "God is in control," no longer strikes my heartstrings in any kind of positive resonance. If God is exhaustively 'in control,' then my experiences of pain and hurt are necessarily included in his directive will for my life as a part of His creation. However, if God's sovereign agency is not the primary culprit behind my suffering, how can I make any sense of the praiseworthy, good gifts in my life for which I desire to give thanks? In other words, if God is not to be blamed for my suffering, or at least exhaustively blamed for all types and instances of suffering, is he responsible for any of the blessings and goodness that I encounter in my journey?

In the end, there is no perfect system with which I can analyze and assess the exact degree to which God's agency is responsible for the diverse events and occurrences that I encounter in this life. Perhaps I ought to trust the idea that James conveys when he explains that God cannot tempt others nor be tempted. In his New Testament epistle, James writes, "Every good gift and every perfect gift is from above, coming down from the Father of lights with whom there is no variation or shadow due to change."[4] I can thank God for everything good in my life, because everything good is from God. It seems as though James instructs his readers to "not be deceived" in the preceding verse because there actually exist evils and temptations which the recipients of the letter falsely ascribe to God.[5] In other words, *that which is not good does not come from God.*

I am unable to rest easily with the claim that there are some things that God is simply unable to do, but I ultimately find myself agreeing with Oord: "We can only trust unreservedly the God in whose nature love is essential, eternal and logically primary."[6] Underneath the uncontrolling love of God, suffering *does not* and *will not* have the final word.

Jesse Thorson is a MN native studying Sustainable Development at Columbia University in NYC. He loves to practice theology in community and is passionate about addressing climate change, making music, and eating plenty of pancakes and other breakfast foods.

Endnotes

1. Nicholas Wolterstorff, *Lament for a Son* (Grand Rapids, Mich: Eerdmans, 1987), 67.

2. Thomas Jay Oord, *The Uncontrolling Love of God: An Open and Relational Account of Providence* (Downers Grove: InterVarsity Press, 2016), 169, 155.

3. Oord, 167.

4. James 1:17 (ESV).

5. James 1:16

6. Oord, 164.

A Decolonial Love of God

Ekaputra Tupamahu

C olonialization is a global phenomenon. Many people groups in Asia, Africa, Latin America, and even the United States, have historically experienced the pain of colonialism and fought to free themselves from it. However, theological discussion has largely missed serious reflection about God in the experience of colonial subjugation, oppression, and exploitation. This exclusion comes because theology as a discourse has been dominated by the voices of the colonizers, primarily white European male thinkers, and consequently, as Grace Ji-Sun Kim correctly points out, it has long been participating in the empire building project.[1] However, in the past few decades, post/de-colonial voices have begun to flourish, not only engaging but also resisting discourses against the dominance of mainstream European theologies. Scholars from many world areas have been pushing their voices, deeply embedded in their socio-political struggle for liberation and equality against colonial rule, into the mainstream global theological discussion. This is truly an encouraging development, because it opens more spaces for people to think critically about God through the particularity of their experiences.

This short reflection considers the possibility of interpreting Thomas Jay Oord's work, *The Uncontrolling Love of God,* through a decolonial lens. In doing so, I will begin with the concern of Frantz Fanon about the role of theology not only in promoting colonial subjugation but also luring the colonized to accept their subjugated condition. Fanon is critical of the way churches in the colonies operate. In *The Wretched of the Earth*, he writes, "The church in the colonies is the white people's Church, the foreigner's church. She does not call the native to God's ways but to the ways of the white man, of the master, of the oppressor."[2]

This is true not only in North Africa, but also in other colonies. For instance, churches in my home country, Indonesia, are basically imitations of European churches ranging from the physical architecture of their buildings, to formation of their liturgies, to the construction of their theologies. European theologians are often perceived as authority figures instead of discussion partners, and college classrooms become a venue for indoctrinating European theological ideas.

Fanon, furthermore, argues that one particular theology that has tremendously shaped the social condition of the colonized, and prevented them from resisting the oppressive power of the colonizer, is that of fatalism—that is, God has predetermined everything from the beginning. After being oppressed for so long, people in the colonies begin to develop a denial and acceptance strategy, persuading themselves "that colonialism does not exist, that everything is going on as before."[3] Fanon argues that theology plays an extremely important role in shaping this social acceptance of colonialism. He explains, "A belief in fatality removes all blame from the oppressor; the cause of misfortunes and poverty is attributed to God: He is the Fate. In this way the individual accepts the disintegration as ordained by God."[4] Fanon apparently sees the concept of God as the prime-cause of all things in the world—a theological model that Oord calls "God is the omni-cause,"—as plain dangerous.[5] If God has (pre)determined everything, then why on earth do we have to do anything to change the unjust social structure? This idea is a pacifier that will put the colonized to sleep in their suppressed condition.

This said, Oord's challenge to the traditional view of God can be well appropriated in the context of colonial struggle from two different angles—the angle of God and the angle of the world. These two angles are directly related to the doctrine of providence, the relationship *between* God and the world.

The all-powerful European God who controls everything is both the product and the promoter of the colonial expansion and subjugation of the world. Thus, it's not a surprise that colonizers often see their mission, to conquer and dominate the world, as doing the work of God. Essential kenosis seriously challenges this picture of God. God does not coerce: God loves. The uncontrolling love of God stands in stark contrast to that of a sovereign ruler. God cannot unilaterally decide on the exception.[6] Hence, the exception is not a space domination, but negotiation. As Giorgio Agamben has pointed out about the "state of exception," essential kenosis will foster the dynamic of biopolitical engagement.[7] It is the site where bare life, in all its nakedness and vulnerabilities, becomes the center of politics. Love that promotes well-being of all must be the motivating force that drives every socio-political interaction. In this way, essential kenosis strips the empire of its total power.

At the heart of Oord's proposal of essential kenosis lies the concept of genuine human freedom. "God's loving nature requires God to create a world with creatures God cannot control," Oord argues.[8] The uncontrolling love of God is the very reason for true freedom. Now, we need to understand that in the colonial context, the term 'freedom' is never taken lightly. It reminds the colonized of their struggle, battle, blood, and death. Hence, Fanon often employs the phrase: "struggle for freedom."[9] Freedom is not a pleasant word. Freedom is a struggle. Essential kenosis opens the door for the possibility of struggle and resistance against subordinating and oppressive social structure in the colonial world. Stating that "some may worry about political or social implications should they rethink their view of God's power," Oord seems to have rightly anticipated the social uncertainty and instability caused by this theological proposal.[10] If God is essentially uncontrolling, then there's no group that can socially and politically claim that they possess an absolute authority over others, nor can they tell others to submit to their authority because God has designed them so. It consequently creates a messy, unstable, and uncertain social space of constant struggle, resistance, and negotiation.

Fanon describes decolonialization as "a program of complete disorder."[11] If we think about essential kenosis from this perspective of struggle for freedom in the colonies, then the eradication of the colonial superstructure is precisely the promise of essential kenosis. Through the absence of the totalitarian power, essential kenosis promises and pushes for the decolonial disorder into the ordered colonial world.

Ekaputra Tupamahu is a Ph.D. candidate in New Testament and Early Christianity at Vanderbilt University. His dissertation research examines the intersectionality of the politics of language, racial-ethnic identity construction, the subjective performativity, and the colonial relations of power in the early Christian movement.

Endnotes

1. Grace Ji-Sun Kim, *Colonialism, Han, and the Transformative Spirit* (New York: Springer, 2013), chap. 1; Grace Ji-Sun Kim, *Embracing the Other: The Transformative Spirit of Love* (Grand Rapids, MI: Eerdmans, 2015), 109

2. Frantz Fanon, *The Wretched of the Earth* (New York: Grove, 2011), 42.

3. Fanon, 54.

4. Ibid.

5. Thomas Jay Oord, *The Uncontrolling Love of God: An Open and Relational Account of Providence* (Downers Grove: InterVarsity Press, 2016), 83-86.

6. Here I am alluding to Carl Schmitt's famous dictum: "Sovereign is he who decides on the exception." See Carl Schmitt, *Political Theology: Four Chapters on the Concept of Sovereignty*, trans. George Schwab (Chicago: University of Chicago Press, 2005), 5.

7. Giorgio Agamben, *State of Exception*, trans. Kevin Attell, Homo Sacer Series, II.1 (Chicago: University of Chicago Press, 2005), 87–88.

8. Oord, 146.

9. Fanon, 47, 56, 58, 75, 233, 235, 237, 245, 246.

10. Oord, 184.

11. Fanon, 36.

A Cosmos Bathed in Love

Paul Wallace

I was raised in a family of scientifically literate Baptists. Dad was a professor at Georgia Tech, and we had science books all over the house. I remember Carl Sagan's *Cosmos*, with its discussion of the deep past and the remote future. For a curious ten-year-old, *Cosmos* was a mind-blowing journey through time and space. The book's illustrations left me in silence, gazing in wonder. It spoke to me on the deepest of levels.

I remember reading another book in our house that offered a highly-organized and detailed timeline of evolution. Life, I learned, started billions of years ago in single-cell mode. After innumerable eons, multicellular organisms appeared. Later came more complex forms of life: trilobites, flowering plants, and jellyfish. Fish grew jaws and insects took to the air. Strange kingdoms rose and fell.

Eventually we humans showed up in evolutionary history. To say human beings are latecomers to the cosmic scene is an understatement. After all, if cosmic time were compressed into a single year, recorded human history would span about 10 seconds!

Dad's influence didn't stop with science. He also took us to church every time the doors were open, which was pretty often in those days.

Evolution and Evil

At church I was handed a different book. It talked about the cosmos too. But the story it told did not match what I had learned from science books. When

I read about six days of creation, I wondered, on what day did God make the dinosaurs?

Sagan's *Cosmos* featured a picture of a tyrannosaur looking over its shoulder at an exploding asteroid. This asteroid was the last thing it and countless other creatures saw before their deaths. That image was haunting.

The thought of a hundred million years of animal suffering overwhelmed my young soul. Why did God let that happen, I wondered. But the Bible offered me no answer. And the science books I read offered no descriptions of Adam and Eve. These books were as different as could be.

I learned later in my life that creatures were related to each other and descended from a single ancestor. In fact, we human creatures are related to all life, past and present. In addition, evolution seemed to operate automatically, randomly, and sometimes brutally. Evolution seemed directionless.

Random, directionless, and brutal evolution was nowhere mentioned in the Bible. By contrast, biblical authors suggested that God created us in love and for love.

As appealing as the biblical writers sounded, I found it hard to believe. In high school, I began to question my Christian faith. I kept going to church with my family, but the whole Christian scheme as I understood it seemed insufficient and irrational in the light of the cosmos I was learning about. My decision to study physics in college only deepened this impression.

Models of Providence

I did not know it at the time, but my religion-and-science problem derived from a faulty view of God's activity in the world. Such activity is called 'providence,' in theological circles. In his book, the *Uncontrolling Love of God*, Thomas Jay Oord distinguishes between several concepts of providence.

During the years I struggled with the apparent incompatibility of religion and science, my view of God's providence was similar to what Oord calls "God empowers and overpowers."[1] In this model, an omnipotent God sustains (empowers) creation and reaches in and adjusts (overpowers) it when necessary. This view says God resides outside the cosmos and intervenes when the divine mind sees fit, to achieve certain ends. These interventions are unilateral moves made by an omnipotent God.

The 'God empowers and overpowers' view of providence makes it hard to see why a perfectly free, all-powerful, and loving God would create through evolution. After all, evolution seems a painful, indirect, and inefficient way to fill a planet with life. Why wouldn't a God capable of overpowering creation just create everything all at once, with no suffering at all?

On this point, Oord's own view of providence is helpful. It solves the problem cleanly and without cutting theological or scientific corners. Oord casts evolution not as a blind series of mechanical events but as a three-billion-year drama of divine love. He sees God not as essentially omni-powerful but as essentially loving and creative. This God "*necessarily* gives the gifts of agency and self-organization to [all] entities capable of them."[2] From the lowest single-celled organism to *Homo sapiens*, God honors creatures by granting them freedoms and possibilities to match their capacities. And God draws creatures gradually forward and upward in love. There is no whiff of divine coercion, manipulation, or micromanaging. The view of God Oord proposes is a view that says God is incapable of such controlling acts.

By the same token, Oord's God is incapable of stopping death and suffering in this life, unilaterally. These things simply cannot be avoided. This view of providence will not satisfy some, I suspect. But a serious study of natural history reveals the problem of matching a fully in-control, omnipotent, and allegedly loving God with the often-brutal and often-inefficient nature of evolution.

We learn a lot about an artist from his or her work. We may learn something true about J.K. Rowling from reading *Harry Potter*, for instance. We may learn something true about Johnny Cash from listening to "Folsom Prison Blues." We may learn something true about Picasso by viewing *Guernica*.

As a young man, I wanted to learn something true about God by studying the cosmos. I wanted to know the Creator by knowing creation. The model of providence I embraced when younger prevented me from learning much about the Creator from studying creation. The mismatch between a controlling God and the suffering and inefficiency of evolution was too great.

By bathing the evolving cosmos in the love of an ever-creating God, Oord's view of providence makes it possible for me to understand much more about God when I study creation. Evolution makes sense in light of God's love.

❧

Paul teaches physics and astronomy at Agnes Scott College in Decatur, Georgia. His first book, Stars Beneath Us: Finding God in the Evolving Cosmos, was released by Fortress Press in March 2016.

Endnotes

1. Thomas Jay Oord, *The Uncontrolling Love of God: An Open and Relational Account of Providence* (Downers Grove: InterVarsity Press, 2016), 83.
2. Oord, 177 (emphasis mine).

Divine Love Trumps Divine Power: The Voice of Sophia

Michel Weatherall

I t is simple. God's love trumps God's power, but what does that really mean? What are the real implications? It means we need to give up a lot. It means we must be willing to let go of many known sacred certainties.

Thomas Jay Oord's book, *The Uncontrolling Love of God*, touches on something close to my heart. It is something I have struggled and wrestled with and have been wounded by, over decades—through a great amount of pain, tears, heartache, and faith crises.

I am going to state one of the rare theological statements that I firmly hold to be true: **God cannot be both omnipotent and omnibenevolent.**

I know. *Ouch.* Now that I have your attention, allow me to continue with a few other statements of belief. I still hold onto the Christian idea of God as not merely *loving,* but *Love* itself. I believe the different world religions sprang from God's general revelations, and what we see is a reflection of their different cultural and historical contexts. Believing this also means accepting Christianity as one of many cultural and historical environments arising from these general revelations. This is where the commonality of religions originates, in the general revelations of God.

I believe God distributes his wisdom (*Sophia*) among all peoples of all nationalities in all geographic locations and all cultures. Whether this *Sophia* speaks their *'cultural language,'* or they hear her voice through their *'cultural filters,'* matters little. The outcome is the same. She meets them where they are. It is not that I believe *all* religions lead to God; I believe *none* do.

Some might say this is something I choose to believe. I, however, don't see it this way; my conscience gives me no other choice. I must trust that God communicates Sophia to all people and cultures. To think otherwise means to accept God as a bigot, even a racist. That is not love. In fact, it would be the polar opposite of love; it would be hatred.

Nowhere does God's love trump God's power more obviously than in God's success in communication. There are over 35,000 denominations dividing Christianity. In addition, Muslims, Jews, Buddhists, Hindus, every spiritual path is fractured based on plurality of human perception. Because of this multiplicity, we have a wellspring of time, experience, and resources at our disposal. If there were one correct way of viewing, or encountering, or experiencing the sacred; in our ever shrinking world it should have been made absolutely evident by now.

If God's message is so simple and unmistakable in its intent, then why is there so much ambiguity? Why don't more people agree? Are we following a supposed omnipotent deity who failed in his endeavor to successfully connect with us? How could an all-powerful and all-loving God have gone so wrong and failed so miserably in his attempts?

Anyone who has ever ventured to communicate has experienced the ways it can go wrong. There are three. First, speakers of a message may not be plain about what they desire to impart.

Second, speakers may not adequately express the idea or message. Third, the listener may not properly interpret or understand the speaker's intent. If any of these occur, then the effort to successfully relate will fail.

However, when dealing with an all-powerful and all-loving entity, there are severe problems. The first two points deal with errors or flaws on the part of the communicator. An omnipotent and omnibenevolent God cannot have a foggy message, unless we allow for deliberate misleading, which would bring God's goodness into question (returning us to the hateful-bigot-god).

Concerning the third error of communication, I struggle with the listener not receiving or understanding the message properly. A perfect God would know how to *successfully* correspond in any situation. This creates a conundrum. Some would say humanity misinterprets God's interactions. I don't buy this. Like a good teacher, God's message—to all people—should be glaring, and I believe it is. Here is what I mean. Even in the midst of human plurality, the message is unmistakable. Among all the world's religions there are overt signs pointing to a process, a direction of growth, a spiritual evolution, without the necessity of a destination. The truth is right before us and we are grasping onto the wrong paradigm—a paradigm of power and belief. All of us know the Golden Rule. In nearly all sacred traditions, we are called to *compassion*. Interestingly it has *always* been made absolutely *crystal clear* how we are to treat one another.

Sophia speaks the loudest in apparent contradictions and paradoxes. Concern for power was our distraction, not God's. Why has God left absolutely no ambiguity as to how we are to treat one another? Why is Compassion the one message or instruction to which we are called to respond?

It is because love trumps power. Love trumps belief. It is not about one right religion. It is not about power. It is about love.

Regardless of our human quest for sacred certainty in all the wrong places, we are given little to no wiggle-room. God's message and wisdom (*Sophia*) to the world was *never* a message of the one true faith. *Sophia's* message was a calling to *compassion*, plain and simple. The voice of Sophia is a voice of love and to hear her is to hear the call to compassion.

Michel Weatherall has published 4 books and is working his fifth. He has an acute interest in spirituality but not religion, marking a distinct difference between the two. He has privately studied Eastern religions, Gnosticism, and the Abrahamic-faiths. http://brokenkeypublishin.wixsite.com/michelweatherall

The Price of Kenosis

Lori Wilson

T he *Giving Tree*, by Shel Silverstein, has haunted my life with its poignant story of selfless giving. Reading it as a child, I was reduced to tears. Later in life, reading it aloud to my own children was more than I could manage. It became almost a game for us, to see how far into the reading I could get before handing the book off to someone else, someone who didn't have a lump in their throat too large to read around. And now, as a mother with an empty nest . . . well, the book gathers dust on a shelf and calls out to my aching heart each time I walk past.

While *The Giving Tree* may look like a children's book, it also disguises profound theological reflections. While much might be (and has been) said about the ungrateful boy, the Tree nevertheless presents a powerful image of kenotic love. At great cost to herself, she gives and gives and gives. In the end, her giving brings about the transformation for which she had longed. The book, in this sense, ends well, but not without new layers of grief at each turn of the page.

The Uncontrolling Love of God tells a story of a God who, in many ways, loves like Silverstein's tree. God gives of God's self without coercion or control, always with the desire to draw us near. But because, like the boy, we remain free to walk away, God's work for our transformation doesn't come with a guarantee of happiness or satisfaction. In fact, deep sorrow is woven into this understanding of God.

We so long for the comfort that everything will work out well, or at the very least that an all-powerful being is 'behind the curtain,' guiding everything for a higher purpose. There is strong emotional incentive to hold onto this classical understanding of providence. But Oord makes a solid case that the traditional model of an all-powerful, controlling God comes at too high a price. At the very least, in light of suffering, it undermines a thoroughgoing belief in a loving God. Given the strong testimony of Scripture and Christian tradition, any doctrine that doesn't point us to a God who 'so loved the world,' who 'loved us first,' who in fact 'is love,' falls short of the mark. Oord's model of *essential kenosis* presents a strong alternative, one that makes better sense of suffering while preserving God's love as primary.

But this model doesn't come without a price of its own. If I accept that God persuades but does not coerce, I have to release my view of a God who controls evil and suffering. I have to accept that some things happen *outside of* God's will. And then, I have to come to terms with God's place in the midst of injustice and pain and loss.

There's some really important theological work out there on these themes (Moltmann & Fiddes come to mind), but what especially has my attention these days is the lived experience of sorrow as a part of kenosis. Silverstein's tree tries to persuade her boy over and again but each time releases him to the path he has chosen, a path that leads away rather than towards her. As she lets him go, and even showers him with her generosity, she experiences profound loss. In her loneliness, "she is happy . . . but not really."[1]

In keeping with this metaphorical picture of kenosis, it doesn't take long to glimpse the suffering of a God who is essentially characterized by "self-giving, others-empowering love."[2] The cruciform love of God sometimes takes the shape of profound sorrow, the grief that comes from rejection, from longings denied. The Old Testament prophets describe in stark terms the depth of divine suffering; Jesus weeps over Jerusalem. The Scriptures bear eloquent witness to God's grief.

If our loving God suffers, so must those of us who follow this God's path. No longer sheltered by the false comfort that 'all things happen for a reason,' we are exposed to the raw grief of God's will thwarted. We walk the path of a kenotic God only insofar as we, too, accept the burden of a world where things go deeply amiss . . . a world where God is at work, but God doesn't always win the day . . . a world where grief is sometimes the only authentic and faithful response.

Our lived experience tells us that even the most sacrificial love sometimes can't 'make it better.' At one time or another, most of us have confronted the fact that the deepest goodness of love is almost inevitably paired with profound grief.

Essential kenosis makes sense of this sad reality. It invites us to walk in the company of the man of sorrows.

This path is not an easy one. Releasing our hold on a God known for power and control comes at no small cost. Much like the tree, we will sometimes find ourselves "happy . . . but not really."[3] But, as the tree shows us, this way is nevertheless a beautiful and faithful one. She grieves, to be sure. Yet her tenacious hope transforms the bitterness of disappointment and the crushing pain of loneliness into an ever-deeper love. And so it is with us. As we allow ourselves to grieve, to follow in God's *kenotic* footsteps, this sorrow can break open our hearts, too, making room to love still more.

Lori is a non-profit consultant based in Denver, Colorado. She holds degrees in Spanish literature (BA, Colorado College) and Systematic Theology (MA, King's College London.) She and her husband enjoy reading, hiking, and traveling.

Endnotes

1. Shel Silverstein, *The Giving Tree.* (New York: HarperCollins, 2004)
2. Thomas Jay Oord, *The Uncontrolling Love of God: An Open and Relational Account of Providence* (Downers Grove: InterVarsity Press, 2016), 159.
3. Silverstein

SECTION THREE

Introduction:
How Creatures Respond

Thomas Jay Oord

My thoughts in the previous introductions influence how I think about my topic here. Some of that influence may be obvious. But I suspect not all.

To begin, if a person believes that God controls all things, it makes no sense to say, "Creatures respond to God." The 'Omni-determiner' view held by some Calvinist theologians allows no room for genuine creaturely response. This is one among many reasons we should avoid saying, "God is in control."

Thankfully, I encounter few believers who think God is all-determining. Belief in free will seems to be on the rise, and I'm happy about that! I could not make sense of my own experience if I were to deny that I have at least some freedom.

Although most believers don't believe God controls everything, my view says God's love *never* controls anything. That view goes beyond common beliefs. Many people think God *usually* doesn't control but will occasionally do so.

The view that God never controls entails some positive implications for how we might think about creaturely response. I want to mention a few . . .

Never Determined Creatures Respond

First, I think many nonhuman creatures can freely respond to God. That's right; your dog is free and can respond to her Creator. Dolphins respond freely to God too, I suspect. I think all complex creatures can respond appropriately or inappropriately to God.

I don't know how 'far down' the creaturely complexity chain we must go before freedom disappears. Are worms free? I don't know. I think they have agency, at least. I join many scholars convinced that self-organization and spontaneity are present at simpler levels of existence. And at least indeterminacy is present at the quantum level of existence.

The idea that nonhuman creatures can respond to God takes John Wesley's view of prevenient grace and extends it wider than Wesley seemed to do. Expanding prevenient grace provides a conceptual framework for affirming the Apostle Paul's hope of the reconciliation of all creation. In fact, I expect to see Wesley's horse in heaven! I've got more ideas about how this plays out in the afterlife, but I'll resist the temptation to follow that train of thought here.

Second, the idea that God's love is *never* controlling implies that humans *always* have the capacity to respond. Most theologians think God sometimes controls creatures in an occasional act of coercion. In other words, they believe God sometimes overrides, withdraws, or does not provide freedom. In those times, however, these creatures cannot *respond* to God.

By contrast, I think creatures *always* have the capacity to respond to God, because God *never* controls. If love does not coerce and requires free response, my view has the advantage of saying God *always* loves, because God *never* controls. And it says creatures can always choose to love in response, because God never takes away from creatures the capacity to respond.

Third, saying God always expresses self-giving, others-empowering, and uncontrolling love means that none of us does good without God's help. God's love makes our love possible. We rely upon God's empowering and inspiring love for any good works we might do in response. As the Apostle John puts it, "We love, because God first loved us."[1]

Because we rely upon God's grace, we have no grounds for the kind of pride that takes all the credit for our good actions. We should give God the lion's share of the credit for any good that emerges when we respond in cooperation. We can feel pleased by our cooperation, however, and we should believe we can be God's co-laborers. We act as God's hands and feet, to use the common phrase, although I sometimes feel as useless as an appendix! But my main point is that God is the source of good, even the good we express in response, but not the sole actor in establishing the common good.

How We Respond Matters

Combining the idea that God never controls with the idea that the future is open provides a framework for an especially important idea: what we do matters. As co-laborers, co-workers, co-creators, or co-operators with God, our actions have real significance. Our choices when responding make a real difference!

Most of us believe this intuitively. But the theology we've sometimes been taught says otherwise. Most of us feel guilty about our sin or happy about the love we share. We think life matters and what we do has real consequences. Consequently when we hear phrases like, "it's all about Jesus," or, "it's not about you," we realize these are at best partially true.

Theologies that say God controls us or imply the future is already settled clash with our intuitions about the genuine worth of our actions. A theology that says God's love is uncontrolling and the future is yet to be decided, by contrast, fits with our intuitions. It fits with our awareness that how we respond matters.

When I talk with audiences about these issues, I'm often struck by their reactions. A sizable portion—usually the majority—seems to perk up, throw back their shoulders, and sit a bit straighter. When they hear that open and relational theology affirms that our choices matter, they think, "That's what I've always thought. What I do makes a difference. It's nice to hear a theologian say so!"

Another portion of my audience, however, reacts differently. Their shoulders slump. They act as if a burden has been placed upon their backs. They seem to be thinking, "Oh no, you mean what I do makes a difference?" For them, this is bad news. It requires a measure of responsibility they had hoped to shirk.

I'm not sure why people have such different responses when hearing that God is not in control, the future is open, and their responses matter. I have some hunches about the differences. But I'm still working through this.

I suspect the essayists writing for this section are among those who think their choices matter. Their essays reflect on how we respond to a God of love. They make a fitting conclusion to this book; they help us reflect on how we might live lives of love in response to the God of uncontrolling love!

In light of my thoughts on responding to God, let me conclude this introduction with Eugene Peterson's translation of 1 Cor. 14:1 . . . "Go after a life of love as if your life depended on it—because it does."[2]

Here's to hoping these essays inspire you to live a life of love!

Endnotes

1. I John 4:19 (NIV).

2. Eugene H. Peterson, *The Message: The New Testament in Contemporary Language* (Colorado Springs, Colo.: Navpress, 1993), 425.

Praying for a Miracle

Donnamie Ali

C ome expecting a miracle," says the huge roadside poster advertising an upcoming miracle healing crusade. Since most people need a miracle in their
lives, people flock to the crusade, all with the expectation that it is their time for
a "miracle."

In my island nation of Trinidad, West Indies, one can see signs and hear ad-
vertisements on radio and television beckoning people with problems to attend
these religious meetings. I often wondered if something was wrong with me, because I am skeptical about these events even though I strongly believe in God's
power to heal. Does God tell us in advance when a miracle is going to occur? Does
God only perform miracles at the behest of certain people known as faith
healers?

A close reading of Oord's chapter entitled "Miracles and God's Providence"
puts into perspective much of what I have been thinking over the years. The author defines a miracle as, "an unusual event that occurs through God's special
action in relation to creation."[1] Yes, I have asked why God heals some people and
not others. I have also heard that if one does not get the miracle prayed for, this
indicates a lack of faith. What a guilt trip has been placed on countless Christians
over and over again!

It is a fact that advancements in medical science allow "health-care workers
to cooperate with God's love in the world."[2] This has been true in the case of my
own illness. I did not only pray but also used natural remedies that detoxed my
entire system. I was made whole again very quickly. Being healed of leprosy in the
time of Jesus was a great miracle, as indicated by the references to Jesus' healing
in the New Testament. Now this condition, known as Hansen's disease, can be

cured medically and is no longer considered a miracle. However, I view all healing as coming from God who uses humans as instruments to effect cures in many.

I bought a special thank you card for the surgeon who removed the tu-
mor from my son's spinal column. I think the skill some doctors have is awesome,
but I also acknowledge healing comes from God. I told the surgeon as much in
the words I penned in the card. I thanked him, but I thanked God so much more!

The idea of a cooperative effort between "God's initiating and empowering
love" and people is noteworthy.[3] Oord mentions that biblical authors often point
to faith as part of this cooperative effort. In fact it is necessary.[4] I endorse the role
of faith and the mind in the healing process. It was upon hearing a sermon about
the bleeding woman who touched the hem of Jesus' cloak that I began letting go
of my situation. Something happened within me when I heard the preacher say,
"Let go and let God!"

I stopped worrying and began to praise God for what was being done in my
life. My de-stressed mind, the herbal remedies, and the prayers of the saints, combined with the measure of faith I had in God, began the healing process in my
body. I was healed to the glory of God.

What about those who exercise faith and still have their loved ones die or
who die themselves? What do we say to them? Oord's essential kenosis theory
helps us to understand that even though God's love is steadfast, God "does not
selectively coerce to enact miracles for some but not for others."[5] God does not
demonstrate favoritism.[6] He loves everyone equally.

The author is clear and affirms the importance of faith in the healing process.
However, he very firmly states that human emotions, state of mind, and expectations all play a role in the healing process.[7] It is therefore reasonable to conclude
that while, in some instances, two individuals may have equally strong faith in
God; cancerous cells, genetic malfunctions, or ingrained unhealthy habits may
prevent bodily healing, even when many prayers are offered for the saints of God
so afflicted. Yes, God does initiate the healing process, but healing rarely occurs
in the absence of "creaturely cooperation."[8]

If the body is already too diseased, prayers of faith may be uttered, but the
mortal body will continue to degenerate until death occurs. Oord points out that
sometimes the body's organs are simply too diseased to cooperate with "God's
healing gifts" and the individual dies.[9]

So, by all means, we should pray for miracles of healing, and we should pray
in faith—believing for ourselves and others. Those prayers should be accompa-

nied by a willingness to alter our lifestyle choices. When we pray, we should at all times remember that while God has the power to heal; God needs the cooperation of the individual as well as the cooperation of their internal organs to effect bodily healing. Since the mind sends signals to the body; our state of mind, even the amount and type of support systems we have, can aid in the healing process. If our emotions are positive, then the chances of bodily healing are greatly increased. The created environment in which God encourages healing is quite the complex system. It helps if we cooperate.

It is cruel to accuse believers of weak faith when the desired healing does not occur. The essential kenosis view of miracles provides those genuinely seeking to understand how God works in people's lives with a credible explanation for why some get their miracles and others do not.

Donnamie Ali lives in Trinidad and Tobago. She earned a M.Div. from Northwest Nazarene University and she teaches occasionally at Caribbean Nazarene College.

Endnotes

1. Thomas Jay Oord, *The Uncontrolling Love of God: An Open and Relational Account of Providence* (Downers Grove: InterVarsity Press, 2016), 196.
2. Oord, 197.
3. Oord, 200.
4. See Oord, 202-203.
5. Oord, 213.
6. See Rom. 2:11 (NIV).
7. See Oord, 203.
8. Oord, 214.
9. Ibid.

The End of the World as We Know It

Chris Baker

W hat happens in the end?" It is one of the 'big questions' people have been wondering about from time immemorial. Many answers have been offered through the years. Some say in the end there is nothing. We live, we die and then we cease to exist. Others say in the end everyone goes to be with God. Still others say in the end earth will be destroyed and humanity will be judged. There are other possibilities and multiple combinations of those listed.

There is an interesting trend, however, among the various answers. Those involving God can usually be summed up in three words, "God takes control." God takes control and brings everyone to live with him. God takes control, destroys the evil creation and brings everyone else to live with him. God takes control and issues judgment. God takes control and fixes what was wrong with creation. Even those who believe in free will tend to believe free will eventually has a stopping point, at which time God takes control. In other words, although there are multiple answers that include God they usually involve God taking control.

In *The Uncontrolling Love of God*, Thomas Jay Oord makes the argument that God's nature is uncontrolling love. Because it goes against God's very nature to unilaterally take control of a situation and coercively guarantee an outcome, Oord says God works through humans who cooperate with his influence and will.

If Oord is right about God's nature, we need to find different answers to the question: "What happens in the end?" If God's nature is uncontrolling love, God cannot 'take control' and do anything, but is there another answer that reflects this nature? How would such an answer look?

In Scripture, Paul says, "Creation waits in eager expectation for the children of God to be revealed . . . in hope that creation itself will be liberated from its bondage to decay and brought into the glorious freedom of the children of God."[1]

In light of the usual answers to our question, this is an interesting passage. According to the status quo, Paul should have written, "Creation waits in eager expectation for God," but Paul says something different. Paul says creation is waiting for God's children, hoping creation itself will be freed from its bondage to decay that it, too, might share in the freedom of God's children.

Paul directly links creation's freedom with the freedom of God's children. When God's children are revealed as God's children, then creation will be freed. Could Paul be saying, in the end creation will be set free as a result of humans co-operating with God? Perhaps when humans cooperate with God, or, as Paul says, when they actually *become* 'children of God,' creation will be freed.

For those of us who are used to the more traditional answers to our question, initially this idea might seem tenuous, but I think it is supported by this passage in Romans. Sandwiched between the idea of creation waiting for the children of God and the concept of creation hoping to join in the freedom of the children of God, Paul says this: "Creation was subjected to frustration, not by its own choice, but by the will of the one who subjected it."[2] In other words, Paul is saying the whole reason creation is in bondage is because of human sin. To use Oord's language, creation is in bondage because humans chose not to cooperate with God.

The original task God gave to humanity in Genesis, before sin entered creation, was twofold – be fruitful and multiply, and take care of creation. Humans chose not to cooperate with God's call. Because we chose not to take care of creation, it makes sense creation would be messed up. If we, as caretakers of creation, chose not to cooperate with that call, it also makes sense creation would be in bondage. Following this line of thinking, the way to fix creation's bondage is for humanity to cooperate with God's original call to care for creation.

The flow of Paul's thought in Romans 8:19-21 goes something like this: Creation waits for God's children to actually act like God's children. Because humanity's lack of cooperation with God is the reason creation is in bondage in the first place, creation longs for God's children to cooperate with God in the hope of creation itself being released to share in the freedom of God's children.

This line of thought also fits well within the larger context of Romans 8. Paul begins by talking about how there is no condemnation for those who are in the Messiah. We are no longer condemned, because what the Law was powerless to do, God did through the Messiah. Those who are not in the Messiah are still governed by sin, but those who *are* in the Messiah are no longer governed by sin but rather by the Spirit.

From here, Paul connects sin to death. Two chapters before, Paul has already said that, "the wages of sin is death . . ."[3] Now in chapter 8, Paul again confirms that those who live in sin will reap death. Paul goes on to say that as followers of the Messiah, we have an obligation to live according to the Spirit rather than according to sin. Then he again reinforces the idea that if we live according to sin we will die, but if we live according to the Spirit we will have life.

Paul continues by saying that if we are in the Messiah, if we live by the Spirit rather than by sin, we are children of God and co-heirs with the Messiah. We share in the Messiah's sufferings and his glory.

It is in this context that Paul talks about sin's effects on creation and creation's restoration. Paul has already been talking about the outcome of living according to sin vs. living according to the Spirit. In talking about the consequences of such a life, Paul brings up the fallen creation.

Paul tells us that creation is fallen because of humanity's sin, but that when the children of God are revealed, creation will be set free from its bondage to decay. It seems to follow naturally that if humanity's sin is the reason creation is in bondage in the first place, the way creation would be set free from bondage is by humanity ceasing to sin. Furthermore, the whole line of thought flows naturally from Paul talking about the differences between life according to the Spirit vs. life according to sin. Life according to sin leads to bondage for creation. Life according to the Spirit leads to life and restoration.

What happens in the end? In the end, all of creation will be set free from its bondage when humans cooperate with God. The question left for us today is, will we live into that future now?

⎯⎯⎯⎯

Chris Baker is a co-pastor at Columbus Community Church of the Nazarene in Columbus, WI, alongside his wife Teresa. He previously served as Associate Pastor involved in worship and discipleship in Upstate New York. Chris enjoys reading, a wide variety of music, and having conversations about big ideas.

Endnotes

1. Rom. 8:19, 21 (NIV).
2. Rom. 8:20
3. Rom 6:23

When God's Plans Aren't in God's Hands

Jared Byas

Am I open?

This question has haunted me since I read *The Uncontrolling Love of God*. In his book, Oord affirms what many recent theologians have said before: God doesn't know the future. God doesn't control the future. Oord then takes it one step further to say that God can't control the future, because love is God's defining and essential characteristic. The future is open.

Are we to believe that God's plans may not come to pass? For instance, when Jeremiah declares that God has plans to prosper those Jews who have been kicked off their land, is God just being hopeful?[1]

Indeed.

But God's control, or lack thereof, over the affairs of humankind aren't disturbing to me. I've made peace with a God who doesn't control, because I am at peace with a relational God who doesn't treat human beings as pawns while God marches all the chess pieces toward a grand finale.

After all, this is the nature of love: having plans disrupted for the sake of relationship. So yes, even God's goals are at-risk because relationships trump plans.

I'll leave trying to understand the God who doesn't control the future to theologians. My question is, "What kind of response might we have in light of such a God?" That is, "Do *I* bear the image of that God?"

The future is open.

God is open.

Am I?

Let's be clear about what we mean by 'openness' here. The future is open *because* God is open: God is open *because* God is love—and not just any kind of love, but here-and-now, freedom-affirming love. Jesus himself, the mirror Christians use to discern the character of this God, says that the Spirit has sent him to, "proclaim freedom for the prisoners and . . . to set the oppressed free."[2] Paul confirms this connection between God's presence and freedom in his letter to the Corinthians: "Now the Lord is the Spirit, and where the Spirit of the Lord is, there is freedom."[3]

So, God is committed to our freedom so much that God is willing to lay down any claim to the future. God is willing to turn a period into a question mark on our behalf, an 'and so it shall come to pass' into a 'perhaps.'

So, I'm compelled to ask again: Am I that open?

Am I willing to lay down my cause, the future I imagine, for the sake of a relationship? Am I willing to embrace the same freedom-affirming love I see in God? Even if it means not accomplishing my vision for a better world?

If God is open, the question on the table is: Am I willing to lay down the future I imagine for the sake of relationships? As we look at this question, I propose we break it down into two different categories. We might phrase them as separate questions:

Am I willing for my future plans to be interrupted for the sake of a relationship?

Am I willing for my vision of a better world to be disrupted for the sake of relationship?

Interruption.

Disruption.

Let's take these one at a time.

On the one hand, there is the very practical application of living in the image of an open God. Am I willing to set aside my goals for the sake of a relationship? From my plans to sit on the couch to watch Netflix to my plans to visit Thailand in the summer, am I willing to be interrupted for the human being in front of me?

But I'm more interested in exploring that second path: Am I willing for my vision of a better world to be disrupted for the sake of relationship?

This is a very relevant question. We live in a world of growing partisanship. Republicans and Democrats and their millions of social media minions (us) keep using apocalyptic language to describe what will happen if the 'other' is in control.

This year it is Trump. In 2008 it was Obama. They both have a vision for the world they think is best. As their devotees, we likely have a similar vision of a better world. It's precisely in this context where we would do well to remember the kenotic God who works for here-and-now, freedom-affirming love.

To follow this God means that *any* vision for the future must submit itself to here-and-now, freedom-affirming love. Otherwise, any vision, whether it's progressive, conservative, libertarian, green, democratic, or republican, will become tyranny. This merging of freedom and love in God is critical.

In her fabulous book, *The Ethics of Ambiguity*, Simone de Beauvoir addresses this very thing—the merging of freedom and love. What would it look like for a person to put their vision for a better world above individual human beings with whom they are face-to-face?

Simone de Beauvoir calls this person the 'serious man,' the person who does not bear the image of the God of freedom-affirming love. This person believes in a cause or goal so strongly that he or she is willing to sacrifice another person's freedom to make it happen. But if the chief end of God is freedom-affirming love, there is no cause that can justify such an action.

The serious person, she goes on, "forgets that . . . human freedom is the ultimate, the unique end to which wo/man should destine him/herself . . . Therefore, the serious person is dangerous. It is natural that s/he makes him/herself a tyrant."[4]

Therefore, if God's love is defined as freedom-affirming, anyone willing to sacrifice individual freedom for a cause, even if that cause is 'to create a more loving world,' ends up a tyrant. If loving relationships are the cause we are fighting for, and if love is defined as freedom-affirming, then the way we fight for that cause must always be freedom-affirming.

This is modeled for us in God.

So, one last time, I ask the question: Are we modeling ourselves after this God? Sometimes, I have worked toward personal goals so intensely that people became things. They became instruments in my plan, and I used them as such. For some, this does bear the image of their God, who also has a goal and will use people however necessary to make it come to pass. But this is not the God of freedom-affirming love.

Sometimes, I have had causes that I believed in so strongly that people became obstacles. If I had the power, perhaps I would have banished them to hell so that I could move forward with my vision of the future, unhindered. For some, this does bear the image of their God, who banishes them to hell in order to move forward without obstructions. But this is not the God of freedom-affirming love.

If we believe God is justified in ignoring our freedom for a higher purpose, we might think we may do this to others, as well. That seems dangerous. If I am to imitate the God of freedom-affirming love, then I must commit to the relationship as the highest cause, the here-and-now, freedom-affirming love over the uncertain, there-and-then vision.

This, of course, doesn't negate dreaming dreams or making plans. We find God doing such again and again in the Bible. It simply gives us an example to follow to make sure those dreams and plans ultimately lead to freedom-affirming love.

Jared Byas is a former professor of philosophy & ethics and current Sunday school teacher. He's the co-author of Genesis for Normal People, co-hosts The Bible for Normal People podcast, and blogs regularly at biblefornormalpeople.com

Endnotes

1. Jer. 29:11 (NIV).
2. Luke 4:18
3. II Cor. 3:17
4. Beauvoir, Simone De, *The Ethics of Ambiguity*, trans. Bernard Frechtman (New York: Philosophical Library, 1949), 52-53

Compassion at Ground Zero

Stephen Carroll

I t was a beautiful, clear morning. I was riding shotgun in a golf cart, placing signs at every tee and hole on one of the most beautiful country clubs in Rockland County, New York. This course was particularly known for its view of the NYC skyline. As we drove, I found myself thinking about how great I had it. Just two months following college graduation; I had an amazing wife, a sixth story condo, a great job as a Youth Pastor that, on this particular day, would require me to sit in the grass and watch the 7th hole while enjoying all the complimentary snacks I could consume over the next 10 hours.

However, our cart never made it as far as the 7th hole that day. By the 4th hole we watched every golf cart with a driver turn off the approved path and head straight for the edge of the course. Curiosity getting the best my Corps Officer (pastor), we followed the golf cart stampede. As we approached the near pile-up of golf carts, the city skyline came into view. The once clear view of Manhattan was quickly filling with smoke. We weren't sure what had happened, but we knew it was big.

My new boss looked at me and said, "Time to get to work."

There would be no sitting in the grass for me. Over the next two and a half days; I ran a mobile feeding truck, poured water into the mouths of people just feet away from the bodies they were sorting, looked into the vacant stares of desperate family members, slept for 4 hours in a shelter next to survivors, and spent time as the de facto Protestant chaplain praying in tandem with a Catholic priest every time a body was pulled from the wreckage.

15 years later, the thing that still impacts me the most are the conversa-

tions I had with grief stricken people whose faith had collapsed under the weight of such overwhelming evil. While the news wanted to point out the spike in church attendance and the unmatched volunteerism and generosity during the days following the attack, the conversations I had with people were not so encouraging.

"Why would God take my son?"

"How could God allow this?"

"There is no God!"

These were the kinds of things I heard.

The day after the attack, well known Christian leaders were calling this an act of divine punishment for our failure to be 'Christian enough' as a nation. When I heard these professional Christians being interviewed, it made me angry. None of them were with us, hacking from the dust, staring into the eyes of these broken people. They had no understanding of the evil around us! I'd like to have seen one of them look someone in the eye and say, "God caused all this death and destruction, killed your husband and friends to draw you closer to Him."

During a quiet conversation with a mom looking for her son, I was asked the same question. I was giving her directions to the nearest hospital when she recognized my uniform and asked, "How can God do this to us?"

It was my turn. I had my answer ready. I was going to explain my understanding of an open God, one who did not stop evil because we were free. I would follow up by quoting my college professor and arguing that in order for God to be loving he cannot control or counter creaturely freedom. If I followed the road map I had created for myself, I would bring the conversation around to Christ's sacrifice—maybe even invite her to become a Christian.

Something broke inside me in that moment. Time stood still. I encountered the divine. I looked this women in the eyes, and as mine filled with tears all I managed to get out was, "God is right here with us. He is heartbroken. He didn't want any of this to happen. And now he is suffering with us."

God is love. God created us to love. God gave us the freedom we need to *really* love. God calls us to love freely and to make loving decisions. When we make decisions that are unloving, the consequences are real and can be disastrous to those around us. But when we answer the call to love, we can be partners with God and change the world.

❧

Captain Stephen Carroll serves alongside his wife, Captain Delia Carroll, together as Commanding Officers (pastors) of The Salvation Army Niagara Falls Citadel Corps. Captain Carroll has also been a frequent guest lecturer in Ohio Christian University's Emergency Management Program.

Are Dreams Regular Appointments with the Source of All Wisdom?

Gloria M. Coffin

Y ou should be a movie producer." "Must have been something you ate." "Stop reading those novels."

These are comments we often hear when sharing our dreams with others, but I never discount the content of my dreams simply because of their relationship to the external. Sure, the baseline for a dream may stem from late night pizza, a science fiction movie, or a painful interaction with a friend, but my dreams have always centered my mind, providing direction and wisdom.

Please do not misunderstand. If a dream was about soaring through the air, I didn't assume it meant I could fly; however, I have been reminded there are ways to rise above what, on the surface, seems impossible terrain.

We are a people of comfort in the certainty of material content. Eventually the juxtaposition of directional thought and related experiences teaches us to respond to God's messages wafting on the breeze during our waking hours.

"Maybe I should clean the kitchen now," prepares us for an unexpected visitor later.

"Call Sally," leads us to discover Sally's battery died and she needs a ride to an appointment.

"Buy that extra pair of gloves," becomes providential on our way home from shopping when we pass a homeless person shivering in the cold.

The song on the radio speaking to our pain, the sign on the fence reminding us to call the insurance agent, and a phrase repeated three times in one day should not order our lives as if God is in control, directing our every move;

however, the transfer of wisdom will inform our options. We begin to pay closer attention to these messages, accepting them as coming from the God of love.

Why couldn't the same God also use the hours we sleep as an avenue for information to help us cooperate with God's efforts for good? After all, once we finally lay to rest the responsibilities and concerns of the day, our sleep hours are the most relaxed times our minds have. Perhaps we are also *most* receptive as we sleep.

In *Windows of the Soul*, Paul Meier, MD and Robert L. Wise, PhD, remove the common fear of opening ourselves to something evil in dream studies.[1] With simple illustrations and advice for recording dreams as soon as we awaken, they include stories from our spiritual ancestors noting biblical truth intentionally revealed, insights God sent for personal guidance, encouragement, protection, and motivation.

My father, a logically thinking civil engineer, was my first dream therapist. One night I woke up sobbing and frantically described the dreaded children's nightmare. I was running as fast as I could with family up ahead and Daddy right behind but too close to the bad guys fiendishly waving their weapons.

"Don't worry," my all-time favorite hero reassured me, "I'm going to outlive all the rest of you!"

On a more recent night, bemused by thoughts of this essay and an unexpected dead end in my ministry journey, I hoped for insight to come in the next eight hours of peaceful slumber. I'm not sure why I am frequently surprised when it happens, but it happened and I was surprised.

In this dream a mother and daughter jogged past our cabin in the woods. They lived so far away I was curious. No one simply passes through on their way somewhere else. If you are on 'my road,' you either live nearby or you have a specific reason for coming. With a friendly wave, the mom said she'd be back and we would chat about why she was there.

On my list of things to do were errands taking me through several towns, including the one where my jogging friends lived. Their street was a mess. Construction made it impassable. Pulling over and backing up to turn around I began spinning my wheels in a rut. That's when I saw my friend's hubby on foot. He told me the family was staying with folks out of town. Grinning, I told him I thought I knew the place!

Half awake, I squeezed my eyes shut to recall the musical segue moving me from subconscious to wide awake. Quickly documenting the memory and re-reading it, I experienced an epiphany. While I know my dream stories often reflect personal concerns and the musical phrases usually provide insightful direction, I had missed the obvious for decades. Transcribed, the written words were messages I could see, direct communication in print from the God of uncontrolling love.

As the day continued, scattered phrases from the song, *Through it All* by Andrae Crouch, continued to play nonstop in my subconscious, telling me I was not alone.

I've had lots of tears and sorrow,
There've been questions for tomorrow,
But I've learned to trust in Jesus;
I've learned to depend upon God's Word.[2]

The verse reminded me of past valleys and storms I had survived just fine. Here was God working for good through a dream that contained words about my life in language I could read and understand. All I had to do was interpret and apply them.

Over the years, many of my dreams revealed hidden anxieties, relieved unknown tensions, and resolved conflicts. The dream about the joggers, road construction, turning around and spinning wheels, contains pieces of my situation. Laugh if you will, but I was convinced there would be more answers in another dream. After all, the joggers were there for a reason and the mom was coming back to reflect with me later.

We read our Bibles. We pray. We seek out good preaching and educated theologians for guidance. Why not also open the window to that peaceful darkened room in our minds where we have designated space and undistracted time to listen to the messages God wants to send?

In the same way dreams may guide us to answers for personal daily living, they may also inform us of action to take in the interest of helping each other. Admittedly, this is a more challenging concept. Most of us feel awkward about accepting other-directed impressions in our sleep as calls from God.

A dream in the night about our neighbor needing help seems coincidental to the subsequent impulse to shovel out his car. When he rushes from his house, worried about running late because he overslept, we observe, "God is good, all the time," which translates, "God is in control," as if the message encouraging our cooperation had nothing to do with it.

If God is always at work for good in the world and we are the partnering voices, hands and feet, why not? Certainly God knows about the snow on the ground. While we sleep creation and our physical bodies may be preparing us for conditions as yet unknown to our conscious minds.

Even when it is true, it is hard to believe.

It was decades before social media networking. The week had been one of the darkest in my life. Isolating myself, I communicated the disappointment with only a few. When a long distance call revealed the voice of my good friend, Pastor Dave, my heart sank. I dreaded telling him of the recent setback on my ministry journey.

"You should probably sit down," he suggested, beginning to explain.

"I had no idea why, but the other night I suddenly sat right up in bed thinking, 'Call Gloria Coffin and ask her to help with music ministry.' I wasn't sure what to do about it until our mutual friend told me your story."

We compared notes. I had received my devastating news the afternoon prior to the night of Pastor Dave's shocking wake up call. Although we considered a working relationship, the phone call was all the assurance I needed of God's timely ability to partner with others for my good.

Not long after that event, I had a terrifying, but sketchy, dream of my own about the family of another close friend I'll call Alice. I didn't know the individual's name or particular relationship to Alice, but I knew the person was afraid, in danger and no one knew. I woke up in a panic.

I, too, spent time wondering if I should share the dream's contents; however, because I was unable to forget it, a day later I called Alice. Crediting God while thanking me profusely, she was instantly aware of the dream's implications. A young relative, attempting to save family embarrassment, had made an unwise solitary decision that could have led to serious ramifications. I was the second friend who had alerted Alice. Either one of our calls would have been a timely catalyst for intervention.

I am convinced such dream stories confirm God's transfer of information in the peaceful darkened room in our minds where we have designated space and undistracted time to listen. What could be more miraculous than a message from God preparing us to work together for good?

❧

A public speaker, writer/editor, minister, and Facebook devotee, Gloria is convinced self-worth, healthy boundaries and universal respect can change the world. She has become an advocate for the marginalized using her voice for the voiceless, offering hope for the hopeless and encouragement for the discouraged.

Endnotes

1. Paul D. Meier and Robert L. Wise, *Windows of the Soul: A Look at Dreams and Their Meanings* (Nashville, TN: Thomas Nelson, 1995).

2. Andrae Crouch, *Through it All* (Manna Music 1971, reprint, The United Methodist Hymnal 1999), 305 (page citation is to reprint edition).

An Invitation to Co-Creation

Noel Cooper

Like most people in my field, I was drawn to be a psychologist because I wanted to help people. As I entered my training and began thinking about how my professional identity was woven into other aspects of myself, I developed an understanding of how my work as a therapist fits in with God's desires for individuals and society. As two of my mentors described it, "The work of psychotherapy is one expression of God's own redemptive work in the world."[1] Oord's model of Essential Kenosis provides a helpful framework for understanding how that works.

As a therapist, I spend every day listening to painful stories from my clients' lives—stories of abuse, tragic deaths, financial losses, broken relationships, miscarriage and infertility, major illness, drug addiction, chronic mental illness, and more. Most of my clients don't spend much time thinking philosophically about the causes of their traumatic experiences. They might blame God, but they are just as likely to blame themselves, other people, or social systems for their troubles. Sometimes they view their situation as simply a result of chance circumstances. Regardless, almost all of them ask the question, "Why?" They're not asking about the *cause* of the events, but about the *meaning* of their experience.

Some take comfort in the idea that all things are ordained by God, so "everything will eventually work itself out for the best."

For others, that idea is no longer tenable in the face of all that they have suffered, or the concept of God has little relevance to their everyday experience. But still they ask, "Why me? What now? How can I make sense of this and move forward with my life?"

The model of Essential Kenosis has something to offer for these questions.

Not a pat and easy answer, but rather an incarnational response. In the act of kenosis, God also became incarnate—Immanuel, "God with us."[2] In becoming enfleshed, Jesus also embraced the suffering that is inevitable in being human, and through him God continues to suffer alongside us in our pain. Rather than looking to the almighty power of God for answers, kenosis opens the way for us to look to the abiding presence of God, in which we can find solace, comfort, and healing. It is not a magical quick fix; but in God's presence, we are invited to move towards wholeness, "for in him we live and move and have our being."[3]

It is this aspect of essential kenosis that gives my work as a therapist significance. God does not enter anyone's life and force healing or wholeness on them. Rather, God works together with individuals to help them heal and grow in the face of tragedy. Oord says, "God's self-giving love invites creaturely cooperation for radically surprising actions that promote overall well-being."[4] God cannot bring wholeness and restoration without the cooperation of the individual; because of the essentially kenotic nature of the deity, God cannot impose well-being on anyone. Sometimes there are obstacles in a person's life that prevent them from fully cooperating with God's desire for their health and well-being. Sometimes the obstacles are obvious—mental illness, addictions, self-destructive behavior, pain and grief from personal tragedy. Other times, the obstacles are more subtle—poor relational skills, insufficient resources for coping with emotions, lack of understanding of their own psyche, self-defeating patterns in relationships because of old hurts. All these things make it difficult for individuals to hear God's 'still, small voice' and fully engage with God's work in them.

God is continually calling to each of us, encouraging and coaxing us towards wholeness, whether we acknowledge God's presence or existence. Psychotherapy is one way that individuals can confront whatever is hindering them from following that path. My goal as a therapist is to help clients move towards God's ultimate goal of transformation for all creation. God cannot do it alone, but depends on our cooperation. I work with my clients to help them uncover new ways of relating to others, new ways of understanding themselves, and new ways of being in the world that are healthier and give more satisfaction to all those involved. In this shift from dysfunction to well-being, they are moving in accordance with God's desires for them.

In this work, I can help my clients answer the question, "Why?" The meaning of a tragedy is not hiding somewhere to be discovered and then adhered to; rather, God invites us to become the co-creators of the meanings in our lives. We can create a negative, nihilistic meaning from an event ("This happened because everything I do is doomed to fail."), or we can create a positive, life-giving meaning from an event ("I have grown stronger and learned this lesson because of this circumstance."). We always choose how we interpret our lives, and with more awareness we can intentionally make better choices. God calls us to view our experiences through the lens of redemption, and I work with my clients to help them consider their hard experiences through that redemptive lens. When we heed that call, God works with us for our transformation.

Noel Cooper is a clinical psychologist and therapist from Pasadena, CA. She graduated from Fuller Theological Seminary in 2013. Her professional website is:

www.drnoelcooper.com.

Endnotes

1. Jennifer Kunst & Siang-Yang Tan, "Psychotherapy as 'Work in the Spirit': Thinking Theologically About Psychotherapy," *Journal of Psychology and Theology*, 24, no. 4 (1996): 289.

2. Matt. 1:23 (NIV).

3. Acts 7:28

4. Thomas Jay Oord, *The Uncontrolling Love of God: An Open and Relational Account of Providence* (Downers Grove: InterVarsity Press, 2016), 200.

Why Do You Speak to Them in Parables?

Nathan Croy

Contrary to popular belief, the parables Jesus used were not designed to solve problems or create more clarity.[1] They were crafted to encourage others to solve their own problems by engaging their minds in a personal way.[2] In practicing therapy, it's rarely a good idea to solve someone's problem for them. Education can be provided on different resources available (this is called case management), but the onus for change and resolution of problems must come from the clients themselves. To simply provide answers without exploring what has prevented clients from finding their own answers defeats the very purpose of therapy. If I give you the answers, it means you are incapable of figuring them out yourself, utterly dependent on others to resolve your issues, ignorant about your situation, and are denied the skill-learning to solve your own problems in the future. However, if time is taken to analyze the origin of the problem and what has prevented resolving it; therapy can move toward empowering, educating, and equipping you to resolve issues on your own.

The goals of empowering, educating, and equipping people to live a more genuine and authentic life are common to therapy, the ministry of Jesus, and Essential Kenosis (EK). Healthy relationships will affirm these three values. I'm reminded of the old saying: if you give a man a fish, you feed him for a day; if you teach him to fish, you feed him for life. Even when Christ was handing out fish, it wasn't about the fish; it was about the way the fish were provided. *That* is the crux of Emmanuel, God with us. There is a message contained within the way God came to be with us. I believe the way (process) in which ministry and evangelism are executed can be more important than the what (content). Again, I think the key to understanding this may lie in EK.

In EK, the existence of freewill evidences God's inability to coerce. This fulfills the first requirement of healthy relationship: Empowering. Some are frightened by the idea God will not force his will on others. For me, it feels like a vote of confidence! Through gifts of the Spirit, community, and sheer force of will, humanity has accomplished incredible feats. Some have been horrible and some have been awe inspiring, but they have been incredible. For God to believe in us is encouraging, especially in times of trial.[3] Evangelicalism, with good intentions, has often assumed others lacked the power to heed the call of the church. This has led to manipulative outreach like offering meals to the homeless, but only after they've listened to the preacher. The way of Christ is inviting and methods that depend on manipulation are inherently not inviting. Invitationalism is an approach that assumes freedom of response without even the hint of coercion. There were many instances where Christ healed others without declaring his divinity or by deferring to their requests.[4] Our desire to convert people to denominations is evidence of hubris and narcissism; this is not the appealing and empowering work of Christ. When the content of Evangelicalism overrules the process of inviting, we have slipped into a legalism whereby the first commandment is utterly demolished.

The process of Education has been capitol in the evangelical movement. Outreach, ministry, and preaching have successfully spread the Gospel to the four corners. At the same time, I fear the evangelical movement has been more focused on conversion (content) rather than invitation (process). Evangelicalism tends to consider ministries successful by counting 'nickels and noses.' This can unintentionally lead to outreach that concentrates on converting people to denominational beliefs rather than The Way. I would suggest an approach more in line with EK and the welcoming technique reflected in the way Christ ministered.

Evangelicalism runs the risk of converting people to specific denominations (content) rather than being instruments that point to God (process). This fits into the process of EK by, not only allowing but, encouraging others to wrestle with the issues and come to their own conclusions. This is *not* moral relativism. Rather, it is a process that affirms our ability to understand and reason with the guidance of God. Otherwise, we would be lost and need moral absolutes. If that were the case, Jesus would have been just like Google: Question | Answer.

Lastly is the goal of Equipping. I don't think it was just a suggestion when

Christ said, "Let those who have ears, hear."[5] Not everyone is equally gifted in hearing, or seeing, or even thinking. We all have deficiencies and gifts in various areas. However, we are called to use the gifts with which we have been equipped. The grace of God, working through, in, and with us, facilitates our ability to participate in an enticing ministry. When the disciples asked for more faith, Jesus instructed them to use the faith they already had.[6] We are called to use our divinely equipped gifts to model God's love to all his creation. Evangelicalism often, but not in all cases, calls us to use our gifts to further a denominational dogma.

This is a scary process to engage in. All humanity seeks a stability and assurance that requires little faith. Even the disciples wanted to understand why Jesus insisted on using parables instead of simply telling them exactly what to do.[7] Clearly, God wants to leave some things open to interpretation. Isn't it nice to know God is empowering, educating, and equipping us to do that very work![8]

Nathan D. Croy is a marriage and family therapist, presenter, and writer living in Kansas City, KS. He graduated from Bethel Seminary in San Diego and enjoys being active in the local church and spending time with his family. You can read more at croymft.com

Endnotes

1. See Mark 4:10-13; John 16:25
2. See Luke 9:44-45
3. See James 1:2-4
4. See John 5:1-13, 18:10; Matthew 20:32
5. See Mark 4:9, Matthew 11:15
6. See Luke 17:6
7. See Matthew 13:10
8. See Philippians 2:13; Ephesians 3:20; Hebrews 13:21; John 5:17

Is Love Enough?
Some Pastoral Reflections
on Prayer, Healing, and
the Uncontrolling Love of God

Simon Hall

I can remember the look on her face. I knew immediately that I had made a terrible, terrible mistake. Words started to pour out of her, warning me that I was on the slippery slope to losing my faith. She was visibly emotionally traumatized by what I had said, and despite the conversation now being about *my* faith; I think everyone in the room knew that I had foolishly said something to undermine *hers*. Her husband kindly intervened and tried to steer the conversation into less emotional territory. Despite our being friends for many years since our college days, I haven't seen her since.

What was it that I had said? After Karen (not her real name) had talked about the heartbreak of losing a baby, she had commented, "All that's keeping me together is knowing that one day God will tell me why he did it."

"I really don't think God killed your baby, Karen," I replied.

Of course, in retrospect, I should have listened to those words, "All that's keeping me together," and realized this wasn't an invitation to a Facebook-style theological debate.

What was I thinking? Some years later when a friend told me that God had taken his daughter to heaven, "because she was too good for this world," I knew to keep my mouth shut.

But in the face of terrible news—a death, a car crash, a cancer diagnosis—do we really want to hold God responsible for everything that happens in life? Is the idea that these terrible events have no divine cause or purpose so discomfiting? Of course, the complicating factor in this story is that my friends prayed . . . fervently. If we pray, and a baby dies, surely that must mean that the death was God's will, right?

I remember hearing a memorable aphorism as a young Christian. It went, "God only answers prayers three ways: Yes, No, or Not Yet."

This stuck with me my whole life, but even as a teenager I had a feeling that God couldn't be reduced to such a limited set of options. Within Scripture, there are other 'answers' staring us in the face. In Daniel, an angel explains that he was sent to aid Daniel but that he was held up by the "Prince of the Kingdom of Persia" for three weeks.[1] God made an immediate response but was delayed by circumstances. We might say that a fourth answer to an intercessory prayer is, "I'm on my way; it might take a little time."

A story from Daniel's dreaming might seem like a poor foundation for pastoral practice (never mind philosophy or theology), so let's look at a moment in the life of Jesus. In Mark, we read that Jesus' ability to perform miracles was limited by the lack of faith of those present.[2] Another answer to prayer might be, "I'm doing my bit; why aren't you doing yours?"

But what is God's 'bit'? A member of my community has just received a diagnosis of terminal cancer. He might have a few months or a few years, according to the doctors. He has called the elders of the church, and we will visit and anoint him with oil. It is unclear what James is promising, but a straight reading of his letter seems to indicate that prayers accompanied by faith and righteousness are somehow more effective.[3] At the very least, James is suggesting that through our faith we are participating in God's healing work.

Pastorally, I have always found verses such as these deeply problematic. I realized only recently that it was because I was still thinking of God as omnipotent. In effect, I imagined God choosing to heal only those whose faith or righteousness met a satisfactory standard, as a kind of reward. A God who withholds healing from those with weak faith does not sound like the Abba whose son promised that even the tiniest seed of faith could invite in the reign of God.

However, if God's work in the world is in any way like that described in *The Uncontrolling Love of God*, then our own partnership with God in bringing about the miraculous starts to make sense. It matters that we engage with the world in every way possible. In the case of ill-health, that can mean medicine, community care, healthy eating, and prayer. If God is present in every atom and cell, lovingly presenting the way of life at every moment, perhaps our own voices can add urgency to God's urging. And when the Spirit woos creation with the possibility of "unusual forms of existence,"[4] we can share in a miracle.

This helps to make some sense of the story of the friend who has a late night visitor and is caught without adequate provision to offer the required standard of hospitality.[5] This story seems to cast God as a sleepy, grumpy neighbor who has to be forced to wake up and offer help. It doesn't seem to connect with Jesus' view of Abba at all. What if the grumpy neighbor represents the thing we are praying about rather than the person we are praying to? The rapidly mutating cancer cells, the job interview, the corrupt politician, the merciless warlord? In this view, God is not the grumpy neighbor but is working inside the heart of the grumpy neighbor to encourage graciousness and generosity. Our persistence is not required to 'change God's mind' about us, but rather to melt away the resistance of cold matter.

The notion of an 'all-in' partnership with God helps me make sense of the funny little story of the two-stage healing of a blind man.[6] Perhaps Jesus was making use of rudimentary medicine *and* praying to Abba for healing? It makes me wonder if the feeding of the five thousand was a miracle of physical multiplication *and* a miracle of kindness, because God was working through all parts of the process, gently nudging in a myriad of places to achieve *shalom*.

If we are spiritual beings, just as much as we are physical, then our prayers matter just as much as our actions. Prayers that attune us to the heart of God. Prayers that lend our voice to God's voice, calling for God's loving will to be done in a situation. Prayers that bless those who are living out the gospel of peace. In fact, if God is not a controlling entity, then our persistence in prayer and action are not the icing on the cake of God's action in the world; they are central to it.

The metaphor of the church as Jesus's body is no longer a lovely image to make us feel good about ourselves but another way of expressing the great commission. God's loving will is continually enticing all of creation to give way to the reign of God, whether by engaging with a human body, a church body, or a cosmic body.

As we anoint this beloved member of our congregation, we can confidently say with James that God wants to 'raise him up,' and that we will join in God's desire for his wholeness. We will speak to the cancer in Jesus' name, calling it to be gone. We will show love, we will enquire after the state of current medical interventions, we will offer help to the household on behalf of the church, and we will no doubt be thinking of children and grandchildren who will someday soon lose this loved one. All of these actions will be influenced by God's uncontrolling love. I will say that death and suffering are not God's will, but even so we cannot know what the outcome of our prayers will be. I will say that prayer is not a magic spell, but sometimes it appears to be, because miracles can happen. I will say that Jesus calls us to be faithful and persistent, because the world doesn't always listen the first time. And I will say that while there is so much that we don't know, there is one thing we do know: God is love.

Is that enough?

There are many Christians who appear to need a god who is in control, a god who will one day make everything right by punishing our enemies. But this is not the way of Jesus—not the way of love. When Paul writes about how all things will be made right, he uses these words: "Follow the way of love"—no force, no violence, and no control.[7] In Jesus, we see this love lived out in human form, but it also gives us a window into the heart of God.

I declare, "Love *is* enough!"

It is enough for all of us: It is *more* than enough! Let us follow the most excellent way.

Simon Hall is Co-minister of Chapel Allerton Baptist Church in Leeds, UK, and of Revive, 'A community for people who like Jesus but aren't too sure about church.' He studied philosophy and theology at Oxford University before training as a youth worker. He is a compulsive starter-upper of things, including three churches, an arts centre, a family support project and Oasis College in London, where he was founding principal. He has written in the fields of spirituality, youth ministry, and applied theology, and edited the UK edition of the NIV Youth Bible. He lives in Leeds with his wife Anna, a TV documentarian, and their three teenage children and a dog. He enjoys soccer, music, literature, box sets, and video games.

Endnotes

1. Dan. 10:13 (NIV).
2. Mark 6:1

3. James. 5:13
4. Thomas Jay Oord, *The Uncontrolling Love of God: An Open and Relational Account of Providence* (Downers Grove, IL: InterVarsity, 2015), 199.
5. Luke 11:5-13
6. Mark 8:22-26
7. I Cor. 13

Navigating Without a Plan

George Hermanson

What do we mean when we talk about 'God's plan?' Planning is big on our agenda, for we want to make the best use of our time, and we want to arrive without too many distractions. In business and life, the role of life coaches is expanding. These professionals sit down with us and lay out what they think is necessary to build a life or a business. In the same way, churches seek out those who will help them grow, as if there is a technique that provides a simple solution, a magic bullet for what ails us.

Planning has become our default position, the narrative that determines our sense of what is crucial as we deal with life. But when we project this planning language onto God, we are left with a serious theological issue. The idea of planning assumes control. The idea of *God's* plan assumes that *God* is in control. This is problematic, because it leads to the further assumption that God has all the power or has determined the future. Too often this theology is left unexamined and leaves us vulnerable to disappointment or criticism when God does not act. Is there another way to frame our understanding of what it means to seek God or to be led by the Spirit without one definitive plan?

As a global society we are faced with many difficult issues. The Brexit referendum is not limited to Europe: it is part of a much larger process of the confusion that underlies the crisis of 'manufacturing democratic consent' in our societies, of the growing gap between political institutions and popular rage. In the US, this rage gave birth to, and provided momentum for, both the Trump and Sanders presidential campaigns. We have the rise of outrage among those who feel left out, resulting in narrow nationalism and distrust of the 'other.' It affects both conservatives and liberals. Signs of chaos are everywhere—is this a reason to despair?

Churches, also, are in a process of imagining what it means to be a congregation, what it means to be a national church, what it means to be a global church, what it means to simply be *the* Church, at all. And it does not stop there, for individual Christians are reevaluating what it means to be a follower of Jesus. We are trying to navigate these questions in a time of unrest.

In such times we worry. We often seek just the right information to move into a far country. We think we can plan our way into the future. The irony is the best laid plans can be a dead end, because each day provides new experiences that we have not anticipated. In fact, planning sometimes causes us to miss the unexpected.

This has created difficult issues for the church regarding how to speak to our culture. We have a history of calling individuals and society to justice and compassion. The problem is: we often phrase this by asking people to 'do the will of God,' or to consider the question, "What would Jesus do?"

Those words fall flat in our secular society and often do not resonate even with people of faith. Simple phrases do not deal with the complexity of action.

A personal moment of transformation came when I wrote a piece for Jesus-JazzBuddhism. The editor pointed out that my use of the term 'God' would not compute for many. I had to search for another term. As it happened, I was reviewing a piece by John Coltrane. In the piece, *Psalm*, he moves to Love Supreme. This made sense because one of his lines was, "I will do all that is worthy of you, Love that is worthy of worship."[1] Thanks to Thomas Jay Oord, I now have made this the *uncontrolling* Love Supreme. Coltrane's prayer is that uncontrolling love supreme will help us resolve our fears and weaknesses.

We know that faith calls us to world care. It is not always easy to discern what is worthy of us or how to make this reality better. Too often, we revert to ideology and shout at those with whom we disagree, but the better move is to search for redemptive ways that are faithful to our insights as opposed to our self-righteous views.

The question, "What has love to do with this?" is compounded when we know that God does not have a plan, that God has not set out a map to follow. It feels good to hold these views, because decision making is easier. If we begin with the realities that this world does not have a straight path, that God has not decided the future, that we live in randomness and chance; we can develop a faith that will guide us without guarantees. The power of a revised faith is to bring to consciousness those beliefs that influence us. It is here that Oord's work on the Uncontrolling Love helps us escape the idea of a meticulously planned future. Although there is no safety net, we can have confidence in our actions and agency, because persons who are open to the prompting of the Spirit of God, who is always transgressing boundaries, find creative ways to bear witness to uncontrolling love.

It takes determination to live out our Christian calling in a world that is so indifferent to values, peace and beauty. Using the idea of the uncontrolling love of God gives us a way of living that any community can mimic—setting one's face toward the future, being spiritually alive, and taking our faith seriously.

The Rev. Dr. George Hermanson, Burnstown Ont., studied at University of British Columbia, Chicago Theological Seminary, and Claremont School of Theology (with John Cobb Jr. and David Griffin). He is a Campus Minister, UBC, director of United Church Education Center, parish minister, and director of the Madawaska Institute for Religion and Culture, ordained in the United Church of Canada.

Endnotes

1. John Coltrane, A *Love Supreme, Part 3: Pursuance / A Love Supreme, Part 4: Psalm* (The Verve Music Group, a Division of UMG Recordings, Inc., 1964).

Civil Disobedience
in the Image of God

Dan Koch

In 1964, civil rights groups exerted nonviolent pressure on then-president Lyndon Johnson, persuading him to push the Civil Rights Act of 1964 through Congress. This move was politically complicated and costly to both LBJ and the Democratic Party. It resulted in a major shift in both parties. Pro-segregation Southern Democrats began leaving the party en masse for the GOP, yet few today would question the moral rightness of this politically difficult move. Martin Luther King, Jr. and associated civil rights groups and leaders exerted pressure on LBJ through televised speeches at the 1964 Democratic National Convention and organized marches, lunch counter sit-ins, and more.

This history is well-worn territory, but what exactly were those activists doing, and what are we doing today, *theologically speaking*, when we peacefully and nonviolently demonstrate or protest? Are we using the most effective or the more loving means available to us as humans to fight against unjust laws, leaders, or practices? Are we imitating God by acting the way He has chosen to act in the world? Are we taking part with God in the only way God *can* act, given His nature?

There are at least three possibilities for mapping different views of God's sovereignty, character, and action in the world: using the best means available to us, imitating God's chosen way of love, or taking part in God's essential nature.

1. The first is simply the traditional view of God as completely omnipotent and omniscient. He can do anything that is not logically impossible, and He knows everything that is knowable, including the future.

2. The second is the view put forward by John Sanders that God voluntarily self-limits His own power. Although He *could* act unilaterally and coercively against his creatures, in love He chooses, before creating the universe, to never do this. ('Before' is used not necessarily in its temporal sense, but more accurately in the sense of *logically prior*.)

3. Essential Kenosis, the view of Thomas Jay Oord, contends that God *cannot* act coercively at all, even if He wanted to, because it is part of God's unchanging, necessary, and *essential* nature to be self-limiting and self-emptying (*kenosis*). Selfless, loving persuasion is the *only means available* to God to act in the world, because it is God's essential and necessary nature to be kenotic.

Applying these three views of God to our scenario above, we find some differences, namely in *what exactly we are doing* when we act non-violently and persuasively toward some end:

1. In the traditional view, God knows everything and can do anything. He *could* unilaterally act to bring an end to segregation by convincing LBJ, supernaturally, that he simply must get the Civil Rights Act passed. Furthermore, God *could* convince enough Senators and Congress people, supernaturally in their own minds, to vote 'yes' on the bill. But, for whatever reason, in God's wisdom, He does not do this. Rather, the mystery of human moral life is that it falls to us, His creatures, to act in accordance with His loving will. Love is at least a major aspect of God's character; on this view, God is also just, holy, and sovereign; perhaps, we could say, in equal measure or status. When King and others acted nonviolently, they were acting in a *loving and moral way*, according to God's will.

2. In Sander's view; before creating the world, God limited Himself to not know the future, to not coerce His creatures to do anything against their will. From that point on (to imperfectly use temporal parlance again), God can only act in non-coercive, lovingly persuasive ways. When the civil rights activists acted in a similar way, they were joined to God, co-workers with Him in this world He created, lovingly acting *in the same way that God has chosen to act*. This is indeed a beautiful picture of cooperation between creator and creature.

3. In Oord's view of essential kenosis, we can take this progression one step further. It isn't that God *chose* to be self-limiting and kenotic. It is that God is *necessarily* kenotic, necessarily self-limiting or selfless. The only way God *can* act toward his creation is through non-coercive persuasion. So, when we act nonviolently toward some end, it isn't simply that we are acting in the only way God acts *today*. Rather, we are *taking part in the divine nature itself*. We are aligning ourselves with the defining characteristic of what it means to be God.

One way of delineating between options (2) and (3) would be to say that in Sanders' view, God does the just and loving thing to limit Himself. Therefore, when humans act in the same manner as God, they too are doing the just and loving thing. In Oord's view, God has no choice but to limit Himself; it flows from his essential nature. And, therefore, when humans act in the same way God acts, yes, we are doing the just and loving thing, insofar as justice and love flow from God. But, additionally, we are acting in *the only way available to God*.

Both views (2) and (3) provide a more robust grounding of nonviolent action than does view (1). It is worth exploring in greater detail the consequences of how we might view human non-coercive action in light of essential kenosis.

Dan Koch earned his Bachelor's in Philosophy from the University of Washington and is the host of the political Depolarize! Podcast. He is also co-host of the theological Reconstruct podcast and lives with his wife in Seattle, WA.

Opening to God through Prayer

Catherine Lawton

My husband and I keep a beehive in our backyard, and I have planted many nectar-producing flowers for the bees. We also grow vegetable and berry gardens. Since we welcomed bees into our gardens; the flowers, berries, and herbs have flourished noticeably more. I'm sure the salvia flower stalks and peppermint blossoms bloom longer than they used to before so many bees were relishing closeness with them. The flowers seem to respond and love the bees as much as the bees delight in the flowers and the nectar they produce. Of course we, also, enjoy seeing the well-being of our gardens and eating the honey that results!

Similarly, I believe our relational God longs to commune with us, to create well-being within us, and to influence the course of the future together with us, as we pray.

Our view of God and his providence affects how we pray. If the future is open to God, our prayers and petitions to him can also be open and answered by him in more possible and creative ways than we can begin to imagine. In *The Uncontrolling Love of God*, Thomas Jay Oord asserts that God has given creatures genuine free will to make choices and to respond to him in ways that affect the future. For that reason, though the future is not pre-determined and known conclusively by God, "the future is full of possibilities, and, being omniscient, God knows them all."[1] We can live and pray in hope and expectancy. The believer's life of prayer can be a life of adventure.

This prayer relationship with God reminds me of the relationship I observe in my garden, between the flowers and the bees. Deep calls to deep as God calls us to intimate prayer and contemplation with him. As we respond and allow him access, he searches our inner being and comes to know us more and more thoroughly. I believe that to be known by God is to be transformed.

If God is Spirit and omnipresent in every moment of time—all the time everywhere—we can and should pray in the spirit everywhere and all the time.

Because, "God lovingly invites creatures and creation to cooperate to enact a future in which well-being is established in surprising and positive ways," we can and should cooperate with him in faith: praying, trusting, and working toward goodness and for his will to be done and his kingdom to come.[2] We can be looking for shalom to blossom and grow.

If God's essence is uncontrolling love, we can and should pray uncontrolling, loving prayers. According to Scripture, God actually shares his nature with us.[3] If this nature is essentially kenotic, 'self-giving, others-empowering love,' we can pray self-giving, others-empowering prayers.

Creator God is far beyond the comfortable boundaries we have set for him in the past. It's overwhelming and unsettling at first to consider this, but God is so much bigger than we have believed. How can he also be personal, hearing our prayers, far bigger *and* far closer than we have imagined? God's essential being is love and he relates to each of us intimately.

Our open and relational God is calling us to:

- Praise him.
- Confess to him our lack of faith, trust, hope, and loving action.
- Give thanks to him for enlarging our hearts and vision.
- Bring supplications to him, interceding on behalf of the people and places we see that are far from the well-being of shalom.
- Listen to and commune with him. Receive and respond.
- Pray in the spirit always.
- Say "yes" to what he is calling forth in and through us.

As we watch and pray that God will call forth cooperation from—and give shalom to—his people and all of creation, the prayers of a righteous person avail much![4] We are co-creators of the future with him! He delights in this.

It is much like the bees that seem to draw out more blooms and fruit from my garden. Through prayer we can work with God to see his kingdom grow. Each one who truly cooperates in prayer and action with the Spirit of God increases his kingdom, his will, his working for good and overcoming evil in this world.

"We know the whole creation has been groaning", kind of like a garden longing to open its petals to sunshine and bees.[5] Perhaps the world is waiting for us to respond to our almighty and ever-present God in open, obedient, watching-for-possibilities prayer. Perhaps the more people respond positively to him, the more grace is available—like in a well-pollinated garden. We have been too passive-aggressive, lazily saying "But God is in control," on one hand, while on the other hand complaining and becoming angry at the way the world is going. God calls us to be active in faith and prayer and love toward him and toward his needy world. I don't think it's irreverent to say he hovers over us like a buzzing bee seeking access to our hearts, waiting for them to open their closed petals to him, to give of the nectar of our lives, to increase goodness, and to sweeten the future.

If it were true that God sees one set future, determined since before time began, we would have a big God. But the open view of God describes a far *bigger* God! He sees every possibility. He sees how our ongoing, potential actions and choices in every instance may cause repercussions that affect those around us.

"When creatures respond well to God's leading, the overall result is that God's will is done 'on earth as it is in heaven.'"[6] Do you want the garden of your heart to flourish? Do you want your life to bear more fruit? Do you want to participate in God's work in this world? Then open to him like a flower to a bee.

Catherine Lawton is owner and editor at Cladach Publishing. Born into a family of Nazarene preachers, she has lived in both California and Colorado. She finds renewal in nature, walking, and contemplation. Author of four books, Cathy blogs at:

http://cladach.com/

Endnotes

1. Thomas Jay Oord, *The Uncontrolling Love of God: An Open and Relational Account of Providence* (Downers Grove, IL: InterVarsity, 2015), 117.

2. Oord, 200.
3. See 2 Pet. 1:3-4 (NIV).
4. See James 5:16 (KJV).
5. Rom 8:22 (NIV).
6. Oord, 180.

Second Comings:
The Religion of Small Things

Jay McDaniel

Two years ago I was looking out my window and saw the second coming of Christ. It only lasted fifteen seconds but was impressive. It came in the form of an action undertaken by my next door neighbor, a fifteen year old teenager named Matthew. Matthew has no readily identifiable religious affiliation. He does not attend church, pray before meals, or read the Bible. If Matthew has a religion it is rock and roll. He once told me music is the closest thing he knows to God; I understood him perfectly. It is one of the closest things I know to God, too.

Something I admire about Matthew is his belief in kindness. Looking outside I saw a very old orange cat crossing the street in front of Matthew's house. The cat was limping slowly as a car full of teenagers was coming very fast. They would have hit the cat if Matthew hadn't stepped in front of them, put out his hand signaling stop, and picked up the cat, taking her across the street petting her along the way. I know this cat very well because she belongs to my family. Matthew was my cat's savior.

Saving a cat is typical of Matthew. He is very tender hearted, loves animals, and does not want to see anything harmed. His act of gentleness exemplifies second comings. Second comings occur whenever human hearts swell with the Spirit of Christ, leading to spontaneous acts of kindness. Some Christians say the only salvation worth having is a happy afterlife provided by Jesus. Maybe so, but it seems to me we can be saved from greed, hatred, and confusion, and for wise and compassionate living, even if there is no life after death. Buddhists tell us there are 84,000 gates to the dharma. Surely one of these gates is kindness. Perhaps this is what it means to be saved by Jesus. It is being saved by the Spirit of Christ, however named. This would truly be good news.

Matthew's act of kindness missed the evening news. The news that day concerned violent deaths in Pakistan. That night when I laid down I had two images in my imagination: one of blood and tears coming from the face of a Pakistani woman and one of Matthew saving the cat. How should I prioritize them? I knew the one coming from the television was more tragic, involving so much suffering and so many human lives, including dead children. I am sad we live in a world where people undergo horrible and untimely deaths leaving others to mourn the rest of their lives. Matthew saving the cat seemed to pale in significance by comparison.

"So much for Second Comings," I pondered.

Then I remembered every life lost and everyone left to mourn was like Matthew. They lived day by day, hour by hour, moment by moment. I sometimes forget this. When I learn about people suffering terrible deaths, I am tempted to think they are defined by those tragedies, as if they are reducible to the worst thing ever happening to them. Then it occurred to me; these people, too, had moments when they enjoyed the poetry of everyday life. They, too, had their songs and stories. The nineteenth century poet Matthew Arnold speaks to this reality when he asks:

"Is it so small a thing, to have enjoyed the sun, to have lived light in the spring, to have loved, to have thought, to have done, to have advanced true friends?"[1]

These small things—the sunshine, the springtime, the process of thinking, the small accomplishments, and the friendships—are the sacraments of daily life. And so is music.

Someone needs to invent a religion called 'The Religion of Small Things.' This religion will not focus on questions of life after death or ultimate salvation. It will not claim to have all the truth or privileged access to something called ultimate reality. Instead it will focus on satisfying relations in this world and be committed to the flourishing of all life. Its sacred texts will include poems, songs and stories speaking to life's beauty and honestly about life's pain. Its touches of transcendence will be found in music, other people, and orange cats. Its spirituality will arise not from an astral plane beyond our world but in the depths of life itself.

It may or may not include belief in God; it will indeed have a sense of God. This sense is connected with what Rabindranath Tagore calls the stream of life—

the one that "runs through my veins night and day runs through the world and dances in rhythmic measures . . . .It is the same life that shoots in joy through the dust of the earth into numberless blades of grass and breaks into tumultuous waves of leaves and flowers."[2] This stream is the uncontrolling love of God as a living presence in the world. It is God's breathing.

Truthfully, this religion, though unnamed, already exists in the hearts of millions on our small planet. When we take surveys of religious affiliation, 'The Religion of Small Things' is not included. The closest we have is 'None,' forcing people to define themselves negatively in terms of what they are not. Members of the Religion of Small Things value many very important things: justice, goodness, hills and rivers, friendships, service, love, and music. They are the Matthews of our world. There are billions everywhere, and more than a few affiliated with the big religions, too. They are Jews, Christians, Muslims, Buddhists, Hindus, and more. Their real religion, the one they live by, is closer to everyday life than anything prescribed. The Religion of Small Things can be included within the big religions and it can also exist apart from them. Second comings happen all the time, within and outside formal religion, if only we have eyes to see.

Jay McDaniel is a Professor of Religion at Hendrix College in Conway, Arkansas.

Endnotes

1. Arnold, Matthew. "The Hymn of Empedocles." In *The Oxford Book of English Verse: 1250-1900*, ed. Arthur Quiller-Couch, 1919.
2. Tagore, Rabindranath. *Gitanjali* (International Pocket Library, 1996).

Now What?

L Michaels

I recently ran across a selection of empathy cards by Emily McDowell. To say the least, they were a little out of the ordinary. This line of cards uses phrases such as, "Please let me be the first to punch the next person who tells you everything happens for a reason,"[1] and, "If this is God's plan, God is a terrible planner."[2] I love these cards, and it's not because I love stirring up controversy or saying horrible things to people who are suffering! I love them, because they express something about what it is to live real, challenging, painful narratives in the midst of a bigger story filled with other people who understand.

In his book, *The Uncontrolling Love of God*, Thomas Jay Oord makes a daring proposal. He has solved the problem of evil. It's a gargantuan claim yet there is much truth to this declaration. Essential kenosis presents us with an image of God that supersedes the prevalent theological debate between a god who coerces evil and a god who allows it, leaving us with a God who is fully love, unable to act unilaterally outside of this primary, defining attribute. If God is legitimately love, then God cannot be anything less. God cannot be culpable for evil, because this would contradict God's very nature, and God would then cease to *be* God. This shifts the blame, and the burden of culpability lands squarely on humanity, on creation, and sometimes even on random chance.

The difficult truth is, as humans we have made God into who we want God to be, and, in humility, we must admit that we have often been wrong. At this juncture, it seems like a good trade-off to shed *both* the controlling, hands in everything, micromanaging god *and* the distant, untouchable, indifferent god for the God of unending love and goodness. There is peace in this. There is comfort. When we accept that God is, indeed, lovingly doing everything God *can* do; we eliminate the temptation to accuse God of causing our suffering or prolonging our pain. Empathy reigns, but the problem of evil persists. People continue to experience pain, loss, and grief. This leaves me asking the question, "Now what?"

God does not desire evil, and God surely didn't create it! God created a world in which people make decisions, on a regular basis, whether to participate in redemption or destruction, and God acts persuasively, through grace, calling us to respond. In many ways, this is cyclical in nature. God calls; we respond. We call; God responds. In the best case scenario, it goes on and on like this over the course of a lifetime.

One question often raised in light of essential kenosis is, "Does prayer matter?"

This question was of great concern to *me* when I began to explore this theology. The answer is a resounding yes! Our good, loving God always responds. God keeps covenant. God participates in our lives on a regular basis when invited to do so. Unfortunately, people are not always so reliable, and the greatest tragedy is when *we* fail to respond to God.

I would venture to say our failure to participate in redemption is deeply connected to our failure to recognize that, "God's power is essentially persuasive and vulnerable, not over powering and aloof . . . cruciform . . . other-oriented love."[3] We need to be more other-oriented, but this does not come naturally. Even those of us who hurt deeply for others who are suffering often lose sight of where the real pain lies.

We talk about social justice and debate how to best become the hands and feet of Jesus, but in all of our discussions we sometimes forget to act. In our zeal to raise awareness or even to be transformed into people who look like Jesus, I fear we risk becoming like those whom James describes as having dead faith when he writes, "Suppose a brother or a sister is without clothes and daily food. If one of you says to them, 'Go in peace; keep warm and well fed,' but does nothing about their physical needs, what good is it?"[4] The right spirit is there, to be sure, but the follow-up is lacking.

Instead, in this world in which an uncontrolling God calls us to partnership, we must take responsibility for pain, even when we are not directly culpable. Interestingly, God appears to do this, as well, for we have certainly blamed God time and time again. Still, God has continued to act in relationship with humanity to squeeze as much good out of genuine evil as possible. Although God's power is limited, God's presence to us in the midst of suffering is not. God offers us the kind of love that moves heaven into our own personal hell, if we will accept it. As followers of Christ, we also are called to embrace Kingdom principles incarnationally and to bring this kind of heaven into the lives of those around us who are suffering. Our partnership with God should look more like the words from the Gospel of Matthew, "For I was hungry and you gave me something to eat, I was thirsty and you gave me something to drink, I was a stranger and you invited me in, I needed clothes and you clothed me, I was sick and you looked after me, I was in prison and you came to visit me."[5]

Perhaps the greatest problem we face is not that we must re-think the probability that we do not serve a magical god who has the power to mysteriously coerce creation in order to bring the narrative of the world into submission to his desired endgame. Almost no one genuinely wants God to be more powerful than loving. No, the challenge is that this theology of an uncontrolling God places a great deal of responsibility on us. When faced with the question of what happens next, we realize we must act, bringing healing to a hurting world.

L Michaels is a follower of Jesus, theology student, author, blogger, editor, educator, wife, mom, and aspiring peacemaker. She has a B.S.M. (business management) from Indiana Wesleyan University and an M.A. and M.Div. (both in theology/spiritual formation) from Northwest Nazarene University. L writes about theology, the sacraments, and ministry to the least of these at Flip Flops, Glitter, and Theology (.com). In her spare time, L sings and dances with babies (AKA teaches early childhood music), plans outlandish vacations, drinks voluminous amounts of Peppermint Bark Mocha (preferably at local coffee shops), and masquerades as Catholic, so she can participate in the Eucharist more often. flipflopsglitterandtheology.com.

Endnotes

1. Emily McDowell. "Everything Happens Empathy™ Card." *Emily McDowell Studio*. Accessed May 24, 2016, https://emilymcdowell.com/products/everything-happens-for-a-reason-card.

2. Emily McDowell. "God's Plan Empathy™ Card." *Emily McDowell Studio*. Accessed May 24, 2016, https://emilymcdowell.com/products/gods-plan-empathy-card.

3. Thomas Jay Oord, *The Uncontrolling Love of God: An Open and Relational Account of Providence* (Downers Grove: InterVarsity Press, 2016), 155.

4. James 2:15-16 (NIV).

5. Matt. 25:35-36

Sticky Love

Bev Mitchell

How should we imagine the love of God? We find ourselves in a wondrous, challenging, and sometimes confusing world, yet as Christians we believe it is all the work of a God who is perfect love. This leads many like me to want to know how perfect love works. However, given the truly unloving, even evil, experiences we and others have had; it is a wonder we can understand love at all. In the book, *The Uncontrolling Love of God*, we are challenged to think hard about divine love and many things directly and indirectly associated with it. I am challenged to explore what love of this kind implies regarding unity. Christ's loving relationship with the Father was so close that he said "the Father and I are one,"[1] and he even prayed regarding those who followed him, "Holy Father, protect them in your name that you have given me, so that they may be one, as we are one."[2] In thinking about relational unity, how can a meditation on love help us grapple with the often unloving experiences we have in this world?

A loving God encourages and challenges us. A loving God convicts us when we act in unloving ways, contrary to who we are called to be in Christ. The Holy Spirit, however, is a gentleman (or a lady) and cannot push us around or override our will. We are free to act in a unified way in cooperation with others. We are also free to imagine we don't need anyone and to live in opposition to Jesus' prayer that we would be one. We become loners believing we can accomplish everything on our own. Additionally, we are free to believe goodness is relative and our actions toward others and creation do not matter. God does not intervene to stop these harmful decisions and behaviors. God cannot but lovingly honor our freedom. It is inconceivable that love would deny freedom to the one loved. Love and freedom are inseparable; they are unified.

If God, who is in God's self a unity of Father, Son, and Holy Spirit, calls us into oneness with each another through a cooperative life, then relational unity in creation is also an expression of God's love. When we consider the biological world, for example, we see relationship everywhere—practically nothing happens without it. Atoms relate to one another to make molecules, molecules relate to one another to make properly functioning cellular systems. The amazing field of developmental biology (how organisms get from a fertilized cell to a fully functioning multi-cellular being) is a glorious symphony of relationships at many levels. Skipping over a great deal of intervening function to observe the highest levels, we are becoming increasingly aware of how whole communities of organisms are absolutely dependent on inter-relationships within forests, fields, rivers and oceans—even within our own bodies. For those who believe this is all made possible and sustained by a loving God, there should be a crystal clear message. Relationships are foundational for living systems. Thinking of and celebrating them as an expression of unity is important.

Relationship and freedom are foundational realities of God's cosmic project of love. God's love is as good as love gets, and we need much help in understanding what it really is. Therefore there is another foundational reality, and the most significant one. It is the incarnation of God, Jesus Christ. If we want to envision perfect love, all we need do is look at him. "Whoever has seen me has seen the Father."[3] Jesus is the best teacher we have in our quest to understand love and its unifying ways of creating and sustaining the universe.

Relationship, freedom, and Christ—these are a strong foundation indeed. But how does it all work? Does divine love look anything like the kind of love we can muster? The ultimate reality is the one we would never imagine. This reality had to be revealed with clarity. He calls himself the Way, the Truth, and the Life. As for his love, if we accept the revelation of his incarnation, life, death, and resurrection, there is no doubt he is the best evidence available that this idea of uncontrolling love is not entirely off track. The fact that we can understand the work of God in Christ, as explained in Scripture through the Spirit, convinces me of this.

Relationship, freedom, and Christ form a unified portrait of God's loving interaction with creation. When taken together, they are supremely efficacious in helping us respond amid the hurtful experiences of life. Indeed, if we embrace the relational unity Christ prayed we would have, if we recognize the interrelated functionality of the created universe and pledge to live in harmony with it, and if we accept Christ as the perfect representation of God's love in action, then we will be empowered to express this same love. We were designed in love to live free and relationally. Will we choose to live in unity? The Spirit of Christ stands at the door knocking, waiting for our response.

Dr. Bev Mitchell is Professor Emeritus of Biological Sciences at University of Alberta.

Endnotes

1. John 10:30 (NIV).
2. John 17:11
3. John 14:9

No Trump Card:
Partisan Politics, Divine Providence, and What the Cross Reveals about Power as Control

T. C. Moore

In 2016, the United States underwent an unprecedented election season. Even journalists who'd spent their entire careers reporting on partisan politics were amazed, sometimes daily, by the candidacy of Donald Trump. One of the most scandalous incidents was the leaking of a recording of Trump making explicit statements about the sexual assaults he had perpetrated upon women and how it was his wealth and celebrity that emboldened him to do so.

And if Donald Trump's actions and statements weren't infuriating enough, there were also the many justifications by 'Conservative' and 'Evangelical' spokespersons. Many of the same figures who seemed to never tired of moral conversations about American 'family values,' 'sexual ethics,' and 'integrity,' were some of the same ones who began performing acrobatics to justify their support of 'The Donald.' But because Trump made certain calculated decisions to align himself with conservative political philosophy (running as 'pro-life' and promising to defend 'religious liberty,' etc.), many Conservative Evangelicals considered themselves unswervingly obliged to support him. However, I believe there's an even deeper issue at work within this strange phenomenon than simple partisan politics. These Christian Trump supporters may not even be aware, but they are guided by a conception of power that the cross of Jesus Christ directly defies.

In their book, *Metaphors We Live By*, linguistic philosophers Johnson and Lakoff explain how the concepts behind our words are formative not only of our beliefs, but of the resulting actions we take.[1] In one example, they detail how we describe argument in terms of warfare.

"He attacked my point."

"I defended my position."

"He shot down all my arguments."

They propose that the conceptual metaphor *"argument as war"* drives not only the way we talk about argument but also how we carry it out.[2] "Imagine a culture where an argument is viewed as a dance, the participants are seen as performers, and the goal is to perform in a balanced and aesthetically pleasing way. In such a culture, people would view arguments differently, experience them differently, carry them out differently, and talk about them differently."[3]

Something similar is going on behind the inexplicable Trump-support of many Evangelical Christians. Rather than the cross of Jesus Christ framing their concept of power, power is conceptualized as totalizing control. Yet, it is precisely this conception of power that the apostle Paul denounces in the New Testament. Paul confronts the Corinthian Christians who are divided along partisan political lines. They have lined up behind their preferred teacher instead of seeking oneness in their shared union with Christ. "For the message about the cross is foolishness to those who are perishing, but to us who are being saved it is the power of God . . . For God's foolishness is wiser than human wisdom, and God's weakness is stronger than human strength."[4]

This is also what Paul teaches the church at Philippi when he uses the term *kenosis* (self-emptying or self-giving) to describe how God is revealed in Jesus' cross. Rather than revealing God as one who exercises totalizing control over others, Jesus' cross reveals that God's character and nature is self-giving love. Jesus' cross, not control, should frame a Christian's perception of power.

It is God's essential nature of *kenosis* that Thomas Jay Oord has described in his book, *The Uncontrolling Love of God*. In a chapter called "Models of God's Providence," Oord confronts the concepts of power that lurk beneath the surface of our thinking about divine providence.[5] Many Christians aren't aware that the concept of *power as control* subtly shows up in how we talk about miracles and justice. Since suffering and injustice are evident in the world, explanations must be provided for how God can be providentially reigning. One of those explanations, which Oord takes on, is the "God is voluntarily self-limited" model.[6] This model holds that God has chosen not to intervene in the world in ways that violate the free agency of creatures or the regularities/natural laws of our world. However, just out of sight, the presence of the concept of *power as control* is still felt as, "This model maintains a view of God's power that says God *could* withdraw, override or fail to offer freedom/agency to creatures. God *could* violate the regularities/natural laws of the universe. God could intervene in these ways if God chose to do so because God can control others."[7]

In this model and others like it, *power as control* is God's 'trump card.' And with this proverbial trump card, God can win the game at any moment.

Yet, this is precisely what God does *not* do on the cross. If ever there were a time to play the 'trump card,' the cross would have been it. But Jesus' revelation of God is decidedly not *power as control* but *power as self-giving love*. And this revelation should be the center of our life together as communities of Christ-followers. As we worship the God who is revealed in Christ crucified, we are being transformed more and more into human beings who live lives of self-giving love—not seeking to *control* others, but, instead, to *serve*. God's love manifested itself in Jesus' servanthood, not coercion. Therefore, it is this 'attitude' or spirit of humility and servanthood that we are empowered to embody in and through our lives.

The 'trump card' concept of power manifests itself in many ways. It's not always as blatant as using one's wealth or celebrity to sexually assault women. In most of our lives it is far subtler. We demand conformity from those around us. Or we only feel powerful when we 'win' an argument. The concept of power as self-giving love demonstrated in Jesus' cross reveals and provides us a better way.

God neither has nor seeks any trump card, so nor should we.

T. C. Moore is the husband of Osheta Moore and together they parent three wonderful school-aged children. He serves as a pastor for an intentionally inclusive, multi-ethnic, multi-socioeconomic, and multi-generational congregation that gathers in Downtown Los Angeles. He is a designer and theology nerd who writes at his blog: TheologicalGraffiti.com, and he graduated from Gordon-Conwell's Center for Urban Ministerial Education.

Endnotes

1. Lakoff, George and Mark Johnson, *Metaphors We Live By* (University of Chicago Press, Chicago, IL, 1980), 4.
2. Lakoff and Johnson, 4.
3. Lakoff and Johnson, 5.
4. I Cor. 1:18, 25 (NIV).
5. Thomas Jay Oord, *The Uncontrolling Love of God: An Open and Relational Account of Providence* (Downers Grove: InterVarsity Press, 2016), 81-106.
6. Oord, 89.
7. Oord, 92.

Flexible Callings

Jonathan Orbell

Allow me to begin with a confession. I often find myself envious of peers whose callings seem clearer than mine. They are budding doctors, lawyers, academics, architects, designers, ministers—the list goes on and on. I admire them; for the surety with which they pursue their vocations conveys a confidence that says, "This is what I was meant to do."

Not all of them believe God exists, but those who do appear confident they are fulfilling a divine purpose laid out long ago.

My path has proved slightly more muddled. Instead of feeling called to a particular vocation and pursuing it with comparable vigor, I bounce from one vision to the next. First I thought God had called me to a career in academe. When that didn't pan out, I thought He might be beckoning me to a career in freelance writing and journalism. Now, while I enjoy and intend to continue writing, I tell people I'm striving for a career in ordained ministry.

Yet, my path is still not set in stone, and I regularly find myself asking God, once again, "To what are you calling me?"

Perhaps you've pondered the same thing.

Being forced to ask this time and time again induces in me a deep-seated anxiety. In the depths of my subconscious, the question evolves from, "What is my calling?" to a more urgent form: "Do I even *have* a calling?"

Subtly and imperceptibly, self-doubt creeps in, and I begin to wonder if I will ever realize the calling God has supposedly placed on my life.

When I picked up Thomas Jay Oord's book, *The Uncontrolling Love of God*, I was caught in the storm of such self-doubt. The book possesses many admirable qualities. It is both rigorous and accessible and offers the most compelling answer to the problem of evil I've yet encountered. It takes substantive steps toward answering some of life's most enduring questions.

Here, however, I want to focus on Oord's particular definition of divine love, examining how this concept may change the way we think about our callings. For Oord, uncontrolling love is God's essential attribute, and "because God's nature is love, God always gives freedom, agency and self-organization to creatures."[1]

Oord's understanding of divine love is rooted in the biblical concept of kenosis. This term, most often discussed in relation to the well-known passage from Philippians 2, has been translated in a number of ways—self-emptying, self-limiting, self-withdrawing, among others. Oord lands on the term "self-giving."[2] To him, kenotic love is that which gives of the self and empowers the other. Jesus' life, ministry, and crucifixion put this kind of selfless love on full display; in doing so, he reveals something fundamental about God's nature.

This is all well and good, but how does it help those of us whose callings and vocations seem unclear?

Most Protestants I know grow up inculcated with a notion of 'calling' that draws from the thought of reformed theologian and pastor, John Calvin. 'We are not our own,' the thinking goes. Ultimately, our lives belong to—and have been predestined by—the Creator of the universe. Because of this, we should attend not to our own wishes and desires, but to uncovering the destiny God laid out in eons past.

This sort of language is, in many ways, quite admirable. It echoes a statement reportedly made by John the Baptist to a curious Jew: "He must increase, but I must decrease."

This tidy theology, however, squares poorly with lived reality—I've always found that disentangling my own will from God's is a trickier endeavor than Calvin makes it out to be.

I much prefer the way Thomas Merton, the 20th century Catholic mystic, thought about calling and vocation. Rather than treating the phenomenon as a one way street—a process in which God calls and we obey—Merton acknowledges the role played by individual will and personal desire. While we earnestly seek signs of God's will for our lives, "the soul that loves [God] dares to make a choice of its own, knowing that its own choice will be acceptable to love."[3] In other words, discerning one's call is often "the work of two wills, not one."[4]

Merton's ideas mesh well with Oord's concept of uncontrolling love. If God's nature compels Him to impart freedom, agency, and self-organization to His creation; it makes sense that we would be afforded some element of self-determination in discerning our calls. After all, a God whose essence is self-giving, others-empowering love does not coerce His people into their vocations. The kenotic God gives of God's self that we might be empowered to choose a path that both satisfies us and honors God. Again, it is "the work of two wills, not one."[5]

Merton and Oord have each helped me come to grips with my somewhat perplexing career path, and I no longer fret over realizing God's predetermined purpose for my life. Rather, I have started to claim the freedom that comes in making "a choice of [my] own, knowing [my] choice will be acceptable to love."[6]

Now that's some seriously good news.

Jonathan Orbell is a writer and seminarian in the San Francisco Bay area. His work has been featured in the United Church Observer, Sojourners, and Religion Dispatches. When he's not reading or studying, he enjoys any combination of food, coffee, and cycling.

Endnotes

1. Thomas Jay Oord, *The Uncontrolling Love of God: An Open and Relational Account of Providence* (Downers Grove: InterVarsity Press, 2016), 95.
2. Oord, 159.
3. Thomas Merton, *No Man Is an Island* (Boston: Houghton Mifflin Harcourt, 2002), 133.
4. Merton, 131.
5. Ibid.
6. Merton, 133.

The Divine Disregard for Boundaries

Bryan Overbaugh

In that day there will be a highway from Egypt to Assyria. The Assyrians will go
to Egypt and the Egyptians to Assyria. The Egyptians and Assyrians will worship together. In that day Israel will be the third, along with Egypt and Assyria, a
blessing on the earth. The LORD Almighty will bless them, saying, "Blessed be Egypt
my people, Assyria my handiwork, and Israel my inheritance."[1]

Those of us who grew up in Evangelical circles were raised in a culture that
rejoiced in the unabandoned embrace of our 'calling' as Christianity's gatekeep-
ers. It is not much of a stretch to say we became experts in defining boundaries
and making pronouncements about who is 'in' and who is 'out.' We act as if we are
divinely appointed oracles who can accurately articulate God's relational prox-
imity to others.

While identifying boundaries helps preserve and protect Christian identity,
for many these boundaries have been the source of hopelessness and despair,
sealing their fate as the religious outsider. A static God, unmovable and predetermined, offers little hope for those who are not included in the blueprint. Sadly,
this kind of determinism is not only reductionistic and hubristic, but robs our
faith of beauty and the ability to be surprised by a God who is beyond our particular religious construct.

In part, our boundary issues surface because of our faulty and often biased
assessments. Our evaluations are often biased because we assume our 'in-out'
language tells the whole story. Usually, our assessments are framed, primarily, in
terms of one's cognitive attestations, propagating determined and homogenous

conclusions. There is usually little discussion about the fruit of one's actions in this conversation. This kind of thinking needs to be challenged. If we engage people across the spectrum, we could position ourselves to observe exceptions to the rule.

Over the past couple of years, some friends and I have had the opportunity to develop and facilitate an ecumenical theological group. We are a diverse group with differences running the spectrum of faith, theology, class, sexuality, and politics. We created a community that clashed with the evangelical value of homogeneity with which I was raised. Where I was raised, we all thought the same, looked the same, and had roughly the same income and political views. The only way we were not allowed to be homogenous concerned who we loved. Despite the evangelical community's heterogeneity on this point, they managed to unanimously resolve to discredit the experience of LGBTQIA people.

Through this new group, different from that of my origins, I discovered heterogeneity was better. Many of the participants in our gathering would have been written off by the evangelical community of my youth and labeled 'devoid of the Spirit' and 'lacking true spiritual wisdom.' Instead, I found the Spirit of God was alive and well. God was extending love, grace and spiritual insight to people I was raised to think had little to offer the spiritual life. Though I knew this for a long time, this group helped me gain a deeper understanding. God's activity is often indifferent to boundaries we assume are determined and static.

I owe much of the philosophical underpinnings of this group to Thomas Jay Oord's scholarship, in general, and his theory of essential kenosis, in particular. I admit it; I'm a bit of an Oordian fanboy. While I have not worked through all the theological particularities surrounding Oord's novel theory of providence, I am certain herein lies a theological framework allowing us to speak about God's radical hope and inclusiveness.

In *The Uncontrolling Love of God*, Oord claims God is fundamentally and essentially love. Since genuine love requires freedom and un-coerced interaction, God's loving nature limits the things God can do. These limitations are contextual, requiring our unique responsiveness to God's call to act. So when God (an incorporeal being) initiates the call of humanity (corporeal beings) and we respond, what results is a risky and participatory divine/human event. Simply put, God trusts humanity enough to allow the world to unfold through our embodiment of God's call forward.

Our participation with God is lived out when, with God's help, we choose the most loving option present in any moment. Individuals are always making decisions unique to their own life experience. The moment we understand the contextual nature of God's activity, we realize there is no blueprint for determining who is 'in' and who is 'out.' This kind of assessment is both clinical and non-relational, allowing us to judge people from a distance. Instead, other-centered love (agape) is the relational assessment tool requiring us to get to know others, especially those with whom we may have little in common.

Oord's open and relational vision of God undoubtedly levels the playing field. Those who have only heard exclusivist propaganda by Christian communities should know that God is at work despite those voices. Those voices, however, are more concerned with maintaining religious purity and Christian identity than with extending love and grace to all God's people.

We must each force ourselves to ask these very important questions: Where is God at work in the world? In whose life is God working? Who can have insight into God's loving plan? Do those people look like you? Are those places only the locations we frequent? If these questions are difficult, perhaps it is a good thing.

When the questioning of our 'in-out' and 'us-them' language leads us into a disorienting liminal space, may we stay long enough to be surprised by a God who is calling us to reflect on the way we assess our boundaries. We may find God having little regard for the boundaries we hold to be self-evident. Now that is Good News!

Bryan Overbaugh resides in Cleveland, Ohio with his wife and three kids. He is the co-founder of The Table, an ecumenical theology group held in bars, coffee shops, and restaurants. Bryan holds a M.Div. from Ashland Theological Seminary. He spends the rest of his time working with underserved kids and teens, nurturing the convergence of skill and imagination. www.poliswoodworking.com

Endnotes

1. Isa. 19:23-24 (NIV).

Death to Power:
Good News for a Power
Hungry World

Michael Palmer

In our world, power is the currency for everything.

We are, daily, weekly, monthly and yearly, bombarded with this message: We are not safe; we should be afraid. We should be suspicious of one other. There is a darkness lurking, and we must sacrifice everything to defeat it.

Power, we're told, is everything. Power, or the ability to take and protect what's ours, is a lie as old as time. Fighting to gain this power, we find ourselves committing acts we never thought possible.

Safety through power, though, is ultimately a lie. In our desperate attempt to conquer, and in our never ending grasp for dominance, such paths quickly take a toll on our souls. Before we know it, power, and our attempts to attain and control it, leads us into a place we never believed we'd go. This realization prompted Lord Acton's famous phrase, "Power tends to corrupt and absolute power corrupts absolutely."

Power Corrupts

Scripture is full of cautionary tales regarding power and the consequences of wielding our power over others.

In the Old Testament, we watched as King Saul descended into madness on the throne; jealous of those who threatened his rule. We watched King David murder in his fight for more; desperate to attain things he was sure were his for the taking. We watched the nation of Israel renounce the calling to be 'a light;' instead, pursuing riches, military might, and prestige over God's call to care for those among them.

The people of Israel, even in the midst of being 'religious' found themselves far from the God who called them. The story of Israel in the Old Testament is the story of a people who forgot their first love because of the siren song of glory and power.

Like Israel, we are tempted to pursue the shadow of power.

The shadow of power demands the removal of the Imago Dei in others. Yet, you cannot destroy what is formed by God. You cannot make bleed what has been bled for.

It's incredibly easy to maim the bodies when they pray to a different god or revere a different city as holy. It's easy to carelessly bomb schools or hospitals when it becomes a matter of 'our kids or theirs.' The things we can justify in our search for power are endless.

"Kill them all," we're told. "Let God sort them out."

"Hate those who look, talk, and love differently." Cling to that which is familiar.

Friends, this 'alternate reality' is a false idol, a dark narrative, and a shadow gospel. It's no wonder Jesus spent his entire ministry teaching people to give power away. From his very birth, Jesus demonstrated what it means to live a holy life. Holiness is the act of relinquishing power.

This is described by Paul in the beautiful kenosis hymn,

> [Jesus], being in very nature God,
> did not consider equality with God
> something to be used to his own advantage;
> rather, he made himself nothing
> by taking the very nature of a servant,
> being made in human likeness.
> And being found in appearance as a man,
> he humbled himself

by becoming obedient to death—
even death on a cross![1]

We serve a God whose very nature places power secondary. We serve a God who chose to take on the form of man—descend into our pain, our hate, our anger—and instead of turning that wrath back upon us, our Messiah chose to die at the hands of his creation. We follow a God who voluntarily submitted to a gruesome death so we might find grace.

The Christian Church is a tribe that has watched the turmoil wrought by power and has chosen to voluntarily surrender it. We are a Church who follows this backwards journey, this upside-down Kingdom, and we're a church who is willing to take this counter-cultural belief all the way to our graves because we know in our graves, we don't find death. No, in the laying down of our lives, in the deepest of graves in which our enemies attempt to bury us, we experience not death but resurrection.

Our world desperately needs to rediscover this good news. Our world needs a new imagination. Our world needs our example. May we defend those under the heel of the powerful. May we name the ways we're sacrificing our humanity in order to get drunk on power, because we can only serve one master. We can only have one king. We can only pledge our heart to one Kingdom.

A Kingdom that serves an uncontrolling God.

A God who invites.

A God who woos.

A God who loves.

❧

Michael R. Palmer is a husband, father, ordained elder, and writer who serves as pastor (along with his wife, Elizabeth) of Living Vine Church of the Nazarene in Napa, California. He is an avid Cardinals fan, lover of blues and jazz, conversational instigator, and deeply passionate about issues of justice and spiritual formation. You can follow him on Twitter at @michaelrpalmer and Facebook at @mryanpalmer85.

Endnotes

1. Phil 2:6-8 (NIV).

Special Delivery

Isaac Petty

The word evangelism scares me.

In the minds of many today, evangelism comes with connotations of preaching at people, trying to coerce them to pray a prayer to avoid the fires of Hell. It gets someone's attention, compels them to conform, then challenges them to continue the cycle. The focus is on converting others, and the primary driving force is fear. It is a scare tactic.

Is this the delivery system that best matches up with the Good News of a God who is self-giving, uncontrolling love?

If we use the Scriptural language of the Church as the Body of Christ, then it would only make sense to say the Church fulfills her duty when she is being the active hands and feet of Jesus in the world. In other words, the Church is most herself when she is fully Christlike in thought, word, and deed. If the Church believes Jesus is God Incarnate, then the Church is to be the tangible sign of Emmanuel, the God-with-us. The mission of the Church is to show Christ to the world.

If we follow the arguments Thomas Jay Oord makes in relation to God's nature, we would conclude God gives God's self for the existence of creation, God is not manipulative, and God is wholly and eternally good. If the Church is to embody the attributes of this God, then the Church is called to give of herself for the sake of all creation. She is to function in such a way as to exist for the outsider, through love, without coercion. If this self-giving, essential kenosis model is followed, then the Church's task of Christlikeness, the Church's mission, is to love and give as if she has no limits or liabilities.

The Apostle Paul prayed for this kind of ministry in Philippi. He calls for an overflowing love that leads to righteousness through Christ Jesus, the virtuous state of corresponding with the will of God in thought, word, and deed.[1] To describe this Christ, Paul employs the Kenosis Hymn, the early confession that Christ was self-giving and others-oriented.[2] This is where we hear that Christ "emptied himself, taking the form of a slave, being born in human likeness. And being found in human form, he humbled himself and became obedient to the point of death—even death on a cross."[3] This is the Christ whom the Church is to model and serve.

The obedience of Christ to the cross shows the greatest model of self-giving, uncontrolling love. However, if the holy Body of Christ is to wholly embody Him, then the Church must remember that death does not have ultimate power. The Church need not have fear nor be compelled by fear. After the ultimate act of self-giving, uncontrolling love on the cross, Christ was raised to new life through the power of resurrection. As Oord argues, the resurrection of Jesus flows from the self-giving, non-coercive love of God.

When the self-giving, uncontrolling power found in the resurrection is factored into the task of Christlikeness, the Church can love and give as if she has no boundaries and nothing to lose. Even death does not stop this Love.

The entire dynamic of evangelism, the bringing of the Good News, is transformed when the Church's ultimate aim is to model the self-giving, uncontrolling love of Christ. No longer is the strategy to convert souls but to proclaim and usher in the Kingdom, which our Lord revealed to us through spoken word and acts of love. When the Church embraces Christlikeness, then the Church actively participates in the Kingdom of God, healing this world in non-coercive ways.

With this in mind, the Church can explore her practice in fulfilling her mission in the self-giving, uncontrolling task of Christlikeness. No longer does evangelism have to be a fear-filled word. Manipulation will find no room in the proclamation of the Gospel. There will be no more deceptive gimmicks to get people into the doors of the Church. No longer will we risk losing our neighbors' trust by inviting them over with a deceitful motive. Sunday morning services can focus more on the praise of God and less on compelling people. We will no longer count conversions in a dehumanizing manner but rather tell the stories of healing and redemption that happen in our very midst. That is what self-giving, uncontrolling love does.

Does this mean the Church should no longer desire to have new members? By no means! The Church should long to include more people. The message of

God's love should still be proclaimed to those who need to hear it. However, if the ultimate aim of the Church is not in converting but being faithful disciples, then our methodology changes. Evangelism has always been a crucial aspect in the role of the Church. Methods may change, but the task of Christlikeness is always the same.

When our primary focus is being the hands and feet of a self-giving and uncontrolling Christ, the Church partners with God in the justification of the world, the making-right of that which is not as it should be. Salvation is tangibly displayed for the world to see instead of written on warning signs along the highway. The poor are clothed, the hungry are fed, the orphan is sheltered, and the widow is comforted. The lost sheep is brought into the fold because the Church follows Christ, the Shepherd who lays His life down for all sheep. This is self-giving, uncontrolling love.

If the Church embodies the self-giving, uncontrolling love of Christ, then the Church has no room for fear.

Isaac Petty has served in church development in Poland and is currently a Master of Arts in Intercultural Studies candidate at Nazarene Theological Seminary.

Endnotes

1. See Phil. 1:9-11 (NRSV).
2. See Phil 2:6-11
3. Phil 2:7-8

Superheroes and
Fantasies of Power

Rick Quinn

S ometimes pop culture sandwiches a little personal introspection between
massive helpings of mindless entertainment. In the recent comic book themed
movie, *Batman v Superman: Dawn of Justice*, the antagonist Lex Luthor expresses
his antipathy toward Superman in the language of a classical dilemma: How can
we call God and God's activity in the life and well-being of all creatures good,
given the presence of evil? During a rooftop encounter, Luthor spits out these
words to the Man of Steel:

"The problem with God is that God is tribal; God takes sides. A God
that is all powerful cannot be all good. A God that is all good cannot be all
powerful."[1]

In the film, the pop culture icon Superman is a metaphor for a certain American fascination with raw absolute power bringing about good through coercive
force. Such fantasies of power are an obsession in a time marked by uncertainty,
rapid change, and a sense of vulnerability. In much of the twentieth century,
American culture wrestled with the implications of rapid growth of technology
and its seductive promise to reach a horizon where humans could perfect, control, and change life for the better. No doubt, human technology has resulted in
important advances improving the quality of life for many. Left mostly unques-
tioned by the general population, however, is the fundamental notion that technology is an attempt to and means of altering nature to bring about certain ends.
It is, in effect, a form of exercising coercive control.

The other legacy of these rapid technological advances is the tenacity of genuine evil. We have not eliminated evil by our advances in subduing nature. To the contrary, we have often implemented horrific new means and methods of destroying life. The morally ambiguous legacy of these technological advancements vexes our cultural psyche and often results in problematic theology.

I often wonder about our cultural fascination with superheroes. On some level it's just entertainment. Viewed through a psychological lens, however, a preoccupation with these mythic characters is indicative of a fear of our own finitude. Our imaginations long for those who transcend our limits and hold back the forces that threaten us.

This longing easily slides into a gravitational pull toward those who promise us impenetrable security. We project this desire onto God when we read back into the biblical and theological tradition a God who is coercive, interventionist power. Insecurity abounds in a world of competing interests. Rather than let that insecurity help us interrogate this notion of coercive power as both biblical and representative of the God revealed in Christ, we all too easily affirm the DC villain's point. We make God tribal.

It is within this cultural context I find the argument of Thomas Jay Oord's, *The Uncontrolling Love of God: An Open and Relational Account of Providence*, timely. It offers not only a needed theological corrective to notions of God's coercive power but also opens up a vision of profoundly countercultural Christian ethics in light of God's nature as uncontrolling love.

The thrust of Oord's work is that God's eternal nature is uncontrolling love. This is revealed in the life, death, and resurrection of Jesus and is called 'essential kenosis.' This theological 'North Star' stands over and against the attempt to divinize coercive power as the primary mode of seeking 'good' in our world. Instead, this love defines God's power rather than being at odds with it. In the movie, Superman is brought before the Senate due to his unilateral use of power. He is told by Holly Hunter's Senator Finch, "In a democracy, good is a conversation and not a unilateral decision."[2] She hints at something Oord's theology makes explicit. Life in and with the God of self-giving, others-empowering love is radically relational.

If, as Oord claims, ". . . love seeks collaboration instead of control, takes risks instead of forcing guarantees and does not force others to comply . . . ," then a life transformed by divine love would necessarily be shaped by its others-empowering trajectory.[3] God then deploys power as servanthood. Enemies are overcome by loving them, not by destroying them. We can now critique our hero worship properly. We are challenged to rethink our culture's view of God's power and its political and social implications.

What of the pervasive fear dominating our cultural landscape? We fear our vulnerability. That is why we worship technology and scientific advancement. We want to believe we can transcend our limits and limit the scope of unpredictability. If we could conquer the unknown and our own constraints we think our fear would be eliminated. That would be useful power. Our desire to reduce or eliminate unpredictability and risk fuels our desire for coercive power. This would come at great cost. We begin to see others as potential threats. Our fear serves as a destroyer of relationships. As Lois Lane tells Clark, "I don't know if it is possible for you to love me and be you (unilateral power)."[4] It is not exercising unilateral coercive power but responding collaboratively to the uncontrolling love of God that is truly transformational of our societies.

If the nature of God is uncontrolling love, then God "creates and enhances good in others" in every moment.[5] This ends the theology of unilateral power, precisely because the nature of coercion is to override autonomy and objectivize humanity. Therefore, a prophetic check to the idolatry of power over love is called for: "Let the same mind be in [us] that was in Christ Jesus."[6] Otherwise that path of unilateral coercive power inevitably requires the silencing of others and is, in light of the self-giving, others-empowering God, un-godly.

The profound relationality of God as uncontrolling love has implications for our life in the world. Those implications require engaging others and recognizing the blessing of the constraint of being collaborative rather than unilateral. This cuts against a culture that worships power, calling it love. We are invited to discover the power of uncontrolling love.

Rick Quinn lives in Nashville, TN, where he is co-architect of The Encounter@Edgehill, a multi-racial, multi-cultural faith movement with a vision of building bridges of hope. He also engages in freelance writing.

Endnotes

1. Goyer, David S., and Chris Terrio. *Batman v Superman: Dawn of Justice*. DVD. Directed by Zack Snyder. Burbank: Warner Brothers, 2016.

2. Ibid.

3. Thomas Jay Oord, *The Uncontrolling Love of God: An Open and Relational Account of Providence* (Downers Grove, IL: InterVarsity, 2015), 148.

4. *Batman v Superman: Dawn of Justice.*

5. Oord, 165.

6. See Phil. 2:5 (NRSV).

A Vision for
Uncontrolling Leadership

Joshua Reichard

I am not, by nature, a servant leader. By virtue of my temperament, I tend to default to a transactional style of leadership: casting vision, establishing and monitoring goals, driving organizational mission, enacting change, disrupting the status quo, and often, meticulously controlling projects to completion. While Western culture would generally regard these as the bedrock of American entrepreneurial-industrial leadership, my experience has taught me otherwise. I've learned that if I have any hope of becoming a servant leader, I must learn to model God's uncontrolling love toward anyone I hope to lead.

I presently serve as a vice president and superintendent of a network of urban, multicultural, nonpublic Christian schools in a city with one of the highest concentrations of children living in poverty per-capita in the United States, with the worst-ranked public school district in the state. The vast majority of the students we serve meet federal poverty guidelines, and about 90% of them are funded with publicly-funded vouchers. About 80% of our students are racial minorities. Nearly 20% of our students have special needs.

We liken our school to the Parable of the Great Banquet in Luke 14. All of the important and powerful people, those who would typically pay private school tuition out-of-pocket, rejected the invitation to the Great Banquet. Instead; the poor, the crippled, the lame, and the blind were offered a privileged place at the table. In fact, Jesus' own interpretation of the parable is that there are some people we explicitly should not invite to dine with us—the rich, the powerful, and the privileged.[1] Instead, we are called to invite those whom the world would see as the least and the lowly, those with the greatest needs.[2] Consequently, we have doubled the enrollment of our school system by operating on this biblical principle: elevate those with the greatest needs to the place of greatest honor.

Leading teachers to meet such needs is just as challenging as meeting the needs of the students themselves. Like most private Christian schools, our teachers are underpaid and overworked. Of the more than 75 instructional staff in our system, most have been called by God to teach at our schools and have committed themselves to our mission at some measure of personal cost. Conventional methods of transactional leadership simply don't work to motivate people in this context. Instead, a servant approach to leadership, grounded in a relational process of self-giving, is a far more effective. But it isn't easy.

Leadership can be reduced to an exercise of power—over others, over an organization, over resources, etc. We equate power with control. The more control we have, the more power we have. Often, the only way to ensure such control is to wield power in controlling, but destructive, ways: fire those who disagree, mandate particular actions, enforce strict rules and consequences, and trust no one. Schools can be among the most brutal battlegrounds for power and control. But such power-plays do not reflect God's priorities.

I believe that God favors the kind of power that God has and condemns the kind of power the world craves. If Thomas Jay Oord's theory of *essential kenosis* is accurate, then God's nature necessitates uncontrolling, others-empowering love—and leaders who profess to lead as agents called by God should strive to lead in ways that honor God's own power. Obviously, this is easier said than done. But Paul's admonition, by which Oord grounds his *essential kenosis* theory, explicitly calls us to "do nothing out of selfish ambition or vain conceit" and to "value others above ourselves."[3] It is impossible to fulfill such a call by leading with controlling power.

Leading those who are not primarily motivated by pay raises, prestige, or authority, such as the teachers whom I have had the privilege to lead, has taught me to curb my own leadership tendencies. Instead of control, I must strive for collaboration and cooperation. Instead, consistent influence and persuasion are far more potent because they lead to heart changes grounded in authentic relationships. More than that, when I lead others in an uncontrolling way, I am transformed in the process, and I've taken one more step toward becoming a servant leader myself.

I strive to see my own leadership as contingent and temporary. I am stewarding people and resources for a season. I'm learning to give power away. To lead consistent with God's love, I must learn to be others-oriented: I must learn to empower others and to relinquish whatever controlling power I still have. This highly relational process elevates the "interests of others" above our own.[4] "Selfish ambition and vain conceit" have no place in uncontrolling leadership.[5]

Now, I am not just leading teachers but leading other leaders. I can do less and less directly. Most of my influence is indirect. I must persuade others to action. Although I think most Americans probably value a 'take charge' style transactional leader, the painful yet rewarding experience of others-empowering servant leadership is far more personally taxing; it takes grit, tenacity, commitment, consistency, and yes, love. In my experience, it's much more difficult to be an uncontrolling leader than to be a controlling one!

As our school system continues to grow and we continue to serve more children and hire more personnel, I know that my leadership challenge will be to exercise less control, not more. As I grow as a leader, I know that I am called to empower others and look to their interests more than my own. To become a serving leader, I will need to continually check my own exercise of power against God's nature of self-giving, others-empowering, uncontrolling love.

Joshua D. Reichard, PhD, EdS is the Vice President for Academic Affairs at Valley Christian Schools, an urban, multicultural, PreK-12 network of nonpublic schools in the Youngstown, Ohio region. Joshua serves on the faculty of the American College of Education, Ashford University's Forbes School of Business, and Oxford Graduate School (American Center for Religion and Society Studies), among others. His scholarly interests include Process-Relational theology in conversation with Pentecostalism, Wesleyan theologies, and the intersections of race, religion, and school choice. His website is http://joshuareichard.com/

Endnotes

1. See Luke 14:12
2. See Luke 14:13
3. Phil. 2:3 (NIV).
4. Phil. 2:4
5. Phil. 2:3

The Uncontrolling Love of God: A Minority Report

Omar Reyes

M an is born free and everywhere he is in chains."[1]
What does it mean to be free? This is a question that both philosophers and theologians have been asking for thousands of years. Unfortunately, the answer has been in the hands of those who have power. More unfortunately, especially if you belong to a minority group, the question of freedom has, until recently, never been in your hands.

Compounding the problem is how the church, particularly in America, has re-shaped a vision of God from a loving, caring creator to a tyrant whose only will is to please himself. Fortunately, theologians like Thomas Jay Oord have striven to recover the Bible's original view of God by reintroducing us to the concept of uncontrolling love.

Before we examine this concept and how it helps the minority community; let's look at how this image of God has been distorted and why this has been especially destructive to the minority community in America. It is important to realize the Church has not always viewed God as all-controlling. In fact, here is a quote from one early church father:

"We have heard from the Scriptures that self-determining choice and refusal have been given by the Lord to men. Therefore, we rest in the infallible criterion of faith, manifesting a willing spirit, since we have chosen life."[2]

The early church viewed the relationship between God and Man through the lens of freedom—freedom to be everything God wants us to be but also freedom to go against our better natures. The church fathers saw in the biblical witness every man and woman freed by God-given decree, so something like slavery went against the very nature of God's created order. Then came St. Augustine.

Augustine believed in the supremacy of God over all things, which differed from many church theologians before him who believed humanity had freedom in cooperating with God and God's plan of redemption. This relationship was called synergism. Augustine had a monergistic view with God as the only active agent—relegating humans, collectively and individually, as only tools and instruments of Gods' grace or wrath.

It's this change in how theologians viewed God's relationship with man that eventually led to the Reformation and laid the foundations for the defense of both slavery and segregation within our own country. Consider this quote defending segregation:

Now, what is the matter? There is an effort today to disturb the established order. Wait a minute. Listen, I am talking straight to you. White folks and colored folks, you listen to me. You cannot run over God's plan and God's established order without having trouble. God never meant to have one race. It was not His purpose at all. God has a purpose for each race. God Almighty may have overruled and permitted the slaves to come over to America so that the colored people could be the great missionaries to the Africans. They could have been. The white people in America would have helped pay their way over there. But the hundred and hundred they could have gone back to Africa and got the Africans converted after the slavery days were over.[3]

Now consider this quote in light of how most reformed theology views the providence of God. If God is truly and totally in control, how can you avoid saying both slavery and segregation are not parts of Gods' manifest plan? And even if you grant, as Oord pointed out when explaining John Sanders' view of open and relational theology, "God cannot be blamed for the actual evil of the creatures, since God did not intend it;"[4] it's a bypass that leads us to the exact same highway: God could have stopped evil, but chose not to. When I read this, it stands in stark opposition to not only the nature of God but the narrative of Scripture. Consider how God demands Justice from his people:

> Seek good, and not evil, that you may live;
> and so the Lord, the God of hosts, will be with you,
> as you have said. Hate evil, and love good,
> and establish justice in the gate;

it may be that the Lord, the God of hosts,
will be gracious to the remnant of Joseph.[5]

The twin pillars of God's universe are love and justice. These pillars uphold God's greatest creation, humanity. Far from existing solely for God's good pleasure, Scripture shows us we are involved in a passionate and uncontrolling love affair with our creator. This love affair can only be real if there is true freedom. Evil cannot be wished on the loved one, or allowed if it is within our power to prevent it. This is why the idea of essential kenosis is so much closer to the Bible's picture of God. Essential Kenosis, "affirms God's pervasive influence but denies that God can control others. Because God providentially gives freedom to creatures complex enough to express it, God gives freedom that creatures use for good or evil (or morally neutral) activities. God acts as a necessary, though partial, cause for all creaturely activity."[6]

To a person of color, this is a God whom we always knew existed. God walks with us, talks with us, and suffers with us. God sees when we can't breathe and mourns when our loved ones are gunned down senselessly. Most importantly, God is not responsible for the evil befalling our communities; wanting instead to work with us to bring true peace and healing through Christ—true Sabbath rest. By introducing us to this uncontrolling love, Oord has shown the minority community they were right all along. God is not the God of the slave owners and slave traders. He is not the God of the segregationist or the white nationalist. God does not have a secret plan to make unimaginable suffering better. God is right here with us, wanting us to use our salvation to bring wholeness to an often broken world. The church is no mere ark of safety; it's a diving board launching us into a world in desperate need of God.

So, while many of my friends see this theology and lament how small it makes God, I retort. Rather than making God small, it makes God's infinite nature immanently accessible: God with us.

The Rev. Omar Reyes was born in Brooklyn, New York to immigrants from the Dominican Republic. He came to faith in Christ while in High School and graduated in 1984. After enlisting in the US Army and then working on Wall Street, he enrolled in Columbia International University and graduated in 1996 with a degree in Psychology and Bible. After years of working with various churches in Boston and South Carolina, Omar

fulfilled his dreams of ministry by graduating from Gordon Conwell Theological Seminary and being ordained in the Anglican Church of Canada and is currently serving 6 parishes in Flowers Cove Newfoundland. He is married to the lovely Jennifer Reyes and has three sons: Azriel who is 15, Tennyson, who is 10, and Vadim who is 7. He loves reading horror stories, especially the one where Donald Trump is elected president, and is praying the series Firefly will come back to network TV. He can be reached at his email address: trueanglican@me.com

Endnotes

1. Attributed to Jean-Jacques Rousseau
2. Attributed to Clement of Alexandria
3. "Is Segregation Scriptural?" Bob Jones Radio Address, April 17, 1960.
4. Thomas Jay Oord, *The Uncontrolling Love of God: An Open and Relational Account of Providence* (Downers Grove: InterVarsity Press, 2016), 138.
5. Amos 5:14-15 (NRSV).
6. Oord, 171.

Church Ministry through Uncontrolling Love

Bo Sanders

As a second-generation minister who is now primarily working to train young women and men for Christian ministry, theology and its implications occupy a significant amount of my time and attention. It has never been more evident that our ideas about God have consequences—serious ramifications in our congregations and communities.

The traditional mechanisms of control and denominational authority that have provided regulation and relative stability—even if they have done so through coercion or fear at times—are diminishing at alarming (and/or exhilarating) rates. I go out of my way to listen to older women and men reflect on their experience of congregational leadership and pastoral ministry. The changes seem to come from every angle: denominational directives *from above,* congregational expectations *from below,* personal questions *from within,* and cultural concerns *from without.*

The reality of being human and ministering *as* a human *with* humans *to* humans is that not everything is always a possibility! There are certain choices that are simply not on the limited menu. This narrowing happens in two definite directions:

1. Not every action is available to everyone in every circumstance. While we are actors with a certain degree of agency within our own circumstances, our past experiences limit the options that we see as 'available' on the menu of possibilities in any given scenario.

2. Even those possibilities we are aware of become limited further when options that do not live up to the model of Christ are eliminated. We are not at liberty to use methods that counter the revealed nature and character of God in order to accomplish things in God's name and to God's glory.

The Uncontrolling Love of God raised questions that impact the way we organize, act as, and lead the church. So, to paraphrase a classic sentiment: if this be true, how then shall we *lead*? How shall we facilitate and model ministry of people to each other and the world around them in a way that honors Christ's model. There are some practical implications of the model that Oord proposes for our understanding of the nature and character of the divine. I want to look at four ramifications for church leadership and ministry.

1. Interpretation
2. Investigation
3. Innovation
4. Impartation

Interpretation: A gift that any leader/mentor/soul-friend can offer is to simply ask the question that will begin the process and open the door to analysis. The question is this: "Talk to me about your options—help me understand why you see *these* as your options."

Investigation: Once an initial menu is created, a second step is to explore. "If you were a different person or had a different personality or skill-set, what do *wish* you could do that you don't feel like you can?"

Innovation: When we partner with *what is*, we provide possibilities for what *can be*. The uncontrolling love of God means that the power of God's spirit is waiting for us in each moment with potentials that were not available to us before. We ask big picture questions about how we want this situation to turn out. "If you had the power, without changing the past, to see this develop into a best-case scenario . . . what would that look like?" Then we ask, "Is there anyway, with the options we have, to move in that direction?"

Impartation: Perhaps the most powerful and underutilized tool in Christian ministry is the ability to impart grace to people. So much religious activity and spirituality has become the conveying of information and not the transfer of insight and wisdom. Every believer has God's spirit within them. That is a grace—a spiritual gift—that you can impart to those you lead.

Uncontrolling church leadership recognizes that we begin with a limited menu and that not all of the options are available to everyone in every circumstance. It then begins to partner with *what is* to bring about *what can be* and to create new possibilities and open up new options. It cannot guarantee a specific outcome, and doing so would require conduct that lacked integrity.

Once you come to terms with the 'bad news' that we are all dealing with limitations and restrictions, you can begin to entertain the 'good news' that there is an ever-expanding set of possibilities where the God of creation and creativity is involved! Partnering with the loving God to minister to, and with, God's people in Jesus' name, by the power of God's Holy Spirit, so that God's name and glory can be spread through the world that God loves *so* much, exponentially expands the menu, opening up options that were simply not available before.

I have grown comfortable with uncontrolling church leadership through two types of humbling experiences. The first type of experience is relational and the second is more conceptual.

My move toward embracing an uncontrolling model of leadership began at the back of the sanctuary after a church service. Early in my ministry I grew to love preaching to *the gathered saints* and the friends that they would bring. There was just one thing that bothered me. That old-school expectation that the pastor would stand by the back door and shake people's hands after the service. I hated it—but maybe not for the reason that you think. I loved meeting the visitors and new people. I also loved the affirming words or lively debates that folks would offer as they passed by. What bothered me was the sheer number and variety of insights and takeaways that people shared with me as they exited. For a few, what they 'got out' of the message was not what I had intended.

I eventually came to the realization that I was not exactly in control . . . and that was a good thing. Uncontrolling ministry is not out-of-control ministry. Uncontrolling ministry embraces influence, preparation, and intentionality but recognizes that we do not control the outcome. It is the condition and price of partnering with God. To paraphrase Archbishop Desmond Tutu "Without God, you cannot; without you, God will not."[1]

Any diverse congregation or audience brings in so many unique experiences, fears, agendas, and insights that it is impossible for any message to ever have a single and uniform takeaway. God's love for creation is multilayered and multifaceted, people are complicated, and language is so complex that in any given presentation or message there is bound be a *"surplus of meaning."*[2] Every message or lesson is overflowing with significance and possibility. Add to that a multiplicity of interpretations and a plurality of applications and we have to grow comfortable with an uncontrolling posture toward leadership and ministry.

The second experience that nudged me down the road toward embracing an uncontrolling model of leadership and ministry came during a 2003 engagement with Keith Ward's *God: A Guide for the Perplexed* that challenged my confidence. In a section on Kierkegaard, Ward asked us to imagine a preacher saying: "I am fifty-six per cent sure there is a God, though the arguments are very finely balanced . . . Let us pray, with a fifty-six per cent probability of being heard" or "Let fifty-six per cent of us pray" or "Let us pray with fifty-six percent of our attention."[3]

There was something both comical and challenging about that scenario. It was completely accurate, of course, but that does not mean that it would ever be feasible to articulate. As much as I bristle at the thought of attracting spectators to the scripted spectacles that we have become comfortable calling a church service, there is something to be said for the expectations that people come in with. However much we talk about being 'authentic' or long for permission to be *real* with each other, there is an inherent level of pageantry and performance when we come together on the weekends. We want to host a space where people can be honest and where we, as a people of God, can bear one another's burdens and doubts.

The art of uncontrolling leadership is to facilitate an atmosphere where people can bring the best of who they are and become all that God has made them to be. Uncontrolling is neither conformist nor is it out-of-control and an unaccountable free-for-all. It is a posture and perspective that says three primary things. First, you are not alone and we are all in this together. Second, there is too much going on any ministry to reduce it down to one thing and attempt to control it. Third, the goal is to be faithful with our end of the equation, making good choices with the limited menu of options that has been provided us.

In the end, our hope is to partner with God in the work that we find God doing. This hope is facilitated by asking the open-ended question, "If the love and nature of this God that we serve and proclaim is un-controlling, how then shall we lead?" The answers and implications are actually far more interesting and profound than the question.

❧

Bo Sanders is a visiting professor of theology at Portland Seminary while he wraps up a PhD in Practical Theology at Claremont. He has almost 20 years of ministry experience with different Methodist and Evangelical denominations, in various regions of North America including NY, the Pacific NW, northern and southern California and Saskatchewan, Canada. He blogs publicly about contemporary theology at: https:// bosanders.wordpress.com/

Endnotes

1. Originally paraphrased from the quote oft attributed to St. Augustine, "We, without God, cannot; God without us, will not."
2. Paul Ricoeur, *Interpretation Theory: Discourse and the Surplus of Meaning* (Texas Christian University Press, 1976).
3. Keith Ward, *God: A Guide for the Perplexed* (Oxford: Oneworld, 2002),189.

Implications of the Uncontrolling Love of God for Preachers, Leaders, and Pastors

Manuel Schmid

The Prodigal Son. He let him go.

Although I've read the story of the prodigal son hundreds of times and preached on it almost as often, I'd never noticed this before.

The father, despite loving his son with all his heart and yearning to be with him, is ready to let him go. Although he knows that his renegade child will probably hurt himself with this flight into supposed freedom, the father consciously decides not to hold his son back.

Many artists' interpretations of this scene picture expulsion from the father's house—the angry patriarch throws his son out, not caring what becomes of him and then throws the money after him—an understandable reaction when one considers the fact that the son's demand to receive his inheritance early was equivalent to wishing his father dead.

And yet, the parable told by Jesus shows us a different picture. It doesn't give the impression that the son is sent away, berated and ashamed, but rather that the father bids him farewell with a heavy heart. He doesn't want to lose him, which is why he waits on the doorstep, desirous of his return; still, he satisfies the wish of his youngest child and lets him leave.

The Uncontrolling Love of God

In his book, *The Uncontrolling Love of God*, Thomas Jay Oord has postulated a model of God's relationship to the world, revolving around essential kenosis. Oord describes a self-sacrificing God—abstaining from any element of control yet untiringly wooing creation, in love.

This love defines everything that God says and does and is embedded throughout Jesus' entire life. Jesus loved people without compromise, accepted them unconditionally and challenged them to become part of the revolutionary movement we call the church. In doing this, he never once used any manipulation, control, or force.

Like the father in the parable of the prodigal son, Jesus too showed a willingness to let go. Yes, he calls people to follow him and establishes authentic friendships, but he refuses to become their sectarian guru, seizing control over their lives. At one point, as most of His followers leave Him after one particularly hard-to-digest sermon, He turns to His twelve closest disciples and gives them also the opportunity to leave Him "You do not want to go away also, do you?"[1]

In view of God's self-revelation, one might say: In Jesus Christ we encounter a God who woos us with an unyielding love; and because He loves us He will never take us by force. He seeks our voluntary agreement to His love and that's why He's also ready to let us go. So, what does this example mean for us, practically, as a church?

Preaching without Manipulation

God's uncontrolling love obliges us neither to push nor to lure people into a relationship with Him, but rather to communicate the gospel in such a way that an encounter with His love is the focus.

If we want to reflect the essence of God's love in our churches, then we must first look at the ways in which we talk about Him and call people into discipleship.

It's difficult to ignore that Jesus was able to brazenly challenge others without ever resorting to threats, fear, or moral pressure. Apparently, Jesus didn't find it necessary to prove to people how sinful and in need of salvation they were in order to convey his message; He didn't lecture society's misfits about their sins to set them straight; rather he stopped for a bite to eat with them, transforming their hearts with unconditional love. The only people who Jesus actually warned about their lifestyle were those specializing in judgement and the application of moral pressure to others.[2]

I fear that evangelicalism has moved far away from this example. As a child of the movement, I am well acquainted with the ways that evangelicals keep their sheep inside their fold—one hand warning of the dangers of this world, threats of a fall from faith, and exhortations to moral integrity; the other promising full and successful lives, rooted in superiority.

It's become common practice in most evangelical tracts, books and courses to begin the communication of the gospel by showing people how lost they really are, making their lives miserable. Many evangelical churches try to make faith more attractive with all sorts of additional promises. We don't appear to trust Jesus, Himself, to reveal to people their brokenness and to awaken their desire for forgiveness and healing through His unconditional love. Apparently, we just can't imagine that an encounter with God's overflowing love is enough to call forth people's fascination and commitment.

There is a significant danger in forcing or manipulating people into a relationship with God. The Son of God who became man didn't try to push people into becoming disciples though warnings of impending disasters, nor did He lure them with guarantees of success.

The gospel is all but missing in scenarios such as these, but proclamation of the gospel that has itself been taken captive by the love of God will put love firmly in focus. It won't need any reinforcement—either from fear factors or guarantees of success.

Leadership without Control

God's uncontrolling love forbids the sort of leadership that instrumentalizes people and leads them into a spiritual dependence. It sets us free to meet people outside of hierarchical barriers and to build life-affirming community with them.

It's not only the way we proclaim the gospel that is affected by the knowledge of the uncontrolling love of God, but also the way in which we as leaders deal with our team members and congregation—not to mention how we understand our responsibilities in the church!

The Jesus described to us by the gospels always met people on their own level. Although He understood Himself to be leader and teacher to His disciples, still Jesus always respected their autonomy and personal dignity. He didn't just put them to work as effectively as possible in order to reach His goals, He built a living, life-changing community with them as His friends. Jesus didn't promote a culture of intimidation and mute obedience. When he gave His followers tasks and spoke out their callings over them, He did it on the precondition that they followed Him freely.

As those with responsibility for the local church, it would do us good to maintain this attitude in our lives today: leadership according to the measure of God's uncontrolling love cannot afford to lead people into spiritual dependency nor to put team members to use to reach the proclaimed vision of the church in a way that underestimates their personal dignity and autonomy, as if they were horses pulling the cart of the church's vision. To clothe leaders in an aura of untouchability and superiority, allowing no room for critique or opposition, is especially contradictory to the essence of God's love revealed by Jesus. If the Son of God Himself meets us on our level, what right do we Christian leaders have to claim any sort of superhuman status?

Whoever takes that love shown to us by the Messiah from Nazareth as his or her role model, that person will refuse to use power-plays and to immunize his or her authority against criticism with spiritually—embellished arguments—he or she will instead find the courage to meet team members and congregants without hierarchy and place his or her own gift of leadership in the service of the community.

Goodbyes without Guilt

God's uncontrolling love sets us free from the pressure to keep everybody and lose no one – it lets people go free in the sure and certain hope that God's love will win back their hearts.

If the latter point gives us, as leaders, certain responsibilities, it also leads to a liberating, unburdening insight. Jesus' behavior with His disciples, those closest to him, as well as with his more distant followers, makes it clear that He didn't weigh Himself down with the need to be able win and keep all those He encountered.

This is truly remarkable.

I've been in church leadership for long enough to know just how much people leaving the church can burden and stress a leader. Members of the church who leave the body or even stop believing; whole families and groups of young people who leave or slowly distance themselves from the community: every departure can feel for some pastors like an accusation against their leadership abilities. "If I'd taken more care of those individuals, if I'd decided this or that in their favor, if I'd trained our small group leaders or welcome team better" they think—then these people might still be with us . . .

That *could* well be the case. I don't want to dispute that certain departures from churches can be explained by the inabilities and mistakes of their leadership. We have to look this reality in the face. At the same time, however, we shouldn't forget that Jesus Himself lost many followers. After a successful start to His public ministry, which bestowed on Him a growing crowd of followers; the Good Shepherd's 'herd' reduced alarmingly as the mood about Him began to change. With increasing pressures, the number of followers shrank—during His last days in Jerusalem even Jesus' closest disciples left Him. Christians will agree very quickly that these losses were not due in any way to inability or mistakes on the part of the Messiah—and we should ponder this fact deeply: According to the example given by Jesus, it's possible to do everything right as a leader (love people with an uncompromising love, make all the right decisions, never miss any opportunity to encourage and promote) and yet still lose people. The reason lies in the essence of an uncontrolling love that doesn't force or manipulate someone into relationship, nor make them dependent on itself, but rather lets the other go free.

And so the circle closes once more back to the parable of the prodigal son: the father lets the son go, just as Jesus let His disciples and followers go. The father's farewell from his renegade son and Jesus' readiness to let His followers go are both accompanied by a broken heart, but God loves us *too much* to force us into relationship with Him. He aches for our voluntary participation and would rather wait for our return than ever forcibly hold us to Him . . .

Hope

Thankfully, this isn't the end of the story.

One day a figure appears on the horizon and the father can no longer hide his excitement: the son is returning! The father's uncontrolling love had let him go—but he had never lost hope and runs towards the returning prodigal: "for this son of mine was dead and has come to life again; he was lost and has been found."[3]

The same applies for Jesus Himself. Even in His darkest hour, abandoned by his followers and closest friends, He was far from giving up hope in them. Life as God's church, according to Jesus as role model, means trusting God's uncontrolling love more than all pressures and attempts at manipulation. It means never giving up hope that God's love will saturate people's hearts and kiss awake their desire to enter freely into relationship with this ever-loving God.

The last picture that God's love paints for us isn't that of the son running away—rather it's of the father embracing his son as he returns.

Manuel Schmid has been the Senior Pastor of ICF Basel, a young and progressive evangelical church in Basel, Switzerland. He is now working as the theologian of the ICF Movement in Europe and as a teaching pastor in ICF Basel, and he is about to finish his dissertation on open theism at the University of Basel. Manuel is married for 18 years now, and he has two wonderful children with his wife Rahel. He would like to thank Nicci Vaughan for the translation from German to English.

Endnotes

1. John 6:67 (LEB).
2. See Matt. 23
3. Luke 15:24

Make Love Not War: Improving the Relationship of Religion and Science

Justin Topp

It was a privilege to be asked by my friend Tom to write an essay interacting with his courageous, remarkable, and eye-opening book, *The Uncontrolling Love of God*.

Courageous, because it challenges a widespread belief held passionately by many American Christians, especially among Evangelicals.

Remarkable, because of how well his thesis and the counterpoints to it are argued.

Eye-opening, because it shows how different theologies can be, even when they share the belief that God is love, a pivot point it would seem in theological construction.

Tom's thesis or model of essential kenosis says that God's love is primary, and because God's love of humans requires free will and the "regularities of existence"[1] that accompany the natural world, "God cannot unilaterally prevent genuine evil."[2] Tom does not claim that God is not sovereign, but that God's sovereignty necessarily flows from God's love and involves creaturely participation such that God cannot completely control others.

In my short piece, I would like to apply this thesis to the broader science and religion discussion. Tom did just that in the last few pages of his book, where he argues that essential kenosis benefits the discussion of miracles (an important topic in science and religion), because it welcomes, if not requires, both scientific and theological explanations. I would like to offer three other benefits of his model. No doubt there are more.

First, I would argue that essential kenosis does more than just impact the conversation on miracles; it influences the entire field of science and religion. One of the founders of this inter-disciplinary field (and all-around stud), Ian Barbour, said that there are four ways in which science and religion can interact: conflict, independence, dialogue, or integration.[3] If Tom's thesis is correct, it supports dialogue or integration because conflict and independence are necessarily incomplete.

Essential kenosis says explanations from science and religion are both required to describe God's interaction with nature. While dialogue and integration are standard models for the interaction of science and religion in academic works, they are rarely promoted in popular books or by the mass media. Rather, conflict and independence reign supreme, which promotes anti-dialogue (see 2016 election and the aftermath) or represents an attempt (perhaps an 'enlightened' attempt) to keep the peace by placing science and religion in separate Ziploc bags, lest one contaminate the other. The model of essential kenosis coupled with the loving hug that *is* Tom and his writing should promote conversation. Good conversation.

Second, essential kenosis represents a standard framework for doing philosophy and theology in the 21st century, because it exemplifies the integration of science and theology. One reason science and theology are seen at odds is because of the philosophical frameworks that accompanied their founding as disciplines. Science is 'bottom up,' and data from discrete experiments are used to construct general theories that apply broadly. Theology, on the other hand, is built layer by layer upon particular logical or biblical foundations that are accepted as true *a priori* (thus the reason for the saltine-level dry prolegomena that initiate any systematic theology).[4] So it *seems* as though you have one discipline that is 'relevant,' because it is always taking account of the data, data that improves in resolution with technological advances, while the other discipline is 'old-fashioned,' because it relies on accepting fanciful, centuries-old ideas built upon pre-modern foundations.

There is no escaping that we live in a world dominated by science. If philosophy and theology are to be relevant and take account of the entirety of our existence, they must at least acknowledge, if not appropriate, scientific findings that describe God's creation. Essential kenosis integrates the best of science and theology by meeting in the middle, which is intellectually challenging since it demands knowledge of multiple fields, and not just their content but also their methods and philosophical foundations. In fact, rarely does a scientist or theologian have the ability to integrate like this, and the best at doing so are the scientist-theologians Ian Barbour, John, Polkinghorne, and Arthur Peacocke, who pursued advanced training in both disciplines. Unfortunately, these authors are not read widely because their prose tends to be academic in nature. Tom has overcome disciplinary boundaries, and it is my hope that his model for doing theology and making it accessible is adopted more broadly.

Third, Tom's ontological placement of love above sovereignty should enable better interfaith dialogue in science and religion. A God who has complete control over others can act capriciously, and different religions thus ascribe different actions and motivations to God. The concept of God's sovereignty combined with the natural human tendency to anthropomorphize God to fit our needs makes identification of common ground difficult and is the key source of religious friction. A God who loves first and uncontrollably *is* a common-ground God, thus improving the potential for interfaith dialogue.

I'm sure there are other ways in which Tom's model of essential kenosis will impact the broader science and religion discussion. Hopefully the three proposed here, and this essay, help to spark the conversation.

Can you think of another example of how God's uncontrollable love could impact science and religion?

Justin Topp is a professor of biology and bioengineering and assistant dean at Endicott College. He maintains an active research lab with undergraduates but also writes on science, religion, and philosophy, with a particular focus on methodological similarities.

Endnotes

1. Thomas Jay Oord, *The Uncontrolling Love of God: An Open and Relational Account of Providence* (Downers Grove, IL: InterVarsity, 2015), 49.

2. Oord, 167.

3. For more information, see https://scienceandtheology.wordpress.com/2010/11/11/science-and-religion-barbours-4-models/

4. I like crackers.

Do You Want to Get Well?

Donna Ward

Every month or so, the kids in Rainbow Kingdom have a new memory verse to learn from the Bible. Currently, it is: "Here I am! I stand at the door and knock. If anyone hears my voice and opens the door, I will come in and eat with that person, and they with me."[1]

During this last segment before the summer break, the folks from the Adult Confirmation Class have been helping out. I got to teach the lesson last night. I showed them one of the famous pictures of Jesus knocking at a door and asked them what was missing. With a little coaxing, they recognized there was no doorknob on this door.

"How is he going to get in?" I asked.

One young girl replied, "He can't!"

"You are right," I said to the girl, "He can't come in without being invited."

One of the young boys said, "Kick the door in!"

"Jesus would never bust in like that," I said to the boy. "Jesus is not a robber. He would only come in if you wanted him to."

We started talking about where the doorknob is on the picture. There must be a doorknob on the inside of the home. We have to open the door from the inside.

In John 5:1-9, we find a story of a man who has been an invalid for 38 years. He is a Jewish man sitting next to a pagan pool—that's how desperate he is. It is a pagan pool close to the Sheep Gate of Jerusalem, but also close to the Roman Fortress of Antonio. He is waiting for the pagan priests of Asclepius, the god of medicine, to release the water from the upper pool to stir up the water in the lower pool.

Jesus approaches this crippled man and asks if he wants to get well. The man gives an answer equivalent to, "Is a frog's bottom waterproof?" The crippled man wouldn't be at the pool if he didn't want to be well.

We find from the passage that no one is present with the man to put him in the water when it stirs. He can't get there acting alone before the healing water dies down.

I find two things amazing about Jesus in this story. The first is that Jesus asked for consent. The second is how little Jesus required of the man.

As I told the kids in my story about Jesus knocking at the door of our hearts, Jesus won't come in uninvited. As evident in Jesus' healing stories, he will not heal uninvited either.

Why is this? Couldn't God snap fingers and everything would be healed?

Evidently not. Evidently God cannot simply snap divine fingers and heal all things unilaterally. After all, we believe a loving God wants to heal all things, and yet all things are not healed. Apparently, God cannot heal without consent, because love never forces its will on another.

It scares some people to think there are things God cannot do. But the Bible tells us that God cannot lie. God also cannot show favoritism. God cannot do anything unloving, because love defines God's character. Thomas Jay Oord puts it this way: God can no more do anything unloving than a mermaid can run a marathon.[2] Think about that a second.

What is required if we want to be made well? Our cooperation. If we want to get well we must be willing to invest.

What do you need to invest? Maybe your investing means spending time with those who can help you experience something new. Maybe it means going ahead with that radiation therapy—an instrument of God's healing. Maybe it means beginning to take a medication every day. Maybe it means joining a support group or getting some counseling. Maybe it means cutting up those credit cards. Maybe it means calling a friend. Maybe it means eating those five green vegetables a day and getting some exercise. Maybe it means reading a book or taking a class. All of these can be instruments of God's healing if we are willing and ready to cooperate.

God desires and is always working for our well-being. But God will not override our will. Love cannot override our will. We must cooperate if we want to avail ourselves to all God wants to give us.

The New Testament uses a word for cooperating or working with God. It is sunergeo. The word synergy comes from that word, and it literally means 'work with.' This is the most quoted scripture where this word is found: God works for good in everything with those who love him, who have been called according to his purpose.[3]

Some translations say God works for the good of those who love him, but these translations misinterpret the word. They make it seem like God does all the work alone. God works with us; and if we love him, we will cooperate.

We find sunergeo in 1 Corinthians 16:16 and 2 Corinthians 6:1. In these instances and others, we are also called to cooperate with those who are cooperating with God.

We also cooperate with God when we receive God's grace and extend it to others. In fact, we are God's preferred method of delivering his grace. John Townsend, in the book Loving People: How to Love and Be *Loved*, describes one husband, Kyle, who had never learned how to be emotionally present with his wife. He had never experienced emotional support from his parents or anyone else. Therefore Townsend, a counselor, sent him to a men's group where he received what God had to give him. God used the men from the retreat to bring healing. In turn, Kyle was able to give his wife what he had received.[4]

"Do you want to get well?" asks Jesus.[5]

By asking this question, Jesus puts the ball in our court. The crippled man was not the epitome of faith. At the time it did not matter to the man where he received his healing, but he was willing to pick up his mat and walk without questioning, even after 38 years of being immobile. God can work wonders with little.

We need not worry about being 'good enough' for God. Our performance isn't the primary issue, but we must cooperate. We must open the door from our side and respond to God's call. Are you willing to take a risk? Do you want to get well?

Donna Ward is an ordained Elder and pastor in the United Methodist Church serving at The Lighthouse UMC, Inc. in Elizabeth, Indiana.

Endnotes

1. Rev 3:20 (NIV).
2. See Thomas Jay Oord, *The Uncontrolling Love of God: An Open and Relational Account of Providence* (Downers Grove: InterVarsity Press, 2016), 180-181.
3. See Rom. 8:28
4. See John Townsend, *Loving People: How to Love and Be Loved* (Nashville: Thomas Nelson, 2010).
5. John 5:6

Nathan on the Beach

Donna Ward

Following is an experience I had earlier this year. It illustrates how my prayer life has been impacted by the book, *The Uncontrolling Love of God*, by Thomas Jay Oord. God is present in the current moment everywhere. In an instance of fear of the unknown, I was able to commune with God who is omnipresent. I held on to God for comfort in a situation when God was there with someone I loved, with whom I wished I could have been in that very moment, when I could not be.

We had walked through town to a beach in Nassau. Nathan, who is 18 years old and can't stay long in one place to save his life, said, "I'm going to walk to the other edge of the beach."

It looked as if it ended at a stone wall that I could see. Because I'm one of those moms who generally always says, "yes," I did, but I turned around and couldn't see him anymore. Fifteen minutes passed before I mentioned to my husband, Ken, one of us really should have gone with him. After another five minutes passed, I nudged, "One of us needs to go find him."

I stayed with the towels and our daughter Rachel. Ken started walking down the beach. Ten minutes later I saw Ken returning without Nathan. There is no terror in the world—no shark, no alien invasion, no maniac with a chainsaw—that could compare with the fear that rose in my flesh at that moment. Panicked, I spouted, "Where's Nathan?"

"I didn't see him. I came back for my shoes. It is rough walking up around the corner."

I've seen the movies, *Taken* and *Vanished*, and I am aware of human trafficking, I have contributed to the ministries combating it, and my churches have hosted the missionaries who educate about it. Sometimes knowledge can be a curse.

"You and Rachel need to stay here. I will be back in a minute," Ken said when he had shoved his shoes on his feet.

In a few minutes I thought aloud, "Rachel, maybe you and I need to follow Ken."

"No. We need to stay here like Ken said," Rachel replied.

I looked at her and marveled at how much more mature, at fifteen, she was than I had been at the same age. I could see the look in her eyes, too. She had never seen me like this. For that matter, *I* had never seen me like this, not even when Nathan was three years old and I lost him in a big room at the Children's Museum in Indianapolis. My own mother was with me then.

"We'll find him," she assured me as we walked around the corner.

That day when Nathan's little body emerged from some crawlspace, I hugged him. "Mommy didn't know where you were, and I was scared."

What would we choose to do in this particular moment of terror? I stood in the sand next to Rachel, reached out and grabbed hold of a chain link fence. If it was the hand of God I was grabbing, I must have broken every bone in it—squeezing so tightly. I could not think. All I could do was pray over and over again in my mind with varying degrees of intonation, "You know where he is right now and I don't. You know where he is right now and I don't."

I stood there and prayed for what seemed like an eternity until Rachel announced, "Here they come!"

"Where was he?" I asked.

"I caught him heading back," said Ken.

"When I walked down the first time, he was in the bathroom and I didn't see him."

Of course he was in the bathroom! Who do we have to stop for every hour on a road trip? Nathan! Who do we ban from drinking Mountain Dews in the car? Nathan!

Then my independent soul of a son said, "I don't see what the big fuss is. I just went for a walk to the end of the beach. Don't you see it right over there?"

"I'm not going to apologize for being a mom," I reminded him, along with the usual, "When you are a parent you will understand but, as for this vacation, no one goes anywhere without a partner again for the rest of this trip. In the words of Forest Gump, 'That's all I have to say about that.'"[1]

Somewhere on the walk back to the cruise ship my heart rate returned to normal! "Don't worry at all then about tomorrow. Tomorrow can take care of itself! One day's trouble is enough for one day."[2]

Donna Ward is an ordained Elder and pastor in the United Methodist Church serving at The Lighthouse UMC, Inc. in Elizabeth, Indiana.

Endnotes

1. Groom, Winston. *Forrest Gump*. DVD. Directed by Robert Zemeckis. Los Angeles: Paramount, 1994.
2. Matt. 6:34 (Phillips).

Take a Walk to Rock Bottom

Adam Watkins

Once, while traveling for business in Phoenix, AZ, I had an extra day before I flew out at 8 p.m. I felt drawn north, to the Grand Canyon. I rented a car, drove three hours to the canyon, paid the entry fee, saw the canyon, took a few photos, drove back, and barely made my return flight. I spent six hours driving and a couple hundred bucks for a few minutes looking at a hole in the ground.

Nearly ten years later, I set out to see the canyon again but took an entire day of my trip to do it. Spontaneously, I decided to hike to the bottom of the canyon and back, all in one day. I got up at 3 a.m. and drove about 45 minutes to the south rim. I forgot a couple things: First, the rim of the canyon is over 7,500 feet above sea level, and in February was bitterly cold with three feet of snow on the ground. Second, the hike to the bottom was fourteen miles of trail and two miles of vertical change. This kind of hike takes a tiny bit of preparation. Nevertheless, armed with my camera, some Gatorade, and—I kid you not—one packet of beef jerky and five rolls of Mentos, I set out to hike to the bottom and back. It is not a difficult walk for the prepared hiker but crazy hard for the idiot who decides the night before to traverse the canyon, taking only a little Gatorade and jerky . . . and Mentos—that unsung energy food. Near the end I was so exhausted I thought I was going to die, but I loved every minute of it.

Again, all for a dirty hole in the ground.

My fellow adventurers, hikers and campers have no problem with these stories. To them it makes sense to see this stuff, to hike it at the last minute, and to enjoy what skeptics would call merely a very deep trench dug by a nasty brown river.

I thought about these stories as I read Thomas Jay Oord's book, The Uncontrolling Love of God. As he attempted to define randomness and chance, he described a religious institution that has, for the most part, denied that randomness and chance can exist alongside the idea of God. Someone must actually be in control of everything at all times if we are to believe that someone is in control of everything at all times.

Tom's book is so welcome for people like me who have issues with established theology. He makes sense of questions most people would call faithless for even asking. It is vindication to have some of the deepest and darkest doubts you've ever had reinforced in this way.

Many of Tom's arguments are triggers for me—topics that have brought about pain or trouble in my life. Years ago, I learned how to deal with those triggers the hard way. I developed the ability to be self-intuitive and find the source of my strong reactions. I eventually managed to avoid the bad effects those reactions had on my relationships. The key for me was walking into the depths of my wounds and completing that healing process by climbing back out and viewing the scars as a source of wisdom and beauty in my life.

To deny randomness at the fundamental level—to gloss over science and even our rough understanding of nature—is like refusing to address those wounds. Instead, we build bridges over them and ignore them. This means we miss the lessons that come from examining them closely by exploring all the way to the bottom and venturing back out again. We'd rather build a bridge than face the shadows we'd find in the depths or the effort of descending and climbing back out.

Bridges are unstable. A mighty river is constantly pulling at the footings with torrents of fear, pain, and uncertainty. These emotions have disastrous effects on faith. They don't fit well within a theology of a God who controls everything yet is supposed to be the very definition of love. Many Christians reinforce their bridges with statements like, "Have more faith," "Let go and let God," or, "God is in control." Time and again when disaster strikes, I have seen these mantras fall apart. The words have no power to describe a hellish descent, a sickening crash into the bottom, and a torturous climb out.

Henri Nouwen said, "But the more I think about loneliness, the more I think that the wound of loneliness is like the Grand Canyon—a deep incision in the surface of our existence that has become an inexhaustible source of beauty and self-understanding."[1] For me, this quote is about more than loneliness. It is about a canyon full of science, doubt, questions, and pain that become rushing waters to wear away at the faith of my childhood.

Thankfully I've learned to see the bottom of the canyon without hitting it. I have taken the hike down there without being forced to do so. I have accepted the pull to visit again and again and understand that those shadows aren't meant to be feared. Overcoming those fears, pains and uncertainties are the foundation from which I was built.

So yeah, Tom's book can vindicate many of my gripes over the years, but the real reason I can read it the way I do now is because I no longer fear to travel down the canyons that it asks me to explore. Though I might lose a superficial sense of control, I gain a deeper and deeper knowledge of the only thing that matters in this life. No matter what I can or cannot comprehend about this world, God loves me.

Adam Watkins is a web developer, hiker, and aspiring photographer from Boise, ID. He has an undergrad and MBA from Northwest Nazarene University.

Endnotes

1. Henri Nouwen, *The Wounded Healer*, (New York: Doubleday, 1979), 92.

The Love of God in Daily Life: One Person's Experience

Jeffrey Wattles

Talk about an idea with implications for how we live! If I believe that God— the good, true, and beautiful universal creator; mightier than all others; the only One who exerts might upon all that exists; the ultimate source of might for all others—*loves* me, then I want to experience this. I want to receive this love more fully, return it more spontaneously, and give it to others more divinely.

In order to speak in a fresh way about the applications to daily life stimulated by Tom's new book, *The Uncontrolling Love of God*, I undertook a project, which I dubbed *"and love."* The idea was to add love to my intention in each task I undertake, small or large, throughout the day. After ten days, this is what I have to report.

My career as a philosopher was based on the idea that learning to live into high concepts of truth, beauty, and goodness would help me to realize the love of God in a new way. Over the years, I learned much about the relationship between those concepts and the love of God. Countless experiences have encouraged me along that path, and this project on love was a special time of integrating and harvesting. Particularly, love led me to a more mature commitment to goodness and thus a new unification of all three supreme values.

Shortly after the strong decision to launch this project, the phrase *"and love"* inserted itself into my stream of consciousness a couple of times, in a spontaneous and timely manner. This was very encouraging, but as time passed it required more effort to refresh the intention.

I began with a brave self-opening to receive the love of God in new fullness.

I waited . . . and waited some more . . . and then some more. Frustration was beginning to set in. Looking back, it strikes me as comical and instructive. I eventually decided to take a different approach. When I want something for myself, I give to others the very thing that I desire, so I began to simply devote myself to being a good host to the Father's spirit within me. Doing so implies faith-trust in the reality of the loving presence of God that is already there. This presence does not have to be requested, only received. As soon as I shifted to the role of a welcoming host (in ways analogous to how I would make a friend feel at home), I found the love that I had been seeking. In fact, the radiant presence of divine value, the flow of my love toward the spirit within, and the flow of divine love to me were indistinguishable currents in a general delight.

One memorable episode was interviewing Sini Lilja, a Finnish teacher and artist, and asking what advice she would give to someone who wants to be good at teaching. She replied, "Love. Love everyone equally. All your students must feel that you are interested in them. Children and adults know intuitively if you have favorites."

That was the perfect lesson for the class that I was about to begin. I also came to a new level of love for someone who has been very difficult for me to love. I envisaged him under the idea that we stand before God as equals. He, too, is a divinely created, infinitely loved, spiritually indwelt, evolutionary, free-will son of God. With another person who has been sometimes difficult for me to love, I broke through her surface and mine to embrace her unbeautiful emotional reactions in love.

Most important during the *"and love"* project was an enhancement of the personal, relational quality of my life. Having developed my mind in religious philosophy and my soul's capacity for recognizing divine value, I would too often rest content in those domains where I could readily find satisfaction. But love is holistic. It does not rest in intellect and even goes beyond soul. It surges forth as a whole to relate with the God who calls to me like Jesus did to Lazarus in the tomb, "Jeff, come forth!"

Worship is not just activation of the mind and soul; it is more than singing or engaging in some gesture of devotion, whether alone or with others. There is a going forth from self, an entry into the space of Presence, a meeting, a relating in love.

Finally, I felt a new heart given to me. It came with a new trust in divine love and a new readiness to love the will of God. For a while, my mantra morphed from *"and love"* to *"love-will."*

Such spiritual experiences are, for the most part, passing phenomena. They nevertheless accumulate, even if the discoveries need to be rediscovered. During the past ten days, I realized above all that love—personal, fully activated *relating*—is an experience of a different order than anything that intellect or soul alone can know. I will always associate this project in my mind with Tom and his book and his invitation to respond to it in terms of applications in daily life. This project joins my cluster of enduring projects along with scientific living and artistic living. There are more stories to tell, but this is plenty to enable you to see the power of a project approach to growth. Happy loving!

Jeff Wattles is a retired professor of philosophy, having published The Golden Rule *and* Living in Truth, Beauty, and Goodness. *He now is starting on a path to become a minister and blogs at http://UniversalFamily.org.*

My Life Is Not My Own

Nathanael Welch

My brother is profoundly intellectually disabled. He has been diagnosed with cerebral palsy, epilepsy, is on the autism spectrum, and has several mood disorders. What all of this means practically is he requires an immense amount of care. He needs assistance with walking and standing (we use a wheelchair for everything not just around the house), he cannot feed himself or provide basic self care (cleaning, bathing, using the restroom), and is unable to communicate linguistically (he can make some noises—grunts, groans, laughter—but cannot use words). I bring all of this up because I want to reflect on some of the central ideas in Thomas Jay Oord's, *The Uncontrolling Love of God*, as it relates to my experience taking care of my brother. Hopefully this will help to bring some of the issues surrounding disability and theology into greater visibility.

"But because God necessarily gives freedom, God could not unilaterally prevent [an evil]. To do so would require removing free will . . . which a loving God who necessarily gives freedom cannot do."[1]

An essentially loving God cannot take away free will, but what about those who are unable to express or utilize their free will? My brother is unable to exercise his God-given free will without the agency of another. That is a big responsibility, especially for people who aren't very good at exercising their free will in self-giving and others-empowering ways.

It is difficult to know if my brother has access to free will in the same way I do. He isn't, because of the limits of his impairments, able to express his free will on his own—he relies on others to do that for him. Is it possible for me to express both my free will and my brother's simultaneously? That is, can I use my free will to help him access his?

In any given moment with my brother, I try to interpret his reactions, facial expressions, noises, as best I can. I am constantly asking him what he wants to do: "Do you want to go outside? Or watch TV?"

Sometimes he responds by crawling to the door; other times he doesn't. So we go outside. "Now what? Do you want to play with the ball, or go for a walk, or go somewhere else?"

Sometimes how I interpret his response to my questions seems to make him happy; other times it doesn't.

I wonder if I ask these questions for his benefit or for mine. Does he really understand what I am asking? Am I really giving him the opportunities he wants, or am I just trying to make myself feel better? I can't know with certainty.

So the question Oord's book brings up for me is, how can I love my brother in a self-giving, others-empowering way? This is the question that keeps me up at night. If God's love is essentially kenotic, what does it mean for my brother? If I were to perfectly manifest God's love, would my brother even know? These are questions I'm sure most people ask, but they take on a significance when considering persons with disabilities.

Oord writes, "Self-giving does not make God literally selfless . . . God doesn't lose the divine self when giving . . . Self-giving love only sometimes involves self-sacrifice . . . Love decenters self-interest, but it does not destroy it."[2]

When I first read this, I must admit, I wasn't so sure I agreed. The idea that self-sacrifice doesn't mean giving up your *self* entirely, but there is a limit to it, contradicts moments I've had with my brother—despite not knowing with certainty how he feels or what he thinks. Those moments are almost impossible to describe, moments where it felt as if the line between us disappeared completely—moments where I stopped being a 'self' in order that he might be. That can sound bad, as if I'm suggesting he wasn't a person already. What I mean is, in some way I emptied myself of my personhood in order for his to come through in a way that isn't possible for him on his own.

So while I was initially turned off by the description of God leaving something behind in the self-giving, perhaps there is some truth to it, but not in a way immediately obvious to me.

There is a better way of explaining the experience than to say I stopped being a 'self' so my brother could be, because clearly that isn't true. Perhaps a better way to say it is, in those moments, my life was not about me—my life was not my own. I didn't exist for me. I was still present in those experiences but in the background.

I'm grateful for a recent exchange after one of my blog posts reminding me of this.[3] Maybe that's why it seemed like I stopped existing—I wasn't focused on me but on someone else completely. This isn't to say I have done, or will ever do, this perfectly. Rather, those moments with my brother have taught me we cannot exercise our free will to love in a self-giving, others-empowering way, without the help of others.

Nathanael Welch is a student at Hatchery LA, musician, lover of trees, and blogger. He is currently working on ways for faith communities to connect with people with disabilities using photography and art. Learn more: nathanaelwelch.com/about

Endnotes

1. Thomas Jay Oord, *The Uncontrolling Love of God: An Open and Relational Account of Providence* (Downers Grove: InterVarsity Press, 2016), 170.
2. Oord, 160.
3. http://nathanaelwelch.wpengine.com/your-body-is-not-your-own

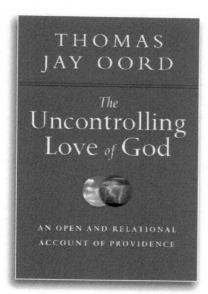

Made in the USA
Las Vegas, NV
11 August 2021

27976390R00236